T0256490

# Hands-On Unsupervised Learning Using Python

*How to Build Applied Machine Learning*
*Solutions from Unlabeled Data*

*Ankur A. Patel*

Beijing · Boston · Farnham · Sebastopol · Tokyo

**Hands-On Unsupervised Learning Using Python**

by Ankur A. Patel

Published by O'Reilly Media, Inc., 1005 Gravenstein Highway North, Sebastopol, CA 95472.

O'Reilly books may be purchased for educational, business, or sales promotional use. Online editions are also available for most titles (*http://oreilly.com*). For more information, contact our corporate/institutional sales department: 800-998-9938 or *corporate@oreilly.com*.

**Development Editor:** Michele Cronin
**Acquisition Editor:** Jonathan Hassell
**Production Editor:** Katherine Tozer
**Copyeditor:** Jasmine Kwityn
**Proofreader:** Christina Edwards

**Indexer:** Judith McConville
**Interior Designer:** David Futato
**Cover Designer:** Karen Montgomery
**Illustrator:** Rebecca Demarest

February 2019:     First Edition

**Revision History for the First Edition**

2019-02-21:   First Release
2019-05-03:   Second Release
2020-03-06:   Third Release
2021-05-21:   Fourth Release
2021-12-10:   Fifth Release

See *http://oreilly.com/catalog/errata.csp?isbn=9781492035640* for release details.

978-1-492-03564-0

[LSI]

# Table of Contents

## Part I.  Fundamentals of Unsupervised Learning

# Part II. Unsupervised Learning Using Scikit-Learn

# Part III. Unsupervised Learning Using TensorFlow and Keras

## Part IV.  Deep Unsupervised Learning Using TensorFlow and Keras

# Preface

## A Brief History of Machine Learning

Machine learning is a subfield of artificial intelligence (AI) in which computers learn from data—usually to improve their performance on some narrowly defined task—without being explicitly programmed. The term *machine learning* was coined as early as 1959 (by Arthur Samuel, a legend in the field of AI), but there were few major commercial successes in machine learning during the twenty-first century. Instead, the field remained a niche research area for academics at universities.

Early on (in the 1960s) many in the AI community were too optimistic about its future. Researchers at the time, such as Herbert Simon and Marvin Minsky, claimed that AI would reach human-level intelligence within a matter of decades:[1]

> Machines will be capable, within twenty years, of doing any work a man can do.
>
> —Herbert Simon, 1965

> From three to eight years, we will have a machine with the general intelligence of an average human being.
>
> —Marvin Minsky, 1970

Blinded by their optimism, researchers focused on so-called *strong AI* or *general artificial intelligence (AGI)* projects, attempting to build AI agents capable of problem solving, knowledge representation, learning and planning, natural language processing, perception, and motor control. This optimism helped attract significant funding into the nascent field from major players such as the Department of Defense, but the problems these researchers tackled were too ambitious and ultimately doomed to fail.

AI research rarely made the leap from academia to industry, and a series of so-called AI winters followed. In these AI winters (an analogy based on the nuclear winter dur-

---

1 Such views inspired Stanley Kubrick in 1968 to create the AI agent HAL 9000 in *2001: A Space Odyssey*.

ing this Cold War era), interest in and funding for AI dwindled. Occasionally, hype cycles around AI occurred but had very little staying power. By the early 1990s, interest in and funding for AI had hit a trough.

## AI Is Back, but Why Now?

AI has re-emerged with a vengeance over the past two decades—first as a purely academic area of interest and now as a full-blown field attracting the brightest minds at both universities and corporations.

Three critical developments are behind this resurgence: breakthroughs in machine learning algorithms, the availability of lots of data, and superfast computers.

First, instead of focusing on overly ambitious strong AI projects, researchers turned their attention to narrowly defined subproblems of strong AI, also known as *weak AI* or *narrow AI*. This focus on improving solutions for narrowly defined tasks led to algorithmic breakthroughs, which paved the way for successful commercial applications. Many of these algorithms—often developed initially at universities or private research labs—were quickly open-sourced, speeding up the adoption of these technologies by industry.

Second, data capture became a focus for most organizations, and the costs of storing data fell dramatically driven by advances in digital data storage. Thanks to the internet, lots of data also became widely and publicly available at a scale never before seen.

Third, computers became increasingly powerful and available over the cloud, allowing AI researchers to easily and cheaply scale their IT infrastructure as required without making huge upfront investments in hardware.

## The Emergence of Applied AI

These three forces have pushed AI from academia to industry, helping attract increasingly higher levels of interest and funding every year. AI is no longer just a theoretical area of interest but rather a full-blown applied field. Figure P-1 shows a chart from Google Trends, indicating the growth in interest in machine learning over the past five years.

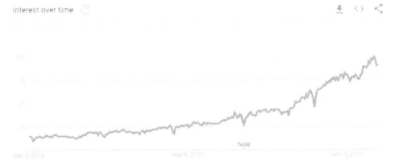

*Figure P-1. Interest in machine learning over time*

AI is now viewed as a breakthrough horizontal technology, akin to the advent of computers and smartphones, that will have a significant impact on every single industry over the next decade.[2]

Successful commercial applications involving machine learning include—but are certainly not limited to—optical character recognition, email spam filtering, image classification, computer vision, speech recognition, machine translation, group segmentation and clustering, generation of synthetic data, anomaly detection, cybercrime prevention, credit card fraud detection, internet fraud detection, time series prediction, natural language processing, board game and video game playing, document classification, recommender systems, search, robotics, online advertising, sentiment analysis, DNA sequencing, financial market analysis, information retrieval, question answering, and healthcare decision making.

## Major Milestones in Applied AI over the Past 20 Years

The milestones presented here helped bring AI from a mostly academic topic of conversation then to a mainstream staple in technology today.

- 1997: Deep Blue, an AI bot that had been in development since the mid-1980s, beats world chess champion Garry Kasparov in a highly publicized chess event.

- 2004: DARPA introduces the DARPA Grand Challenge, an annually held autonomous driving challenge held in the desert. In 2005, Stanford takes the top prize. In 2007, Carnegie Mellon University performs this feat in an urban setting. In 2009, Google builds a self-driving car. By 2015, many major technology giants, including Tesla, Alphabet's Waymo, and Uber, have launched well-funded programs to build mainstream self-driving technology.

---

2 According to McKinsey Global Institute, over half of all the professional activities people are paid to do could be automated by 2055.

- 2006: Geoffrey Hinton of the University of Toronto introduces a fast learning algorithm to train neural networks with many layers, kicking off the deep learning revolution.

- 2006: Netflix launches the Netflix Prize competition, with a one million dollar purse, challenging teams to use machine learning to improve its recommendation system's accuracy by at least 10%. A team won the prize in 2009.

- 2007: AI achieves superhuman performance at checkers, solved by a team from the University of Alberta.

- 2010: ImageNet launches an annual contest—the ImageNet Large Scale Visual Recognition Challenge (ILSVRC)—in which teams use machine learning algorithms to correctly detect and classify objects in a large, well-curated image dataset. This draws significant attention from both academia and technology giants. The classification error rate falls from 25% in 2011 to just a few percent by 2015, backed by advances in deep convolutional neural networks. This leads to commercial applications of computer vision and object recognition.

- 2010: Microsoft launches Kinect for Xbox 360. Developed by the computer vision team at Microsoft Research, Kinect is capable of tracking human body movement and translating this into gameplay.

- 2010: Siri, one of the first mainstream digital voice assistants, is acquired by Apple and released as part of iPhone 4S in October 2011. Eventually, Siri is rolled out across all of Apple's products. Powered by convolutional neural networks and long short-term memory recurrent neural networks, Siri performs both speech recognition and natural language processing. Eventually, Amazon, Microsoft, and Google enter the race, releasing Alexa (2014), Cortana (2014), and Google Assistant (2016), respectively.

- 2011: IBM Watson, a question-answering AI agent developed by a team led by David Ferrucci, beats former *Jeopardy!* winners Brad Rutter and Ken Jennings. IBM Watson is now used across several industries, including healthcare and retail.

- 2012: Google Brain team, led by Andrew Ng and Jeff Dean, trains a neural network to recognize cats by watching unlabeled images taken from YouTube videos.

- 2013: Google wins DARPA's Robotics Challenge, involving trials in which semi-autonomous bots perform complex tasks in treacherous environments, such as driving a vehicle, walking across rubble, removing debris from a blocked entryway, opening a door, and climbing a ladder.

- 2014: Facebook publishes work on DeepFace, a neural network-based system that can identify faces with 97% accuracy. This is near human-level performance and is a more than 27% improvement over previous systems.

- 2015: AI goes mainstream, and is commonly featured in media outlets around the world.

- 2015: Google DeepMind's AlphaGo beats world-class professional Fan Hui at the game Go. In 2016, AlphaGo defeats Lee Sedol, and in 2017, AlphaGo defeats Ke Jie. In 2017, a new version called AlphaGo Zero defeats the previous AlphaGo version 100 to zero. AlphaGo Zero incorporates unsupervised learning techniques and masters Go just by playing itself.

- 2016: Google launches a major revamp to its language translation, Google Translate, replacing its existing phrase-based translation system with a deep learning-based neural machine translation system, reducing translation errors by up to 87% and approaching near human-level accuracy.

- 2017: Libratus, developed by Carnegie Mellon, wins at head-to-head no-limit Texas Hold'em.

- 2017: OpenAI-trained bot beats professional gamer at Dota 2 tournament.

# From Narrow AI to AGI

Of course, these successes in applying AI to narrowly defined problems are just a starting point. There is a growing belief in the AI community that—by combining several weak AI systems—we can develop strong AI. This strong AI or AGI agent will be capable of human-level performance at many broadly defined tasks.

Soon after AI achieves human-level performance, some researchers predict this strong AI will surpass human intelligence and reach so-called *superintelligence*. Estimates for attaining such superintelligence range from as little as 15 years to as many as 100 years from now, but most researchers believe AI will advance enough to achieve this in a few generations. Is this inflated hype once again (like what we saw in previous AI cycles), or is it different this time around?

Only time will tell.

# Objective and Approach

Most of the successful commercial applications to date—in areas such as computer vision, speech recognition, machine translation, and natural language processing—have involved supervised learning, taking advantage of labeled datasets. However, most of the world's data is *unlabeled*.

In this book, we will cover the field of *unsupervised learning* (which is a branch of machine learning used to find hidden patterns) and learn the underlying structure in unlabeled data. According to many industry experts, such as Yann LeCun, the Director of AI Research at Facebook and a professor at NYU, unsupervised learning is the next frontier in AI and may hold the key to AGI. For this and many other reasons, unsupervised learning is one of the trendiest topics in AI today.

The book's goal is to outline the concepts and tools required for you to develop the intuition necessary for applying this technology to everyday problems that you work on. In other words, this is an applied book, one that will allow you to build real-world systems. We will also explore how to efficiently label unlabeled datasets to turn unsupervised learning problems into semisupervised ones.

The book will use a hands-on approach, introducing some theory but focusing mostly on applying unsupervised learning techniques to solving real-world problems. The datasets and code are available online as Jupyter notebooks on GitHub (*http:// bit.ly/2Gd4v7e*).

Armed with the conceptual understanding and hands-on experience you'll gain from this book, you will be able to apply unsupervised learning to large, unlabeled datasets to uncover hidden patterns, obtain deeper business insight, detect anomalies, cluster groups based on similarity, perform automatic feature engineering and selection, generate synthetic datasets, and more.

# Prerequisites

This book assumes that you have some Python programming experience, including familiarity with NumPy and Pandas.

For more on Python, visit the official Python website (*https://www.python.org/*). For more on Jupyter Notebook, visit the official Jupyter website (*http://jupyter.org/ index.html*). For a refresher on college-level calculus, linear algebra, probability, and statistics, read Part I of the *Deep Learning* textbook (*http://www.deeplearning book.org/*) by Ian Goodfellow and Yoshua Bengio. For a refresher on machine learning, read *The Elements of Statistical Learning* (*https://stanford.io/2Tju4al*).

# Roadmap

The book is organized into four parts, covering the following topics:

*Part I, "Fundamentals of Unsupervised Learning"*
Differences between supervised and unsupervised learning, an overview of popular supervised and unsupervised algorithms, and an end-to-end machine learning project

*Part II, "Unsupervised Learning Using Scikit-Learn"*
Dimensionality reduction, anomaly detection, and clustering and group segmentation

For more information on the concepts discussed in Parts I and II, refer to the Scikit-learn documentation (*https://scikit-learn.org/stable/modules/classes.html*).

*Part III, "Unsupervised Learning Using TensorFlow and Keras"*
Representation learning and automatic feature extraction, autoencoders, and semisupervised learning

*Part IV, "Deep Unsupervised Learning Using TensorFlow and Keras"*
Restricted Boltzmann machines, deep belief networks, and generative adversarial networks

# Conventions Used in This Book

The following typographical conventions are used in this book:

*Italic*
Indicates new terms, URLs, email addresses, filenames, and file extensions.

`Constant width`
Used for program listings, as well as within paragraphs to refer to program elements such as variable or function names, databases, data types, environment variables, statements, and keywords.

**`Constant width bold`**
Shows commands or other text that should be typed literally by the user.

*`Constant width italic`*
Shows text that should be replaced with user-supplied values or by values determined by context.

This element signifies a tip or suggestion.

This element signifies a general note.

This element indicates a warning or caution.

# Using Code Examples

Supplemental material (code examples, etc.) is available for download on GitHub (*http://bit.ly/2Gd4v7e*).

This book is here to help you get your job done. In general, if example code is offered with this book, you may use it in your programs and documentation. You do not need to contact us for permission unless you're reproducing a significant portion of the code. For example, writing a program that uses several chunks of code from this book does not require permission. Selling or distributing a CD-ROM of examples from O'Reilly books does require permission. Answering a question by citing this book and quoting example code does not require permission. Incorporating a significant amount of example code from this book into your product's documentation does require permission.

We appreciate, but do not require, attribution. An attribution usually includes the title, author, publisher, and ISBN. For example: "*Hands-On Unsupervised Learning Using Python* by Ankur A. Patel (O'Reilly). Copyright 2019 Ankur A. Patel, 978-1-492-03564-0."

If you feel your use of code examples falls outside fair use or the permission given above, feel free to contact us at *permissions@oreilly.com*.

# O'Reilly Online Learning

 For almost 40 years, *O'Reilly Media* has provided technology and business training, knowledge, and insight to help companies succeed.

Our unique network of experts and innovators share their knowledge and expertise through books, articles, conferences, and our online learning platform. O'Reilly's online learning platform gives you on-demand access to live training courses, in-depth learning paths, interactive coding environments, and a vast collection of text and video from O'Reilly and 200+ other publishers. For more information, please visit *http://oreilly.com*.

# How to Contact Us

Please address comments and questions concerning this book to the publisher:

O'Reilly Media, Inc.
1005 Gravenstein Highway North
Sebastopol, CA 95472
800-998-9938 (in the United States or Canada)
707-829-0515 (international or local)
707-829-0104 (fax)

We have a web page for this book, where we list errata, examples, and any additional information. You can access this page at *http://bit.ly/unsupervised-learning*.

To comment or ask technical questions about this book, send email to *bookquestions@oreilly.com*.

For more information about our books, courses, conferences, and news, see our website at *http://www.oreilly.com*.

Find us on Facebook: *http://facebook.com/oreilly*

Follow us on Twitter: *http://twitter.com/oreillymedia*

Watch us on YouTube: *http://www.youtube.com/oreillymedia*

# Acknowledgments

This entire past year—2018—has been an incredible journey, occasionally frustrating but mostly full of joy. I would like to thank my former ThetaRay colleagues for helping me explore unsupervised learning. In particular, Mark Gazit, Amir Averbuch, David Segev, Gil Shabat, Ovad Harari, and Udi Menkes have been instrumental to this process.

I also want to thank my current colleagues at 7Park Data—in particular, Brian Lichtenberger, Alex Nephew, and Rishit Shah—for giving me the opportunity to take my machine learning background and apply it to dozens of very interesting alternative datasets. And I want to thank Vista Equity Partners for providing me with a massive platform to have incredible impact in the AI space.

Special thanks to Sarah Nagy, Charles Givre, Matthew Harrison, and Eric Perkins. I am incredibly grateful to these generous people that spent countless hours to review my book and my code in such great detail. Without them, this book would not be nearly as polished as it is today.

I thoroughly enjoyed working with the O'Reilly team and look forward to collaborating with them in the years to come. They made the entire writing process a breeze, everything from the initial conceptualization of the work to the final production of it. In particular, my editors, Michele Cronin and Nicole Tache, were very thoughtful and patient throughout the process, shepherding the project every step of the way.

Big thanks to Rachel Roumeliotis for believing in this project from the very beginning and providing the original green light for it. Melanie Yarbrough, Katherine Tozer, Jasmine Kwityn, Jonathan Hassell, Eszter Schoell, Daisy Wizda, and Scott Murray all played highly meaningful roles in making both the book and all the additional online materials possible. I am so thankful for their collaboration on this work.

Last but not least, I am so fortunate to have wonderful people in my life supporting me every step of the way; in particular, I want to thank my parents, Amrat and Ila, my sister, Bhavini, and my brother, Jigar. And, of course, I am ever grateful to my girlfriend, Maria Koval, who is my constant champion. I am so happy to have her in my life.

# PART I

# Fundamentals of Unsupervised Learning

To start, let's explore the current machine learning ecosystem and where unsupervised learning fits in. We will also build a machine learning project from scratch to cover basics such as setting up the programming environment, acquiring and preparing data, exploring data, selecting machine learning algorithms and cost functions, and evaluating the results.

# CHAPTER 1

# Unsupervised Learning in the Machine Learning Ecosystem

Most of human and animal learning is unsupervised learning. If intelligence was a cake, unsupervised learning would be the cake, supervised learning would be the icing on the cake, and reinforcement learning would be the cherry on the cake. We know how to make the icing and the cherry, but we don't know how to make the cake. We need to solve the unsupervised learning problem before we can even think of getting to true AI.

—Yann LeCun

In this chapter, we will explore the difference between a rules-based system and machine learning, the difference between supervised learning and unsupervised learning, and the relative strengths and weaknesses of each.

We will also cover many popular supervised learning algorithms and unsupervised learning algorithms and briefly examine how semisupervised learning and reinforcement learning fit into the mix.

## Basic Machine Learning Terminology

Before we delve into the different types of machine learning, let's take a look at a simple and commonly used machine learning example to help make the concepts we introduce tangible: the email spam filter. We need to build a simple program that takes in emails and correctly classifies them as either "spam" or "not spam." This is a straightforward classification problem.

Here's a bit of machine learning terminology as a refresher: the *input variables* into this problem are the text of the emails. These input variables are also known as *features* or *predictors* or *independent variables*. The *output variable*—what we are trying to predict—is the *label* "spam" or "not spam." This is also known as the *target variable*, *dependent variable*, or *response variable* (or *class* since this is a classification problem).

The set of examples the AI trains on is known as the *training set*, and each individual example is called a training *instance* or *sample*. During the training, the AI is attempting to minimize its *cost function* or *error rate*, or framed more positively, to maximize its *value function*—in this case, the ratio of correctly classified emails. The AI actively optimizes for a minimal error rate during training. Its error rate is calculated by comparing the AI's predicted label with the true label.

However, what we care about most is how well the AI generalizes its training to never-before-seen emails. This will be the true test for the AI: can it correctly classify emails that it has never seen before using what it has learned by training on the examples in the training set? This *generalization error* or *out-of-sample error* is the main thing we use to evaluate machine learning solutions.

This set of never-before-seen examples is known as the *test set* or *holdout set* (because the data is held out from the training). If we choose to have multiple holdout sets (perhaps to gauge our generalization error as we train, which is advisable), we may have intermediate holdout sets that we use to evaluate our progress before the final test set; these intermediate holdout sets are called *validation sets*.

To put all of this together, the AI trains on the training data (*experience*) to improve its error rate (*performance*) in flagging spam (*task*), and the ultimate success criterion is how well its experience generalizes to new, never-before-seen data (*generalization error*).

# Rules-Based vs. Machine Learning

Using a rules-based approach, we can design a spam filter with explicit rules to catch spam such as flag emails with "u" instead of "you," "4" instead of "for," "BUY NOW," etc. But this system would be difficult to maintain over time as bad guys change their spam behavior to evade the rules. If we used a rules-based system, we would have to frequently adjust the rules manually just to stay up-to-date. Also, it would be very expensive to set up—think of all the rules we would need to create to make this a well-functioning system.

Instead of a rules-based approach, we can use machine learning to train on the email data and automatically engineer rules to correctly flag malicious email as spam. This machine learning-based system could be automatically adjusted over time as well. This system would be much cheaper to train and maintain.

In this simple email problem, it may be possible for us to handcraft rules, but, for many problems, handcrafting rules is not feasible at all. For example, consider designing a self-driving car—imagine drafting rules for how the car should behave in each and every single instance it ever encounters. This is an intractable problem unless the car can learn and adapt on its own based on its experience.

We could also use machine learning systems as an exploration or data discovery tool to gain deeper insight into the problem we are trying to solve. For example, in the email spam filter example, we can learn which words or phrases are most predictive of spam and recognize newly emerging malicious spam patterns.

# Supervised vs. Unsupervised

The field of machine learning has two major branches—*supervised learning* and *unsupervised learning*—and plenty of sub-branches that bridge the two.

In supervised learning, the AI agent has access to labels, which it can use to improve its performance on some task. In the email spam filter problem, we have a dataset of emails with all the text within each and every email. We also know which of these emails are spam or not (the so-called *labels*). These labels are very valuable in helping the supervised learning AI separate the spam emails from the rest.

In unsupervised learning, labels are not available. Therefore, the task of the AI agent is not well-defined, and performance cannot be so clearly measured. Consider the email spam filter problem—this time without labels. Now, the AI agent will attempt to understand the underlying structure of emails, separating the database of emails into different groups such that emails within a group are similar to each other but different from emails in other groups.

This unsupervised learning problem is less clearly defined than the supervised learning problem and harder for the AI agent to solve. But, if handled well, the solution is more powerful.

Here's why: the unsupervised learning AI may find several groups that it later tags as being "spam"—but the AI may also find groups that it later tags as being "important" or categorize as "family," "professional," "news," "shopping," etc. In other words, because the problem does not have a strictly defined task, the AI agent may find interesting patterns above and beyond what we initially were looking for.

Moreover, this unsupervised system is better than the supervised system at finding new patterns in future data, making the unsupervised solution more nimble on a go-forward basis. This is the power of unsupervised learning.

## The Strengths and Weaknesses of Supervised Learning

Supervised learning excels at optimizing performance in well-defined tasks with plenty of labels. For example, consider a very large dataset of images of objects, where each image is labeled. If the dataset is sufficiently large enough and we train using the right machine learning algorithms (i.e., convolutional neural networks) and with powerful enough computers, we can build a very good supervised learning-based image classification system.

As the supervised learning AI trains on the data, it will be able to measure its performance (via a cost function) by comparing its predicted image label with the true image label that we have on file. The AI will explicitly try to minimize this cost function such that its error on never-before-seen images (from a holdout set) is as low as possible.

This is why labels are so powerful—they help guide the AI agent by providing it with an error measure. The AI uses the error measure to improve its performance over time. Without such labels, the AI does not know how successful it is (or isn't) in correctly classifying images.

However, the costs of manually labeling an image dataset are high. And, even the best curated image datasets have only thousands of labels. This is a problem because supervised learning systems will be very good at classifying images of objects for which it has labels but poor at classifying images of objects for which it has no labels.

As powerful as supervised learning systems are, they are also limited at generalizing knowledge beyond the labeled items they have trained on. Since the majority of the world's data is unlabeled, with supervised learning, the ability of AI to expand its performance to never-before-seen instances is quite limited.

In other words, supervised learning is great at solving narrow AI problems but not so good at solving more ambitious, less clearly defined problems of the strong AI type.

## The Strengths and Weaknesses of Unsupervised Learning

Supervised learning will trounce unsupervised learning at narrowly defined tasks for which we have well-defined patterns that do not change much over time and sufficiently large, readily available labeled datasets.

However, for problems where patterns are unknown or constantly changing or for which we do not have sufficiently large labeled datasets, unsupervised learning truly shines.

Instead of being guided by labels, unsupervised learning works by learning the underlying structure of the data it has trained on. It does this by trying to represent the data it trains on with a set of parameters that is significantly smaller than the number of examples available in the dataset. By performing this representation learning, unsupervised learning is able to identify distinct patterns in the dataset.

In the image dataset example (this time without labels), the unsupervised learning AI may be able to identify and group images based on how similar they are to each other and how different they are from the rest. For example, all the images that look like chairs will be grouped together, all the images that look like dogs will be grouped together, etc.

Of course, the unsupervised learning AI itself cannot label these groups as "chairs" or "dogs" but now that similar images are grouped together, humans have a much simpler labeling task. Instead of labeling millions of images by hand, humans can manually label all the distinct groups, and the labels will apply to all the members within each group.

After the initial training, if the unsupervised learning AI finds images that do not belong to any of the labeled groups, the AI will create separate groups for the unclassified images, triggering a human to label the new, yet-to-be-labeled groups of images.

Unsupervised learning makes previously intractable problems more solvable and is much more nimble at finding hidden patterns both in the historical data that is available for training and in future data. Moreover, we now have an AI approach for the huge troves of unlabeled data that exist in the world.

Even though unsupervised learning is less adept than supervised learning at solving specific, narrowly defined problems, it is better at tackling more open-ended problems of the strong AI type and at generalizing this knowledge.

Just as importantly, unsupervised learning can address many of the common problems data scientists encounter when building machine learning solutions.

# Using Unsupervised Learning to Improve Machine Learning Solutions

Recent successes in machine learning have been driven by the availability of lots of data, advances in computer hardware and cloud-based resources, and breakthroughs in machine learning algorithms. But these successes have been in mostly narrow AI problems such as image classification, computer vision, speech recognition, natural language processing, and machine translation.

To solve more ambitious AI problems, we need to unlock the value of unsupervised learning. Let's explore the most common challenges data scientists face when building solutions and how unsupervised learning can help.

### Insufficient labeled data

> I think AI is akin to building a rocket ship. You need a huge engine and a lot of fuel. If you have a large engine and a tiny amount of fuel, you won't make it to orbit. If you have a tiny engine and a ton of fuel, you can't even lift off. To build a rocket you need a huge engine and a lot of fuel.
>
> —Andrew Ng

If machine learning were a rocket ship, data would be the fuel—without lots and lots of data, the rocket ship cannot fly. But not all data is created equal. To use supervised algorithms, we need lots of labeled data, which is hard and costly to generate.[1]

With unsupervised learning, we can automatically label unlabeled examples. Here is how it would work: we would cluster all the examples and then apply the labels from labeled examples to the unlabeled ones within the same cluster. Unlabeled examples would receive the label of the labeled ones they are most similar to. We will explore clustering in Chapter 5.

## Overfitting

If the machine learning algorithm learns an overly complex function based on the training data, it may perform very poorly on never-before-seen instances from hold-out sets such as the validation set or test set. In this case, the algorithm has overfit the training data—by extracting too much from the noise in the data—and has very poor generalization error. In other words, the algorithm is memorizing the training data rather than learning how to generalize knowledge based off of it.[2]

To address this, we can introduce unsupervised learning as a *regularizer*. *Regularization* is a process used to reduce the complexity of a machine learning algorithm, helping it capture the signal in the data without adjusting too much to the noise. Unsupervised pretraining is one such form of regularization. Instead of feeding the original input data directly into a supervised learning algorithm, we can feed a new representation of the original input data that we generate.

This new representation captures the essence of the original data—the true underlying structure—while losing some of the less representative noise along the way. When we feed this new representation into the supervised learning algorithm, it has less noise to wade through and captures more of the signal, improving its generalization error. We will explore feature extraction in Chapter 7.

## Curse of dimensionality

Even with the advances in computational power, big data is hard for machine learning algorithms to manage. In general, adding more instances is not too problematic because we can parallelize operations using modern map-reduce solutions such as Spark. However, the more features we have, the more difficult training becomes.

---

1 There are startups such as Figure Eight that explicitly provide this *human in the loop* service.

2 Underfitting is another problem that may occur in building machine learning applications, but this is easier to solve. Underfitting occurs because the model is too simple—the algorithm cannot build a complex enough function approximation to make good decisions for the task at hand. To solve this, we can allow the algorithm to grow in size (have more parameters, perform more training iterations, etc.) or apply a more complicated machine learning algorithm.

---

In a very high-dimensional space, supervised algorithms need to learn how to separate points and build a function approximation to make good decisions. When the features are very numerous, this search becomes very expensive, both from a time and compute perspective. In some cases, it may be impossible to find a good solution fast enough.

This problem is known as the *curse of dimensionality*, and unsupervised learning is well suited to help manage this. With dimensionality reduction, we can find the most salient features in the original feature set, reduce the number of dimensions to a more manageable number while losing very little important information in the process, and then apply supervised algorithms to more efficiently perform the search for a good function approximation. We will cover dimensionality reduction in Chapter 3.

### Feature engineering

Feature engineering is one of the most vital tasks data scientists perform. Without the right features, the machine learning algorithm will not be able to separate points in space well enough to make good decisions on never-before-seen examples. However, feature engineering is typically very labor-intensive; it requires humans to creatively hand-engineer the right types of features. Instead, we can use representation learning from unsupervised learning algorithms to automatically learn the right types of feature representations to help solve the task at hand. We will explore automatic feature extraction in Chapter 7.

### Outliers

The quality of data is also very important. If machine learning algorithms train on rare, distortive outliers, their generalization error will be lower than if they ignored or addressed the outliers separately. With unsupervised learning, we can perform outlier detection using dimensionality reduction and create a solution specifically for the outliers and, separately, a solution for the normal data. We will build an anomaly detection system in Chapter 4.

### Data drift

Machine learning models also need to be aware of drift in the data. If the data the model is making predictions on differs statistically from the data the model trained on, the model may need to retrain on data that is more representative of the current data. If the model does not retrain or does not recognize the drift, the model's prediction quality on current data will suffer.

By building probability distributions using unsupervised learning, we can assess how different the current data is from the training set data—if the two are different enough, we can automatically trigger a retraining. We will explore how to build these types of data discriminators in Chapter 12.

# A Closer Look at Supervised Algorithms

Before we delve into unsupervised learning systems, let's take a look at supervised learning algorithms and how they work. This will help frame where unsupervised learning fits within the machine learning ecosystem.

In supervised learning, there are two major types of problems: *classification* and *regression*. In classification, the AI must correctly classify items into one of two or more classes. If there are just two classes, the problem is called *binary classification*. If there are three or more classes, the problem is classed *multiclass classification*.

Classification problems are also known as *discrete* prediction problems because each class is a discrete group. Classification problems also may be referred to as *qualitative* or *categorical* problems.

In regression, the AI must predict a *continuous* variable rather than a discrete one. Regression problems also may be referred to as *quantitative* problems.

Supervised machine learning algorithms span the gamut, from very simple to very complex, but they are all aimed at minimizing some cost function or error rate (or maximizing a value function) that is associated with the labels we have for the dataset.

As mentioned before, what we care about most is how well the machine learning solution generalizes to never-before-seen cases. The choice of the supervised learning algorithm is very important at minimizing this generalization error.

To achieve the lowest possible generalization error, the complexity of the algorithmic model should match the complexity of the true function underlying the data. We do not know what this true function really is. If we did, we would not need to use machine learning to create a model—we would just solve the function to find the right answer. But since we do not know what this true function is, we choose a machine learning algorithm to test hypotheses and find the model that best approximates this true function (i.e., has the lowest possible generalization error).

If what the algorithm models is less complex than the true function, we have *underfit* the data. In this case, we could improve the generalization error by choosing an algorithm that can model a more complex function. However, if the algorithm designs an overly complex model, we have *overfit* the training data and will have poor performance on never-before-seen cases, increasing our generalization error.

In other words, choosing more complex algorithms over simpler ones is not always the right choice—sometimes simpler is better. Each algorithm comes with its set of strengths, weaknesses, and assumptions, and knowing what to use when given the data you have and the problem you are trying to solve is very important to mastering machine learning.

In the rest of this chapter, we will describe some of the most common supervised algorithms (including some real-world applications) before doing the same for unsupervised algorithms.[3]

# Linear Methods

The most basic supervised learning algorithms model a simple linear relationship between the input features and the output variable that we wish to predict.

## Linear regression

The simplest of all the algorithms is *linear regression*, which uses a model that assumes a linear relationship between the input variables (x) and the single output variable (y). If the true relationship between the inputs and the output is linear and the input variables are not highly correlated (a situation known as *collinearity*), linear regression may be an appropriate choice. If the true relationship is more complex or nonlinear, linear regression will underfit the data.[4]

Because it is so simple, interpreting the relationship modeled by the algorithm is also very straightforward. *Interpretability* is a very important consideration for applied machine learning because solutions need to be understood and enacted by both technical and nontechnical people in industry. Without interpretability, the solutions become inscrutable black boxes.

*Strengths*
> Linear regression is simple, intrepretable, and hard to overfit because it cannot model overly complex relationships. It is an excellent choice when the underlying relationship between the input and output variables is linear.

*Weaknesses*
> Linear regression will underfit the data when the relationship between the input and output variables is nonlinear.

*Applications*
> Since the true underlying relationship between human weight and human height is linear, linear regression is great for predicting weight using height as the input variable or, vice versa, for predicting height using weight as the input variable.

---

3 This list is by no means exhaustive but does include the most commonly used machine learning algorithms.

4 There may be other potential issues that might make linear regression a poor choice, including outliers, correlation of error terms, and nonconstant variance of error terms.

### Logistic regression

The simplest classification algorithm is *logistic regression*, which is also a linear method but the predictions are transformed using the logistic function. The outputs of this transformation are *class probabilities*—in other words, the probabilities that the instance belongs to the various classes, where the sum of the probabilities for each instance adds up to one. Each instance is then assigned to the class for which it has the highest probability of belonging in.

*Strengths*
> Like linear regression, logistic regression is simple and interpretable. When the classes we are trying to predict are nonoverlapping and linearly separable, logistic regression is an excellent choice.

*Weaknesses*
> When classes are not linearly separable, logistic regression will fail.

*Applications*
> When classes are mostly nonoverlapping—for example, the heights of young children versus the heights of adults—logistic regression will work well.

## Neighborhood-Based Methods

Another group of very simple algorithms are neighborhood-based methods. Neighborhood-based methods are *lazy learners* since they learn how to label new points based on the proximity of the new points to existing labeled points. Unlike linear regression or logistic regression, neighborhood-based models do not learn a set model to predict labels for new points; rather, these models predict labels for new points based purely on distance of new points to preexisting labeled points. Lazy learning is also referred to as *instance-based learning* or *nonparametric methods*.

### k-nearest neighbors

The most common neighborhood-based method is *k-nearest neighbors (KNN)*. To label each new point, KNN looks at a $k$ number (where $k$ is an integer value) of nearest labeled points and has these already labeled neighbors vote on how to label the new point. By default, KNN uses Euclidean distance to measure what is closest.

The choice of $k$ is very important. If $k$ is set to a very low value, KNN becomes very flexible, drawing highly nuanced boundaries and potentially overfitting the data. If $k$ is set to a very high value, KNN becomes inflexible, drawing a too rigid boundary and potentially underfitting the data.

*Strengths*
> Unlike linear methods, KNN is highly flexible and adept at learning more complex, nonlinear relationships. Yet, KNN remains simple and interpretable.

*Weaknesses*

KNN does poorly when the number of observations and features grow. KNN becomes computationally inefficient in this highly populated, high-dimensional space since it needs to calculate distances from the new point to many nearby labeled points in order to predict labels. It cannot rely on an efficient model with a reduced number of parameters to make the necessary prediction. Also, KNN is very sensitive to the choice of $k$. When $k$ is set too low, KNN can overfit, and when $k$ is set too high, KNN can underfit.

*Applications*

KNN is regularly used in recommender systems, such as those used to predict taste in movies (Netflix), music (Spotify), friends (Facebook), photos (Instagram), search (Google), and shopping (Amazon). For example, KNN can help predict what a user will like given what similar users like (known as *collaborative filtering*) or what the user has liked in the past (known as *content-based filtering*).

# Tree-Based Methods

Instead of using a linear method, we can have the AI build a *decision tree* where all the instances are *segmented* or *stratified* into many regions, guided by the labels we have. Once this segmentation is complete, each region corresponds to a particular class of label (for classification problems) or a range of predicted values (for regression problems). This process is similar to having the AI build rules automatically with the explicit goal of making better decisions or predictions.

## Single decision tree

The simplest tree-based method is a *single decision tree*, in which the AI goes once through the training data, creates rules for segmenting the data guided by the labels, and uses this tree to make predictions on the never-before-seen validation or test set. However, a single decision tree is usually poor at generalizing what it has learned during training to never-before-seen cases because it usually overfits the training data during its one and only training iteration.

## Bagging

To improve the single decision tree, we can introduce *bootstrap aggregation* (more commonly known as *bagging*), in which we take *multiple random samples of instances* from the training data, create a decision tree for each sample, and then predict the output for each instance by averaging the predictions of each of these trees. By using *randomization* of samples and averaging results from multiple trees—an approach that is also known as the *ensemble method*—bagging will address some of the overfitting that results from a single decision tree.

### Random forests

We can improve overfitting further by sampling not only the instances but also the predictors. With *random forests*, we take multiple random samples of instances from the training data like we do in bagging, but, for each split in each decision tree, we make the split based not on all the predictors but rather a *random sample of the predictors*. The number of predictors we consider for each split is usually the square root of the total number of predictors.

By sampling the predictors in this way, the random forests algorithm creates trees that are even less correlated with each other (compared to the trees in bagging), reducing overfitting and improving the generalization error.

### Boosting

Another approach, known as *boosting*, is used to create multiple trees like in bagging but to *build the trees sequentially*, using what the AI learned from the previous tree to improve results on the subsequent tree. Each tree is kept pretty shallow, with only a few decision splits, and the learning occurs slowly, tree by tree. Of all the tree-based methods, *gradient boosting machines* are among the best-performing and are commonly used to win machine learning competitions.[5]

*Strengths*
> Tree-based methods are among the best-performing supervised-learning algorithms for prediction problems. These methods are able to capture complex relationships in the data by learning many simple rules, one rule at a time. They are also capable of handling missing data and categorical features.

*Weaknesses*
> Tree-based methods are difficult to interpret, especially if many rules are needed to make a good prediction. Performance also becomes an issue as the number of features increase.

*Applications*
> Gradient boosting and random forests are excellent for prediction problems.

## Support Vector Machines

Instead of building trees to separate data, we can use algorithms to create hyperplanes in space that separate the data, guided by the labels that we have. The approach is known as *support vector machines (SVMs)*. SVMs allow some violations to this separation—not all the points within an area in hyperspace need to have the same label—

---

5 For more on gradient boosting in machine learning competitions, consult Ben Gorman's blog post (*http://bit.ly/2S1C8Qy*).

but the distance between boundary-defining points of a certain label and the boundary-defining points of another label should be maximized as much as possible. Also, the boundaries do not have to be linear—we can use nonlinear kernels to more flexibly separate the data.

## Neural Networks

We can learn representations of the data using neural networks, which are composed of an input layer, several hidden layers, and an output layer.[6] The input layer uses the features, and the output layer tries to match the response variable. The hidden layers are a nested hierarchy of concepts—each layer (or concept) is trying to understand how the previous layer relates to the output layer.

Using this hierarchy of concepts, the neural network is able to learn complicated concepts by building them out of simpler ones. Neural networks are one of the most powerful approaches to function approximation but are prone to overfitting and are hard to interpret, shortcomings that we will explore in greater detail later in the book.

# A Closer Look at Unsupervised Algorithms

We will now turn our attention to problems where we do not have labels. Instead of trying to make predictions, unsupervised learning algorithms will try to learn the underlying structure of the data.

## Dimensionality Reduction

One family of algorithms—known as *dimensionality reduction algorithms*—projects the original high-dimensional input data to a low-dimensional space, filtering out the not-so-relevant features and keeping as much of the interesting ones as possible. Dimensionality reduction allows unsupervised learning AI to more effectively identify patterns and more efficiently solve large-scale, computationally expensive problems (often involving images, video, speech, and text).

### Linear projection

There are two major branches of dimensionality—linear projection and nonlinear dimensionality reduction. We will start with linear projection first.

**Principal component analysis (PCA).** One approach to learning the underlying structure of data is to identify which features out of the full set of features are most important in explaining the variability among the instances in the data. Not all features are equal

---

6 For more on neutral networks, check out *Deep Learning* (*http://www.deeplearningbook.org/*) by Ian Goodfellow, Yoshua Bengio, and Aaron Courville (MIT Press).

—for some features, the values in the dataset do not vary much, and these features are less useful in explaining the dataset. For other features, the values might vary considerably—these features are worth exploring in greater detail since they will be better at helping the model we design separate the data.

In *PCA*, the algorithm finds a low-dimensional representation of the data while retaining as much of the variation as possible. The number of dimensions we are left with is considerably smaller than the number of dimensions of the full dataset (i.e., the number of total features). We lose some of the variance by moving to this low-dimensional space, but the underlying structure of the data is easier to identify, allowing us to perform tasks like clustering more efficiently.

There are several variants of PCA, which we will explore later in the book. These include mini-batch variants such as *incremental PCA*, nonlinear variants such as *kernel PCA*, and sparse variants such as *sparse PCA*.

**Singular value decomposition (SVD).** Another approach to learning the underlying structure of the data is to reduce the rank of the original matrix of features to a smaller rank such that the original matrix can be recreated using a linear combination of some of the vectors in the smaller rank matrix. This is known as *SVD*. To generate the smaller rank matrix, SVD keeps the vectors of the original matrix that have the most information (i.e., the highest singular value). The smaller rank matrix captures the most important elements of the original feature space.

**Random projection.** A similar dimensionality reduction algorithm involves projecting points from a high-dimensional space to a space of much lower dimensions in such a way that the scale of distances between the points is preserved. We can use either a *random Gaussian matrix* or a *random sparse matrix* to accomplish this.

## Manifold learning

Both PCA and random projection rely on projecting the data linearly from a high-dimensional space to a low-dimensional space. Instead of a linear projection, it may be better to perform a nonlinear transformation of the data—this is known as *manifold learning* or *nonlinear dimensionality reduction*.

**Isomap.** *Isomap* is one type of manifold learning approach. This algorithm learns the intrinsic geometry of the data manifold by estimating the *geodesic* or *curved distance* between each point and its neighbors rather than the Euclidean distance. Isomap uses this to then embed the original high-dimensional space to a low-dimensional one.

**t-distributed stochastic neighbor embedding (t-SNE).** Another nonlinear dimensionality reduction—known as *t-SNE*—embeds high-dimensional data into a space of just two or three dimensions, allowing the transformed data to be visualized. In this two- or three-dimensional space, similar instances are modeled closer together and dissimilar instances are modeled further away.

**Dictionary learning.**  An approach known as *dictionary learning* involves learning the representation of the underlying data. These representative elements are simple vectors, and each instance in the dataset is represented as the weight vector and can be reconstructed as a weighted sum of the representative elements. The representative elements that this unsupervised learning generates is called the *dictionary*.

By creating such a dictionary, this algorithm is able to efficiently identify the most salient representative elements of the original feature space—these are the ones that have the most nonzero weights. The representative elements that are less important will have few nonzero weights. As with PCA, dictionary learning is excellent for learning the underlying structure of the data, which will be helpful in separating the data and in identifying interesting patterns.

## Independent component analysis

One common problem with unlabeled data is that there are many independent signals embedded together into the features we are given. Using *independent component analysis (ICA)*, we can separate these blended signals into their individual components. After the separation is complete, we can reconstruct any of the original features by adding together some combination of the individual components we generate. ICA is commonly used in signal processing tasks (for example, to identify the individual voices in an audio clip of a busy coffeehouse).

## Latent Dirichlet allocation

Unsupervised learning can also explain a dataset by learning why some parts of the dataset are similar to each other. This requires learning unobserved elements within the dataset—an approach known as *latent Dirichlet allocation (LDA)*. For example, consider a document of text with many, many words. These words within a document are not purely random; rather, they exhibit some structure.

This structure can be modeled as unobserved elements known as topics. After training, LDA is able to explain a given document with a small set of topics, where for each topic there is a small set of frequently used words. This is the hidden structure the LDA is able to capture, helping us better explain a previously unstructured corpus of text.

Dimensionality reduction reduces the original set of features to a smaller set of just the most important features. From here, we can run other unsupervised learning algorithms on this smaller set of features to find interesting patterns in the data (see the next section on clustering), or, if we have labels, we can speed up the training cycle of supervised learning algorithms by feeding in this smaller matrix of features instead of using the original feature matrix.

# Clustering

Once we have reduced the set of original features to a smaller, more manageable set, we can find interesting patterns by grouping similar instances of data together. This is known as clustering and can be accomplished with a variety of unsupervised learning algorithms and be used for real-world applications such as market segmentation.

## k-means

To cluster well, we need to identify distinct groups such that the instances within a group are similar to each other but different from instances in other groups. One such algorithm is *k-means clustering*. With this algorithm, we specify the number of desired clusters $k$, and the algorithm will assign each instance to exactly one of these $k$ clusters. It optimizes the grouping by minimizing the *within-cluster variation* (also known as *inertia*) such that the sum of the within-cluster variations across all $k$ clusters is as small as possible.

To speed up this clustering process, $k$-means randomly assigns each observation to one of the $k$ clusters and then begins to reassign these observations to minimize the Euclidean distance between each observation and its cluster's center point, or *centroid*. As a result, different runs of $k$-means—each with a randomized start—will result in slightly different clustering assignments of the observations. From these different runs, we can choose the one that has the best separation, defined as the lowest total sum of within-cluster variations across all $k$ clusters.[7]

## Hierarchical clustering

An alternative clustering approach—one that does not require us to precommit to a particular number of clusters—is known as *hierarchical clustering*. One version of hierarchical clustering called *agglomerative clustering* uses a tree-based clustering method, and builds what is called a *dendrogram*. A dendrogram can be depicted graphically as an upside-down tree, where the leaves are at the bottom and the tree trunk is at the top.

---

7 There are faster variants of $k$-means clustering such as mini-batch $k$-means, which we cover later in the book.

The leaves at the very bottom are individual instances in the dataset. Hierarchical clustering then joins the leaves together—as we move vertically up the upside-down tree—based on how similar they are to each other. The instances (or groups of instances) that are most similar to each other are joined sooner, while the instances that are not as similar are joined later. With this iterative process, all the instances are eventually linked together forming the single trunk of the tree.

This vertical depiction is very helpful. Once the hierarchical clustering algorithm has finished running, we can view the dendrogram and determine where we want to cut the tree—the lower we cut, the more individual branches we are left with (i.e., more clusters). If we want fewer clusters, we can cut higher on the dendrogram, closer to the single trunk at the very top of this upside-down tree. The placement of this horizontal cut is similar to choosing the number of $k$ clusters in the $k$-means clustering algorithm.[8]

## DBSCAN

An even more powerful clustering algorithm (based on the density of points) is known as *DBSCAN* (density-based spatial clustering of applications with noise). Given all the instances we have in space, DBSCAN will group together those that are packed closely together, where close together is defined as a minimum number of instances that must exist within a certain distance. We specify both the minimum number of instances required and the distance.

If an instance is within this specified distance of multiple clusters, it will be grouped with the cluster to which it is most densely located. Any instance that is not within this specified distance of another cluster is labeled an outlier.

Unlike $k$-means, we do not need to prespecify the number of clusters. We can also have arbitrarily shaped clusters. DBSCAN is much less prone to the distortion typically caused by outliers in the data.

# Feature Extraction

With unsupervised learning, we can learn new representations of the original features of data—a field known as *feature extraction*. Feature extraction can be used to reduce the number of original features to a smaller subset, effectively performing dimensionality reduction. But feature extraction can also generate new feature representations to help improve performance on supervised learning problems.

---

8 Hierarchical clustering uses Euclidean distance by default, but it can also use other similarity metrics such as correlation-based distance, which we will explore in greater detail later in the book.

## Autoencoders

To generate new feature representations, we can use a feedforward, nonrecurrent neural network to perform representation learning, where the number of nodes in the output layer matches the number of nodes in the input layer. This neural network is known as an *autoencoder* and effectively reconstructs the original features, learning a new representation using the hidden layers in between.[9]

Each hidden layer of the autoencoder learns a representation of the original features, and subsequent layers build on the representation learned by the preceding layers. Layer by layer, the autoencoder learns increasingly complicated representations from simpler ones.

The output layer is the final newly learned representation of the original features. This learned representation can then be used as an input into a supervised learning model with the objective of improving the generalization error.

## Feature extraction using supervised training of feedforward networks

If we have labels, an alternate feature extraction approach is to use a feedforward, nonrecurrent neural network where the output layer attempts to predict the correct label. Just like with autoencoders, each hidden layer learns a representation of the original features.

However, when generating the new representations, this network is explicitly *guided by the labels*. To extract the final newly learned representation of the original features in this network, we extract the penultimate layer—the hidden layer just before the output layer. This penultimate layer can then be used as an input into any supervised learning model.

# Unsupervised Deep Learning

Unsupervised learning performs many important functions in the field of deep learning, some of which we will explore in this book. This field is known as *unsupervised deep learning*.

Until very recently, the training of deep neural networks was computationally intractable. In these neural networks, the hidden layers learn internal representations to help solve the problem at hand. The representations improve over time based on how the neural network uses the *gradient of the error function* in each training iteration to update the weights of the various nodes.

---

9 There are several types of autoencoders, and each learns a different set of representations. These include denoising autoencoders, sparse autoencoders, and variational autoencoders, all of which we will explore later in the book.

These updates are computationally expensive, and two major types of problems may occur in the process. First, the gradient of the error function may become very small, and, since *backpropagation* relies on multiplying these small weights together, the weights of the network may update very slowly or not at all, preventing proper training of the network.[10] This is known as the *vanishing gradient problem*.

Conversely, the other issue is that the gradient of the error function might become very large; with backprop, the weights throughout the network may update in huge increments, making the training of the network very unstable. This is known as the *exploding gradient problem*.

## Unsupervised pretraining

To address these difficulties in training very deep, multilayered neural networks, machine learning researchers train neural networks in multiple, successive stages, where each stage involves a shallow neural network. The output of one shallow network is then used as the input of the next neural network. Typically, the first shallow neural network in this pipeline involves an unsupervised neural network, but the later networks are supervised.

This unsupervised portion is known as *greedy layer-wise unsupervised pretraining*. In 2006, Geoffrey Hinton demonstrated the successful application of unsupervised pretraining to initialize the training of deeper neural network pipelines, kicking off the current deep learning revolution. Unsupervised pretaining allows the AI to capture an improved representation of the original input data, which the supervised portion then takes advantage of to solve the specific task at hand.

This approach is called "greedy" because each portion of the neural network is trained independently, not jointly. "Layer-wise" refers to the layers of the network. In most modern neural networks, pretraining is usually not necessary. Instead, all the layers are trained jointly using backpropagation. Major computer advances have made the vanishing gradient problem and the exploding gradient problem much more manageable.

Unsupervised pretraining not only makes supervised problems easier to solve but also facilitates *transfer learning*. Transfer learning involves using machine learning algorithms to store knowledge gained from solving one task to solve another related task much more quickly and with considerably less data.

---

10 Backpropagation (also known as *backward propagation of errors*) is a gradient descent-based algorithm used by neural networks to update weights. In backprop, the weights of the final layer are calculated first and then used to update the weights of the preceding layers. This process continues until the weights of the very first layer are updated.

## Restricted Boltzmann machines

One applied example of unsupervised pretraining is the *restricted Boltzmann machine (RBM)*, a shallow, two-layer neural network. The first layer is the input layer, and the second layer is the hidden layer. Each node is connected to every node in the other layer, but nodes are not connected to nodes of the same layer—this is where the restriction occurs.

RBMs can perform unsupervised tasks such as dimensionality reduction and feature extraction and provide helpful unsupervised pretraining as part of supervised learning solutions. RBMs are similar to autoencoders but differ in some important ways. For example, autoencoders have an output layer, while RBMs do not. We will explore these and other differences in detail later in the book.

## Deep belief networks

RBMs can be linked together to form a multistage neural network pipeline known as a *deep belief network (DBN)*. The hidden layer of each RBM is used as the input for the next RBM. In other words, each RBM generates a representation of the data that the next RBM then builds upon. By successively linking this type of representation learning, the deep belief network is able to learn more complicated representations that are often used as *feature detectors*.[11]

## Generative adversarial networks

One major advance in unsupervised deep learning has been the advent of *generative adversarial networks (GANs)*, introduced by Ian Goodfellow and his fellow researchers at the University of Montreal in 2014. GANs have many applications; for example, we can use GANs to create near-realistic synthetic data, such as images and speech, or perform anomaly detection.

In GANs, we have two neural networks. One network—known as the generator—generates data based on a model data distribution it has created using samples of real data it has received. The other network—known as the discriminator—discriminates between the data created by the generator and data from the true data distribution.

As a simple analogy, the generator is the counterfeiter, and the discriminator is the police trying to identify the forgery. The two networks are locked in a zero-sum game. The generator is trying to fool the discriminator into thinking the synthetic data comes from the true data distribution, and the discriminator is trying to call out the synthetic data as fake.

---

11 Feature detectors learn good representations of the original data, helping separate distinct elements. For example, in images, feature detectors help separate elements such as noses, eyes, mouths, etc.

---

GANs are unsupervised learning algorithms because the generator can learn the underlying structure of the true data distribution even when there are no labels. GANs learn the underlying structure in the data through the training process and efficiently capture the structure using a small, manageable number of parameters.

This process is similar to the representation learning that occurs in deep learning. Each hidden layer in the neutral network of a generator captures a representation of the underlying data—starting very simply—and subsequent layers pick up more complicated representations by building on the simpler preceding layers.

Using all these layers together, the generator learns the underlying structure of the data and, using what it has learned, the generator attempts to create synthetic data that is nearly identical to the true data distribution. If the generator has captured the essence of the true data distribution, the synthetic data will appear real.

## Sequential Data Problems Using Unsupervised Learning

Unsupervised learning can also handle sequential data such as time series data. One such approach involves learning the hidden states of a *Markov model*. In the *simple Markov model*, states are fully observed and change stochastically (in other words, randomly). Future states depend only on the current state and are not dependent on previous states.

In a *hidden Markov model*, the states are only partially observable, but, like with simple Markov models, the outputs of these partially observable states are fully observable. Since the observations that we have are insufficient to determine the state completely, we need unsupervised learning to help discover these hidden states more fully.

Hidden Markov model algorithms involve learning the probable next state given what we know about the sequence of previously occurring, partially observable states and fully observable outputs. These algorithms have had major commercial applications in sequential data problems involving speech, text, and time series.

# Reinforcement Learning Using Unsupervised Learning

Reinforcement learning is the third major branch of machine learning, in which an *agent* determines its optimal behavior (*actions*) in an *environment* based on feedback (*reward*) that it receives. This feedback is known as the *reinforcement signal*. The agent's goal is to maximize its cumulative reward over time.

While reinforcement learning has been around since the 1950s, it has made mainstream headline news only in recent years. In 2013, DeepMind—now owned by Google—applied reinforcement learning to achieve superhuman-level performance at playing many different Atari games. DeepMind's system achieved this with just raw sensory data as input and no prior knowledge of the rules of the games.

In 2016, DeepMind again captured the imagination of the machine learning community—this time the DeepMind reinforcement learning-based AI agent AlphaGo beat Lee Sedol, one of the world's best Go players. These successes have cemented reinforcement learning as a mainstream AI topic.

Today, machine learning researchers are applying reinforcement learning to solve many different types of problems including:

- Stock market trading, in which the agent buys and sells (actions) and receives profits or losses (rewards) in return
- Video games and board games, in which the agent makes game decisions (actions) and wins or loses (rewards)
- Self-driving cars, in which the agent directs the vehicle (actions) and either stays on course or crashes (rewards)
- Machine control, in which the agent moves about its environment (actions) and either completes the course or fails (rewards)

In the simplest reinforcement learning problems, we have a finite problem—with a finite number of states of the environment, a finite number of actions that are possible at any given state of the environment, and a finite number of rewards. The action taken by the agent given the current state of the environment determines the next state, and the agent's goal is to maximize its long-term reward. This family of problems is known as finite *Markov decision processes.*

However, in the real world, things are not so simple—the reward is unknown and dynamic rather than known and static. To help discover this unknown reward function and approximate it as best as possible, we can apply unsupervised learning. Using this approximated reward function, we can apply reinforcement learning solutions to increase the cumulative reward over time.

# Semisupervised Learning

Even though supervised learning and unsupervised learning are two distinct major branches of machine learning, the algorithms from each branch can be mixed together as part of a machine learning pipeline.[12] Typically, this mix of supervised and unsupervised is used when we want to take full advantage of the few labels that we have or when we want to find new, yet unknown patterns from unlabeled data in

---

[12] Pipeline refers to a system of machine learning solutions that are applied in succession to achieve a larger objective.

addition to the known patterns from the labeled data. These types of problems are solved using a hybrid of supervised and unsupervised learning known as semisupervised learning. We will explore this area in greater detail later in the book.

# Successful Applications of Unsupervised Learning

In the last ten years, most successful commercial applications of machine learning have come from the supervised learning space, but this is changing. Unsupervised learning applications have become more commonplace. Sometimes, unsupervised learning is just a means to make supervised applications better. Other times, unsupervised learning achieves the commercial application itself. Here is a closer look at two of the biggest applications of unsupervised learning to date: anomaly detection and group segmentation.

## Anomaly Detection

Performing dimensionality reduction can reduce the original high-dimensional feature space into a transformed lower-dimensional space. In this lower-dimensional space, we find where the majority of points densely lie. This portion is the *normal space*. Points that lie much farther away are called *outliers*—or *anomalies*—and are worth investigating in greater detail.

Anomaly detection systems are commonly used for fraud detection such as credit card fraud, wire fraud, cyber fraud, and insurance fraud. Anomaly detection is also used to identify rare, malicious events such as hacking of internet-connected devices, maintenance failures in mission-critical equipment such as airplanes and trains, and cybersecurity breaches due to malware and other pernicious agents.

We can use these systems for spam detection, such as the email spam filter example we used earlier in the chapter. Other applications include finding bad actors to stop activity such as terrorist financing, money laundering, human and narcotics trafficking, and arms dealing, identifying high risk events in financial trading, and discovering diseases such as cancer.

To make the analysis of anomalies more manageable, we can use a clustering algorithm to group similar anomalies together and then hand-label these clusters based on the types of behavior they represent. With such a system, we can have an unsupervised learning AI that is able to identify anomalies, cluster them into appropriate groups, and, using the cluster labels provided by humans, recommend to business analysts the appropriate course of action.

With anomaly detection systems, we can take an unsupervised problem and eventually create a semisupervised one with this cluster-and-label approach. Over time, we can run supervised algorithms on the labeled data alongside the unsupervised algorithms. For successful machine learning applications, unsupervised systems and supervised systems should be used in conjunction, complementing one another.

The supervised system finds the known patterns with a high level of accuracy, while the unsupervised system discovers new patterns that may be of interest. Once these patterns are uncovered by the unsupervised AI, the patterns are labeled by humans, transitioning more of the data from unlabeled to labeled.

### Group segmentation

With clustering, we can segment groups based on similarity in behavior in areas such as marketing, customer retention, disease diagnosis, online shopping, music listening, video watching, online dating, social media activity, and document classification. The amount of data that is generated in each of these areas is massive, and the data is only partially labeled.

For patterns that we already know and want to reinforce, we can use supervised learning algorithms. But often we want to discover new patterns and groups of interest—for this discovery process, unsupervised learning is a natural fit. Again, it is all about synergy. We should use supervised and unsupervised learning systems in conjunction to build a stronger machine learning solution.

# Conclusion

In this chapter, we explored the following:

- The difference between a rules-based system and machine learning
- The difference between supervised and unsupervised learning
- How unsupervised learning can help address common problems in training machine learning models
- Common algorithms for supervised, unsupervised, reinforcement, and semisupervised learning
- Two major applications of unsupervised learning—anomaly detection and group segmentation

In Chapter 2, we'll explore how to build machine learning applications. Then, we will cover dimensionality reduction and clustering in detail, building an anomaly detection system and a group segmentation system in the process.

# End-to-End Machine Learning Project

Before we begin exploring unsupervised learning algorithms in detail, we will review how to set up and manage machine learning projects, covering everything from acquiring data to building and evaluating a model and implementing a solution. We will work with supervised learning models in this chapter—an area most readers should have some experience in—before jumping into unsupervised learning models in the next chapter.

## Environment Setup

Let's set up the data science environment before going further. This environment is the same for both supervised and unsupervised learning.

 These instructions are optimized for the Windows operating system but installation packages are available for Mac and Linux, too.

## Version Control: Git

If you have not already, you will need to install Git (*https://git-scm.com/*). Git is a version control system for code, and all the coding examples in this book are available as Jupyter notebooks from the GitHub repository (*http://bit.ly/2Gd4v7e*). Review Roger Dudler's Git guide (*http://rogerdudler.github.io/git-guide/*) to learn how to clone repositories; add, commit, and push changes; and maintain version control with branches.

## Clone the Hands-On Unsupervised Learning Git Repository

Open the command-line interface (i.e., command prompt on Windows, terminal on Mac, etc.). Navigate to the directory where you will store your unsupervised learning projects. Use the following prompt to clone the repository associated with this book from GitHub:

```
$ git clone https://github.com/aapatel09/handson-unsupervised-learning.git
$ pip install git-lfs
$ git lfs install
$ git lfs pull
```

Alternatively, you can visit the repository (*http://bit.ly/2Gd4v7e*) on the GitHub website and manually download the repository for your use. You can *watch* or *star* the repository to stay updated on changes.

Once the repository has been pulled or manually downloaded, use the command-line interface to navigate into the *handson-unsupervised-learning* repository.

```
$ cd handson-unsupervised-learning
```

For the rest of the installations, we will continue to use the command-line interface.

## Scientific Libraries: Anaconda Distribution of Python

To install Python and the scientific libraries necessary for machine learning, download the Anaconda distribution (*https://www.anaconda.com/download/*) of Python (version 3.6 is recommended because version 3.7 is relatively new as of the writing of this book and not supported by all the machine libraries we will use).

Create an isolated Python environment so that you can import different libraries for each project separately:

```
$ conda create -n unsupervisedLearning python=3.6 anaconda
```

This creates an isolated Python 3.6 environment—with all of the scientific libraries that come with the Anaconda distribution—called unsupervisedLearning.

Now, activate this for use:

```
$ conda activate unsupervisedLearning
```

## Neural Networks: TensorFlow and Keras

Once unsupervisedLearning is activated, you will need to install TensorFlow and Keras to build neutral networks. TensorFlow is an open source project by Google and is not part of the Anaconda distribution:

```
$ pip install tensorflow
```

Keras is an open source netural network library that offers a higher-level API for us to use the lower-level functions in TensorFlow. In other words, we will use Keras on top of TensorFlow (the backend) to have a more intuitive set of API calls to develop our deep learning models:

```
$ pip install keras
```

## Gradient Boosting, Version One: XGBoost

Next, install one version of gradient boosting known as XGBoost. To make this simple (for Windows users, at least), you can navigate into the *xgboost* folder in the *handson-unsupervised-learning* repository and find the package there.

To install the package, use `pip install`:

```
cd xgboost
pip install xgboost-0.6+20171121-cp36-cp36m-win_amd64.whl
```

Alternatively, download the correct version of XGBoost (*http://bit.ly/2G1jBxs*) based on your system—either the 32-bit or the 64-bit version.

In the command-line interface, navigate to the folder with this newly downloaded file. Use `pip install`:

```
$ pip install xgboost-0.6+20171121-cp36-cp36m-win_amd64.whl
```

Your XGBoost WHL filename may be slightly different as newer versions of the software are released publicly.

Once XGBoost has been successfully installed, navigate back to the *handson-unsupervised-learning* folder.

## Gradient Boosting, Version Two: LightGBM

Install another version of gradient boosting, Microsoft's LightGBM:

```
$ pip install lightgbm
```

## Clustering Algorithms

Let's install a few clustering algorithms we will use later in the book. One clustering package, *fastcluster*, is a C++ library with an interface in Python/SciPy.[1]

---

1 For more on fastcluster, consult the documentation (*https://pypi.org/project/fastcluster/*).

This fastcluster package can be installed with the following command:

```
$ pip install fastcluster
```

Another clustering algorithm is *hdbscan*, which can also be installed via pip:

```
$ pip install hdbscan
```

And, for time series clustering, let's install *tslearn*:

```
$ pip install tslearn
```

## Interactive Computing Environment: Jupyter Notebook

Jupyter notebook is part of the Anaconda distribution, so we will now activate it to launch the environment we just set up. Make sure you are in the *handson-unsupervised-learning* repository before you enter the following command (for ease of use):

```
$ jupyter notebook
```

You should see your browser open up and launch the *http://localhost:8888/* page. Cookies must be enabled for proper access.

We are now ready to build our first machine learning project.

 On Mac, you may need to install libomp before running $ jupyter notebook. Use the following command to install libomp:

```
$ brew install libomp
```

# Overview of the Data

In this chapter, we will use a real dataset of anonymized credit card transactions made by European cardholders from September 2013.[2] These transactions are labeled as fraudulent or genuine, and we will build a fraud detection solution using machine learning to predict the correct labels for never-before-seen instances.

This dataset is highly imbalanced. Of the 284,807 transactions, only 492 are fraudulent (0.172%). This low percentage of fraud is pretty typical for credit card transactions.

---

2 This dataset is available via Kaggle (*https://www.kaggle.com/dalpozz/creditcardfraud*) and was collected during a research collaboration by Worldline and the Machine Learning Group of Universite Libre de Bruxelles. For more information, see Andrea Dal Pozzolo, Olivier Caelen, Reid A. Johnson and Gianluca Bontempi, "Calibrating Probability with Undersampling for Unbalanced Classification" in Symposium on Computational Intelligence and Data Mining (CIDM), IEEE, 2015.

There are 28 features, all of which are numerical, and there are no categorical variables.[3] These features are not the original features but rather the output of principal component analysis, which we will explore in Chapter 3. The original features were distilled to 28 principal components using this form of dimensionality reduction.

In addition to the 28 principal components, we have three other variables—the time of the transaction, the amount of the transaction, and the true class of the transaction (one if fraud, zero if genuine).

# Data Preparation

Before we can use machine learning to train on the data and develop a fraud detection solution, we need to prepare the data for the algorithms.

## Data Acquisition

The first step in any machine learning project is data acquisition.

### Download the data

Download the dataset and, within the *handson-unsupervised-learning* directory, place the CSV file in a folder called */datasets/credit_card_data/*. If you downloaded the GitHub repository earlier, you already have this file in this folder in the repository.

### Import the necessary libraries

Import the Python libraries that we will need to build our fraud detection solution:

```
'''Main'''
import numpy as np
import pandas as pd
import os

'''Data Viz'''
import matplotlib.pyplot as plt
import seaborn as sns
color = sns.color_palette()
import matplotlib as mpl

%matplotlib inline

'''Data Prep'''
from sklearn import preprocessing as pp
from scipy.stats import pearsonr
```

---

3 Categorical variables take on one of a limited number of possible qualitative values and often have to be encoded for use in machine learning algorithms.

```
from sklearn.model_selection import train_test_split
from sklearn.model_selection import StratifiedKFold
from sklearn.metrics import log_loss
from sklearn.metrics import precision_recall_curve, average_precision_score
from sklearn.metrics import roc_curve, auc, roc_auc_score
from sklearn.metrics import confusion_matrix, classification_report

'''Algos'''
from sklearn.linear_model import LogisticRegression
from sklearn.ensemble import RandomForestClassifier
import xgboost as xgb
import lightgbm as lgb
```

### Read the data

```
current_path = os.getcwd()
file = file = os.path.sep.join(['', 'datasets', 'credit_card_data', 'credit_card.csv'])
data = pd.read_csv(current_path + file)
```

### Preview the data

Table 2-1 shows the first five rows of the dataset. As you can see, the data has been properly loaded:

```
data.head()
```

*Table 2-1. Preview of the data*

|   | Time | V1 | V2 | V3 | V4 | V5 |
|---|------|------|------|------|------|------|
| 0 | 0.0 | −1.359807 | −0.072781 | 2.536347 | 1.378155 | −0.338321 |
| 1 | 0.0 | 1.191857 | 0.266151 | 0.166480 | 0.448154 | 0.060018 |
| 2 | 1.0 | −1.358354 | −1.340163 | 1.773209 | 0.379780 | −0.503198 |
| 3 | 1.0 | −0.966272 | −0.185226 | 1.792993 | −0.863291 | −0.010309 |
| 4 | 2.0 | −1.158233 | 0.877737 | 1.548718 | 0.403034 | −0.407193 |

5 rows x 31 columns

# Data Exploration

Next, let's get a deeper understanding of the data. We will generate summary statistics for the data, identify any missing values or categorical features, and count the number of distinct values by feature.

### Generate summary statistics

Table 2-2 describes the data, column by column. The block of code that follows lists all the column names for easy reference.

```
data.describe()
```

*Table 2-2. Simple summary statistics*

| | Time | V1 | V2 | V3 | V4 |
|---|---|---|---|---|---|
| count | 284807.000000 | 2.848070e+05 | 2.848070e+05 | 2.848070e+05 | 2.848070e+05 |
| mean | 94813.859575 | 3.919560e−15 | 5.688174e−16 | −8.769071e−15 | 2.782312e−15 |
| std | 47488.145955 | 1.958696e+00 | 1.651309e+00 | 1.516255e+00 | 1.415869e+00 |
| min | 0.000000 | −5.640751e+01 | −7.271573e+01 | −4.832559e+01 | −5.683171e+00 |
| 25% | 54201.500000 | −9.203734e−01 | −5.985499e−01 | −8.903648e−01 | −8.486401e−01 |
| 50% | 84692.000000 | 1.810880e−02 | 6.548556e−02 | 1.798463e−01 | −1.984653e−02 |
| 75% | 139320.500000 | 1.315642e+00 | 8.037239e−01 | 1.027196e+00 | 7.433413e−01 |
| max | 172792.000000 | 2.454930e+00 | 2.205773e+01 | 9.382558e+00 | 1.687534e+01 |

8 rows x 31 columns

```
data.columns

Index(['Time', 'V1,' 'V2', 'V3', 'V4', 'V5', 'V6', 'V7', 'V8', 'V9', 'V10',
'V11', 'V12', 'V13', 'V14', 'V15', 'V16', 'V17', 'V18', 'V19', 'V20', 'V21',
'V22', 'V23', 'V24', 'V25', 'V26', 'V27', 'V28', 'Amount', 'Class'],
dtype='object')

data['Class'].sum()
```

The total number of positive labels, or fraudulent transactions, is 492. There are 284,807 instances and 31 columns as expected—28 numerical features (V1 through V28), Time, Amount, and Class.

The timestamps range from 0 to 172,792, the amounts range from 0 to 25,691.16, and there are 492 fraudulent transactions. These fraudulent transactions are also referred to as positive cases or positive labels (labeled as one); the normal transactions are negative cases or negative labels (labeled as zero).

The 28 numerical features are not standardized yet, but we will standardize the data soon. *Standardization* rescales the data to have a mean of zero and standard deviation of one.

Some machine learning solutions are very sensitive to the scale of the data, so having all the data on the same relative scale—via standardization—is a good machine learning practice.

Another common method to scale data is *normalization*, which rescales the data to a zero to one range. Unlike the standardized data, all the normalized data is on a positive scale.

### Identify nonnumerical values by feature

Some machine learning algorithms cannot handle nonnumerical values or missing values. Therefore, it is best practice to identify nonnumerical values (also known as *not a number*, or *NaNs*).

In the case of missing values, we can impute the value—for example, by replacing the missing points with the mean, median, or mode of the feature—or substitute with some user-defined value. In the case of categorical values, we can encode the data such that all the categorical values are represented with a sparse matrix. This sparse matrix is then combined with the numerical features. The machine learning algorithm trains on this combined feature set.

The following code shows that none of the observations have NaNs, so we will not need to impute or encode any of the values:

```
nanCounter = np.isnan(data).sum()

Time      0
V1        0
V2        0
V3        0
V4        0
V5        0
V6        0
V7        0
V8        0
V9        0
V10       0
V11       0
V12       0
V13       0
V14       0
V15       0
V16       0
V17       0
V18       0
V19       0
V20       0
V21       0
V22       0
V23       0
V24       0
V25       0
V26       0
V27       0
V28       0
Amount    0
Class     0
dtype:    int64
```

### Identify distinct values by feature

To develop a better understanding of the credit card transactions dataset, let's count the number of distinct values by feature.

The following code shows that we have 124,592 distinct timestamps. But we know from earlier that we have 284,807 observations in total. That means that there are multiple transactions at some timestamps.

And, as expected, there are just two classes—one for fraud, zero for not fraud:

```
distinctCounter = data.apply(lambda x: len(x.unique()))
```

```
Time    124592
V1      275663
V2      275663
V3      275663
V4      275663
V5      275663
V6      275663
V7      275663
V8      275663
V9      275663
V10     275663
V11     275663
V12     275663
V13     275663
V14     275663
V15     275663
V16     275663
V17     275663
V18     275663
V19     275663
V20     275663
V21     275663
V22     275663
V23     275663
V24     275663
V25     275663
V26     275663
V27     275663
V28     275663
Amount  32767
Class   2
dtype:  int64
```

# Generate Feature Matrix and Labels Array

Let's create and standardize the feature matrix X and isolate the labels array y (one for fraud, zero for not fraud). Later on we will feed these into the machine learning algorithms during training.

### Create the feature matrix X and the labels array Y

```
dataX = data.copy().drop(['Class'],axis=1)
dataY = data['Class'].copy()
```

### Standardize the feature matrix X

Let's rescale the feature matrix so that each feature, except for time, has a mean of zero and standard deviation of one:

```
featuresToScale = dataX.drop(['Time'],axis=1).columns
sX = pp.StandardScaler(copy=True)
dataX.loc[:,featuresToScale] = sX.fit_transform(dataX[featuresToScale])
```

As shown in Table 2-3, the standardized features now have a mean of zero and a standard deviation of one.

*Table 2-3. Summary of scaled features*

|  | Time | V1 | V2 | V3 | V4 |
|---|---|---|---|---|---|
| count | 284807.000000 | 2.848070e+05 | 2.848070e+05 | 2.848070e+05 | 2.848070e+05 |
| mean | 94813.859575 | −8.157366e−16 | 3.154853e−17 | −4.409878e−15 | −6.734811e−16 |
| std | 47488.145955 | 1.000002e+00 | 1.000002e+00 | 1.000002e+00 | 1.000002e+00 |
| min | 0.000000 | −2.879855e+01 | −4.403529e+01 | −3.187173e+01 | −4.013919e+00 |
| 25% | 54201.500000 | −4.698918e−01 | −3.624707e−01 | −5.872142e−01 | −5.993788e−01 |
| 50% | 84692.000000 | 9.245351e−03 | 3.965683e−02 | 1.186124e−02 | −1.401724e−01 |
| 75% | 139320.500000 | 6.716939e−01 | 4.867202e−01 | 6.774569e−01 | 5.250082e−01 |
| max | 172792.000000 | 1.253351e+00 | 1.335775e+01 | 6.187993e+00 | 1.191874e+01 |

8 rows x 30 columns

## Feature Engineering and Feature Selection

In most machine learning projects, we should consider *feature engineering* and *feature selection* as part of the solution. Feature engineering involves creating new features—for example, calculating ratios or counts or sums from the original features—to help the machine learning algorithm extract a stronger signal from the dataset.

Feature selection involves selecting a subset of the features for training, effectively removing some of the less relevant features from consideration. This may help prevent the machine learning algorithm from overfitting to the noise in the dataset.

For this credit card fraud dataset, we do not have the original features. We have only the principal components, which were derived from PCA, a form of dimensionality reduction that we will explore in Chapter 3. Since we do not know what any of the features represent, we cannot perform any intelligent feature engineering.

Feature selection is not necessary either since the number of observations (284,807) vastly outnumbers the number of features (30), which dramatically reduces the chances of overfitting. And, as Figure 2-1 shows, the features are only slightly correlated to each other. In other words, we do not have redundant features. If we did, we could remove or reduce the redundancy via dimensionality reduction. Of course, this is not a surprise. PCA was already performed on this credit card dataset, removing the redundancy for us.

## Check correlation of features

```
correlationMatrix = pd.DataFrame(data=[],index=dataX.columns,
columns=dataX.columns)
for i in dataX.columns:
    for j in dataX.columns:
        correlationMatrix.loc[i,j] = np.round(pearsonr(dataX.loc[:,i],
            dataX.loc[:,j])[0],2)
```

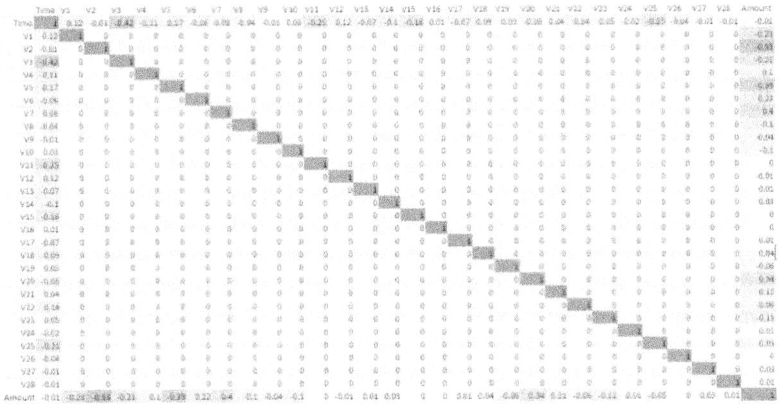

*Figure 2-1. Correlation matrix*

# Data Visualization

As a final step, let's visualize the data to appreciate just how imbalanced the dataset is (Figure 2-2). Since there are so few cases of fraud to learn from, this is a difficult problem to solve; fortunately, we have labels for the entire dataset:

```
count_classes = pd.value_counts(data['Class'],sort=True).sort_index()
ax = sns.barplot(x=count_classes.index, y=[tuple(count_classes/len(data))[0], \
                tuple(count_classes/l...
ax.set_title('Frequency Percentage by Class')
ax.set_xlabel('Class')
ax.set_ylabel('Frequency Percentage')
```

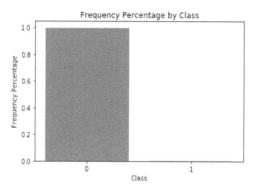

*Figure 2-2. Frequency percentage of labels*

# Model Preparation

Now that the data is ready, let's prepare for the model. We need to split the data into a training and a test set, select a cost function, and prepare for *k*-fold cross-validation.

## Split into Training and Test Sets

As you may recall from Chapter 1, machine learning algorithms learn from data (i.e., train on the data) to have good performance (i.e., accurately predict) on never-before-seen cases. The performance on these never-before-seen cases is known as the generalization error—this is the most important metric in determining the goodness of a machine learning model.

We need to set up our machine learning project so that we have a training set from which the machine learning algorithm learns. We also need a test set (the never-before-seen cases) the machine learning algorithm can make predictions on. The performance on this test set will be the ultimate gauge of success.

Let's go ahead and split our credit card transactions dataset into a training set and a test set.

```
X_train, X_test, y_train, y_test = train_test_split(dataX,
                           dataY, test_size=0.33,
                           random_state=2018, stratify=dataY)
```

We now have a training set with 190,280 instances (67% of the original dataset) and a test set with 93,987 instances (the remaining 33%). To preserve the percentage of fraud (~0.17%) for both the training and the test set, we have set the stratify parameter. We also fixed the random state to 2018 to make it easier to reproduce results.[4]

We will use the test set for a final evaluation of our generalization error (also known as out-of-sample error).

## Select Cost Function

Before we train on the training set, we need a cost function (also referred to as the error rate or value function) to pass into the machine learning algorithm. The machine learning algorithm will try to minimize this cost function by learning from the training examples.

Since this is a supervised classification problem—with two classes—let's use *binary classification log loss* (as shown in Equation 2-1), which will calculate the cross-entropy between the true labels and the model-based predictions.

*Equation 2-1. Log loss function*

$$\text{log loss} = -\frac{1}{N} \sum_{i=1}^{N} \sum_{j=1}^{M} y_{i,j} \log(p_{i,j})$$

Where $N$ is the number of observations; $M$ is the number of class labels (in this case, two); log is the natural logarithm; $y_{i,j}$ is 1 if observation $i$ is in class $j$ and 0 otherwise; and $p_{i,j}$ is the predicted probability that observation $i$ is in class $j$.

The machine learning model will generate the fraud probability for each credit card transaction. The closer the fraud probabilities are to the true labels (i.e., one for fraud or zero for not fraud), the lower the value of the log loss function. This is what the machine learning algorithm will try to minimize.

## Create k-Fold Cross-Validation Sets

To help the machine learning algorithm estimate what its performance will be on the never-before-seen examples (the test set), it is best practice to further split the training set into a training set and a validation set.

For example, if we split the training set into fifths, we can train on four-fifths of the original training set and evaluate the newly training model by making predictions on the fifth slice of the original training set, known as the validation set.

---

4 For more on how the stratify parameter preserves the ratio of positive labels, visit the official website (*http://bit.ly/2NiKWfi*). To reproduce the same split in your experiments, set the random state to 2018. If you set this to another number or don't set it at all, the results will be different.

It is possible to train and evaluate like this five times—leaving aside a different fifth slice as the validation set each time. This is known as *k-fold cross-validation*, where *k* in this case is five. With this approach, we will have not one estimate but five estimates for the generalization error.

We will store the training score and the cross-validation score for each of the five runs, and we will store the cross-validation predictions each time. After all five runs are complete, we will have cross-validation predictions for the entire dataset. This will be the best all-in estimate of the performance the test set.

Here's how to set up for the *k*-fold validation, where *k* is five:

```
k_fold = StratifiedKFold(n_splits=5, shuffle=True, random_state=2018)
```

# Machine Learning Models (Part I)

Now we're ready to build the machine learning models. For each machine algorithm we consider, we will set hyperparameters, train the model, and evaluate the results.

## Model #1: Logistic Regression

Let's start with the most basic classification algorithm, logistic regression.

### Set hyperparameters

```
penalty = 'l2'
C = 1.0
class_weight = 'balanced'
random_state = 2018
solver = 'liblinear'

logReg = LogisticRegression(penalty=penalty, C=C,
            class_weight=class_weight, random_state=random_state,
                        solver=solver, n_jobs=n_jobs)
```

We will set the penalty to the default value L2 instead of L1. Compared to L1, L2 is less sensitive to outliers and will assign nonzero weights to nearly all the features, resulting in a stable solution. L1 will assign high weights to the most important features and near-zero weights to the rest, essentially performing feature selection as the algorithm trains. However, because the weights vary so much feature to feature, the L1 solution is not as stable to changes in data points as the L2 solution.[5]

C is the regularization strength. As you may recall from Chapter 1, regularization helps address overfitting by penalizing complexity. In other words, the stronger the

---

5 For more on L1 versus L2, refer to the blog post "Differences Between L1 and L2 as Loss Function and Regularization." (*http://bit.ly/2Bcx413*)

regularization, the greater the penalty the machine learning algorithm applies to complexity. Regularization nudges the machine learning algorithm to prefer simpler models to more complex ones, all else equal.

This regularization constant, C, must be a positive floating number. The smaller the value, the stronger the regularization. We will keep the default 1.0.

Our credit card transactions dataset is very imbalanced—out of all the 284,807 cases, only 492 are fraudulent. As the machine learning algorithm trains, we want the algorithm to focus more attention on learning from the positive labeled transactions—in other words, the fraudulent transactions—because there are so few of them in the dataset.

For this logistic regression model, we will set the `class_weight` to balanced. This signals to the logistic regression algorithm that we have an imbalanced class problem; the algorithm will need to weigh the positive labels more heavily as it trains. In this case, the weights will be inversely proportional to the class frequencies; the algorithm will assign higher weights to the rare positive labels (i.e., fraud) and lower weights to the more frequent negative labels (i.e., not fraud).

The random state is fixed to 2018 to help others—such as you, the reader—reproduce results. We will keep the default solver liblinear.

## Train the model

Now that the hyperparameters are set, we will train the logistic regression model on each of the five $k$-fold cross-validation splits, training on four-fifths of the training set and evaualting the performance on the fifth slice that is held aside.

As we train and evaluate like this five times, we will calculate the cost function—log loss for our credit card transactions problem—for the training (i.e., the four-fifths slice of the original training set) and for the validation (i.e., the one-fifth slice of the original training set). We will also store the predictions for each of the five cross-validation sets; by the end of the fifth run, we will have predictions for the entire training set:

```
trainingScores = []
cvScores = []
predictionsBasedOnKFolds = pd.DataFrame(data=[],
                                index=y_train.index,columns=[0,1])

model = logReg

for train_index, cv_index in k_fold.split(np.zeros(len(X_train))
                                ,y_train.ravel()):
    X_train_fold, X_cv_fold = X_train.iloc[train_index,:], \
        X_train.iloc[cv_index,:]
    y_train_fold, y_cv_fold = y_train.iloc[train_index], \
```

```
        y_train.iloc[cv_index]

    model.fit(X_train_fold, y_train_fold)
    loglossTraining = log_loss(y_train_fold,
                        model.predict_proba(X_train_fold)[:,1])
    trainingScores.append(loglossTraining)

    predictionsBasedOnKFolds.loc[X_cv_fold.index,:] = \
        model.predict_proba(X_cv_fold)
    loglossCV = log_loss(y_cv_fold,
                    predictionsBasedOnKFolds.loc[X_cv_fold.index,1])
    cvScores.append(loglossCV)

    print('Training Log Loss: ', loglossTraining)
    print('CV Log Loss: ', loglossCV)

loglossLogisticRegression = log_loss(y_train,
                        predictionsBasedOnKFolds.loc[:,1])
print('Logistic Regression Log Loss: ', loglossLogisticRegression)
```

### Evaluate the results

The training log loss and cross-validation log loss are shown for each of the five runs in the following code. Generally (but not always) the training log loss will be lower than the cross-validation log loss. Because the machine learning algorithm has learned directly from the training data, its performance (i.e., log loss) should be better on the training set than on the cross-validation set. Remember, the cross-validation set has the transactions that were explicitly held out from the training exercise.

```
Training Log Loss:      0.10080139188958696
CV Log Loss:            0.10490645274118293
Training Log Loss:      0.12098957040484648
CV Log Loss:            0.11634801169793386
Training Log Loss:      0.1074616029843435
CV Log Loss:            0.10845630232487576
Training Log Loss:      0.10228137039781758
CV Log Loss:            0.10321736161148198
Training Log Loss:      0.11476012373315266
CV Log Loss:            0.1160124452312548
```

For our credit card transactions dataset, it is important to keep in mind that we are building a fraud detection solution. When we refer to the *performance* of the machine learning model, we mean how good the model is at predicting fraud among the transactions in the dataset.

The machine learning model outputs a prediction probability for each transaction, where one is fraud and zero is not fraud. The closer the probability is to one, the more likely the transaction is fraudulent; the closer the probability is to zero, the more likely the transaction is normal. By comparing the model's probabilities with the true labels, we can assess the goodness of the model.

For each of the five runs, their training and cross-validation log losses are similar. The logistic regression model does not exhibit severe overfitting; if it did, we would have a low training log loss and comparably high cross-validation log loss.

Since we stored the predictions for each of the five cross-validation sets, we can combine the predictions into a single set. This single set is the same as the original training set, and we can now calculate the overall log loss for this entire training set. This is the best estimate for the logistic regression model's log loss on the test set:

```
Logistic Regression Log Loss: 0.10978811472134588
```

## Evaluation Metrics

Although the log loss is a great way to estimate the performance of the machine learning model, we may want a more intuitive way to understand the results. For example, of the fraudulent transactions in the training set, how many did we catch? This is known as the *recall*. Or, the transactions that were flagged as fraudulent by the logistic regression model, how many were truly fraudulent? This is known as the *precision* of the model.

Let's take a look at these and other similar evaluation metrics to help us more intuitively grasp the results.

These evaluation metrics are very important because they empower data scientists to intuitively explain results to business people, who may be less familiar with log loss, cross-entropy, and other cost functions. The ability to convey complex results as simply as possible to nondata scientists is one of the essential skills for applied data scientists to master.

## Confusion Matrix

In a typical classification problem (without class imbalance) we can evaluate the results using a confusion matrix, which is a table that summarizes the number of true positives, true negatives, false positives, and false negatives (Figure 2-3).[6]

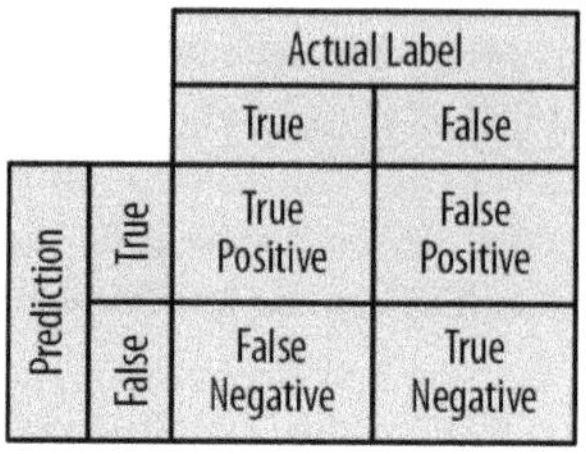

| | | Actual Label | |
|---|---|---|---|
| | | True | False |
| Prediction | True | True Positive | False Positive |
| | False | False Negative | True Negative |

*Figure 2-3. Confusion matrix*

Given that our credit card transactions dataset is highly imbalanced, using the confusion matrix would not be meaningful. For example, if we predict that every transaction is not fraudulent, we would have 284,315 true negatives, 492 false negatives, zero true positives, and zero false positives. We would have a 0% accuracy in identifying the truly fraudulent transactions. The confusion matrix does a poor job of capturing this suboptimal outcome given this imbalanced class problem.

For problems involving more balanced classes (i.e., the number of positives is roughly similar to the number of negatives), the confusion matrix may be a good, straightforward evaluation metric. We need to find a more appropriate evaluation metric given our imbalanced dataset.

## Precision-Recall Curve

For our imbalanced credit card transactions dataset, a better way to evaluate the results is to use precision and recall. *Precision* is the number of true positives over the number of total positive predictions. In other words, of the total positive predictions the model makes, how many are true positives?

Precision = True Positives / (True Positives + False Positives)

---

6 True positives are instances where the prediction and the actual label are both positive. True negatives are instances where the prediction and the actual label are both negative. False positives are instances where the prediction is positive but the actual label is negative (also known as a false alarm or Type I error). False negatives are instances where the prediction is negative but the actual label is positive (also known as a miss or Type II error).

A high precision means that—of all our positive predictions—many are true positives (in other words, it has a low false positive rate).

*Recall* is the number of true positives over the number of total actual positives in the dataset. In other words how many of the fraudulent transactions does the model catch?[7]

Recall = True Positives / (True Positives + False Negatives)

A high recall means that the model has captured most of the total actual positives (in other words, it has a low false negative rate).

A solution with high recall but low precision returns many results—capturing many of the positives—but with many false alarms. A solution with high precision but low recall is the exact opposite; it returns few results—capturing a fraction of all the positives in the dataset—but most of its predictions are correct.

To put this into context, if our solution had high precision but low recall, there would be a very small number of fraudulent transactions found but most would be truly fraudulent.

However, if the solution had low precision but high recall it would flag many of the transactions as fraudulent, thus catching a lot of the fraud, but most of the flagged transactions would not be fraudulent.

Obviously, both solutions have major problems. In the high precision–low recall case, the credit card company would lose a lot of money due to fraud, but it would not antagonize customers by unnecessarily rejecting transactions. In the low precision–high recall case, the credit card company would catch a lot of the fraud, but it would most certainly anger customers by unnecessarily rejecting a lot of normal, non-fraudulent transactions.

An optimal solution needs to have high precision and high recall, rejecting only those transactions that are truly fraudulent (i.e., high precision) and catching most of the fraudulent cases in the dataset (high recall).

There is generally a trade-off between precision and recall, which is usually determined by the threshold set by the algorithm to separate the positive cases from the negative cases; in our example, positive is fraud and negative is not fraud. If the threshold is set too high, very few cases are predicted as positive, resulting in high

---

7 Recall is also known as sensitivity or true positive rate. Related to sensitivity is a concept called specificity, or the true negative rate. This is defined as the number of true negatives over the total number of total actual negatives in the dataset. Specificity = true negative rate = true negatives / (true negatives + false positives).

precision but low recall. As the threshold is lowered, more cases are predicted as positive, generally decreasing the precision and increasing the recall.

For our credit card transactions dataset, think of the threshold as the sensitivity of the machine learning model in rejecting transactions. If the threshold is too high/strict, the model will reject few transactions, but the ones it does reject will be very likely to be fraudulent.

As the threshold moves lower (i.e., becomes less strict), the model will reject more transactions, catching more of the fraudulent cases but also unnecessarily rejecting more of the normal cases as well.

A graph of the trade-off between precision and recall is known as the precision-recall curve. To evaluate the precision-recall curve, we can calculate the average precision, which is the weighted mean of the precision achieved at each threshold. The higher the average precision, the better the solution.

The choice of the threshold is a very important one and usually involves the input of business decision makers. Data scientists can present the precision-recall curve to these business decision makers to figure out where the threshold should be.

For our credit card transactions dataset, the key question is how do we balance customer experience (i.e., avoid rejecting normal transactions) with fraud detection (i.e., catch the fraudulent transactions)? We cannot answer this without business input, but we can find the model with the best precision-recall curve. Then, we can present this model to business decision makers to set the appropriate threshold.

# Receiver Operating Characteristic

Another good evaluation metric is the area under the receiver operating characteristic (auROC). The receiver operating characteristic (ROC) curve plots the true positive rate on the Y axis and the false positive rate on the X axis. The true positive rate can also be referred to as the sensitivity, and the false positive rate can also be referred to as the 1-specificity. The closer the curve is to the top-left corner of the plot, the better the solution—with a value of (0.0, 1.0) as the absolute optimal point, signifying a 0% false positive rate and a 100% true positive rate.

To evaluate the solution, we can compute the area under this curve. The larger the auROC, the better the solution.

### Evaluating the logistic regression model

Now that we understand some of the evaluation metrics used, let's use them to better understand the logistic regression model's results.

First, let's plot the precision-recall curve and calculate the average precision:

```
preds = pd.concat([y_train,predictionsBasedOnKFolds.loc[:,1]], axis=1)
preds.columns = ['trueLabel','prediction']
predictionsBasedOnKFoldsLogisticRegression = preds.copy()

precision, recall, thresholds = precision_recall_curve(preds['trueLabel'],
                                                        preds['prediction'])

average_precision = average_precision_score(preds['trueLabel'],
                                            preds['prediction'])

plt.step(recall, precision, color='k', alpha=0.7, where='post')
plt.fill_between(recall, precision, step='post', alpha=0.3, color='k')

plt.xlabel('Recall')
plt.ylabel('Precision')
plt.ylim([0.0, 1.05])
plt.xlim([0.0, 1.0])

plt.title('Precision-Recall curve: Average Precision = {0:0.2f}'.format(
            average_precision))
```

Figure 2-4 shows the plot of the precision-recall curve. Putting together what we discussed earlier, you can see that we can achieve approximately 80% recall (i.e., catch 80% of the fraudulent transactions) with approximately 70% precision (i.e., of the transactions the model flags as fraudulent, 70% are truly fraudulent while the remaining 30% were incorrectly flagged as fraudulent).

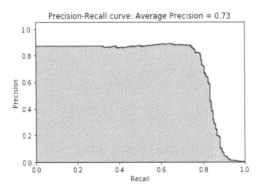

*Figure 2-4. Precision-recall curve of logistic regression*

We can distill this precision-recall curve into a single number by calculating the average precision, which is 0.73 for this logistic regression model. We cannot yet tell whether this is good or bad average precision yet since we have no other models to compare our logistic regression against.

Now, let's measure the auROC:

```
fpr, tpr, thresholds = roc_curve(preds['trueLabel'],preds['prediction'])

areaUnderROC = auc(fpr, tpr)

plt.figure()
plt.plot(fpr, tpr, color='r', lw=2, label='ROC curve')
plt.plot([0, 1], [0, 1], color='k', lw=2, linestyle='--')
plt.xlim([0.0, 1.0])
plt.ylim([0.0, 1.05])
plt.xlabel('False Positive Rate')
plt.ylabel('True Positive Rate')
plt.title('Receiver operating characteristic:
        Area under the curve = {0:0.2f}'.format(areaUnderROC))
plt.legend(loc="lower right")
plt.show()
```

As shown in Figure 2-5, the auROC curve is 0.97. This metric is just another way to evaluate the goodness of the logistic regression model, allowing you to determine how much of the fraud you can catch while keeping the false positive rate as low as possible. As with the average precision, we do not know whether this auROC curve of 0.97 is good or not, but we will once we compare it with those of other models.

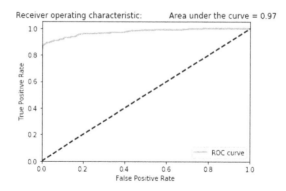

*Figure 2-5. auROC curve of logistic regression*

# Machine Learning Models (Part II)

To compare the goodness of the logistic regression model, let's build a few more models using other supervised learning algorithms.

## Model #2: Random Forests

Let's start with random forests.

As with logistic regression, we will set the hyperparameters, train the model, and evaluate the results using the precision-recall curve and the auROC.

---

## Set the hyperparameters

```
n_estimators = 10
max_features = 'auto'
max_depth = None
min_samples_split = 2
min_samples_leaf = 1
min_weight_fraction_leaf = 0.0
max_leaf_nodes = None
bootstrap = True
oob_score = False
n_jobs = -1
random_state = 2018
class_weight = 'balanced'

RFC = RandomForestClassifier(n_estimators=n_estimators,
        max_features=max_features, max_depth=max_depth,
        min_samples_split=min_samples_split, min_samples_leaf=min_samples_leaf,
        min_weight_fraction_leaf=min_weight_fraction_leaf,
        max_leaf_nodes=max_leaf_nodes, bootstrap=bootstrap,
        oob_score=oob_score, n_jobs=n_jobs, random_state=random_state,
        class_weight=class_weight)
```

Let's start with the default hyperparameters. The number of estimators is set at 10; in other words, we will build 10 trees and average the results across these 10 trees. For each tree, the model will consider the square root of the total number of features (in this case, the square root of 30 total features, which is 5 features, rounded down).

By setting the max_depth to none, the tree will grow as deep as possible, splitting as much as possible given the subset of features. Similar to what we did for logistic regression, we set the random state to 2018 for reproducibility of results and class weight to balanced given our imbalanced dataset.

## Train the model

We will run k-fold cross-validation five times, training on four-fifths of the training data and predicting on the fifth slice. We will store the predictions as we go:

```
trainingScores = []
cvScores = []
predictionsBasedOnKFolds = pd.DataFrame(data=[],
                                index=y_train.index,columns=[0,1])

model = RFC

for train_index, cv_index in k_fold.split(np.zeros(len(X_train)),
                                y_train.ravel()):
    X_train_fold, X_cv_fold = X_train.iloc[train_index,:], \
        X_train.iloc[cv_index,:]
    y_train_fold, y_cv_fold = y_train.iloc[train_index], \
        y_train.iloc[cv_index]
```

```
model.fit(X_train_fold, y_train_fold)
loglossTraining = log_loss(y_train_fold, \
                    model.predict_proba(X_train_fold)[:,1])
trainingScores.append(loglossTraining)

predictionsBasedOnKFolds.loc[X_cv_fold.index,:] = \
    model.predict_proba(X_cv_fold)
loglossCV = log_loss(y_cv_fold, \
    predictionsBasedOnKFolds.loc[X_cv_fold.index,1])
cvScores.append(loglossCV)

print('Training Log Loss: ', loglossTraining)
print('CV Log Loss: ', loglossCV)

loglossRandomForestsClassifier = log_loss(y_train,
                            predictionsBasedOnKFolds.loc[:,1])
print('Random Forests Log Loss: ', loglossRandomForestsClassifier)
```

### Evaluate the results

The training and cross-validation log loss results are as follows:

```
Training Log Loss:      0.0003951763883952557
CV Log Loss:            0.014479198936303003
Training Log Loss:      0.0004501221178398935
CV Log Loss:            0.005712702421375242
Training Log Loss:      0.00043128813023860164
CV Log Loss:            0.00908372752510077
Training Log Loss:      0.0004341676022058672
CV Log Loss:            0.013491161736979267
Training Log Loss:      0.0004275530435950083
CV Log Loss:            0.009963232439211515
```

Notice that the training log losses are considerably lower than the cross-validation log losses, suggesting that the random forests classifier—with the mostly default hyperparameters—overfits the data during the training somewhat.

The following code shows the log loss over the entire training set (using cross-validation predictions):

```
Random Forests Log Loss: 0.010546004611793962
```

Even though it overfits the training data somewhat, the random forests has a validation log loss that is about one-tenth that of the logistic regression—significant improvement over the previous machine learning solution. The random forests model is better at correctly flagging the fraud among credit card transactions.

Figure 2-6 shows the precision-recall curve of random forests. As you can see from the curve, the model can catch approximately 80% of all the fraud with approximately 80% precision. This is more impressive than the approximately 80% of all the fraud the logistic regression model caught with 70% precision.

---

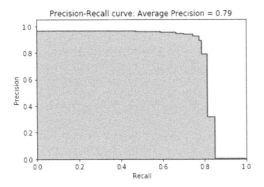

*Figure 2-6. Precision-recall curve of random forests*

The average precision of 0.79 of the random forests model is a clear improvement over the 0.73 average precision of the logistic regression model. However, the auROC, shown in Figure 2-7, is somewhat worse—0.93 for random forests versus 0.97 for logistic regression.

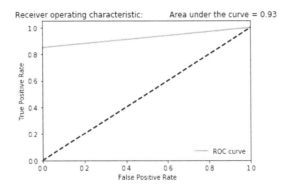

*Figure 2-7. auROC curve of random forests*

# Model #3: Gradient Boosting Machine (XGBoost)

Now let's train using gradient boosting and evaluate the results. There are two popular versions of gradient boosting—one known as XGBoost and another, much faster version by Microsoft called LightGBM. Let's build a model using each one, starting with XGBoost.[8]

---

8 For more on XGBoost gradient boosting, consult the GitHub repository (*https://github.com/dmlc/xgboost*).

## Set the hyperparameters

We will set this up as a binary classification problem and use log loss as the cost function. We will set the max depth of each tree to the default six and a default learning rate of 0.3. For each tree, we will use all the observations and all the features; these are the default settings. We will set a random state of 2018 to ensure the reproducibility of the results:

```
params_xGB = {
    'nthread':16, #number of cores
    'learning rate': 0.3, #range 0 to 1, default 0.3
    'gamma': 0, #range 0 to infinity, default 0
        # increase to reduce complexity (increase bias, reduce variance)
    'max_depth': 6, #range 1 to infinity, default 6
    'min_child_weight': 1, #range 0 to infinity, default 1
    'max_delta_step': 0, #range 0 to infinity, default 0
    'subsample': 1.0, #range 0 to 1, default 1
        # subsample ratio of the training examples
    'colsample_bytree': 1.0, #range 0 to 1, default 1
        # subsample ratio of features
    'objective':'binary:logistic',
    'num_class':1,
    'eval_metric':'logloss',
    'seed':2018,
    'silent':1
}
```

## Train the model

As before, we will use *k*-fold cross-validation, training on a different four-fifths of the training data and predicting on the fifth slice for a total of five runs.

For each of the five runs, the gradient boosting model will train for as many as two thousand rounds, evaluating whether the cross-validation log loss is decreasing as it goes. If the cross-validation log loss stops improving (over the previous two hundred rounds), the training process will stop to avoid overfitting. The results of the training process are verbose, so we will not print them here, but they can be found via the code on GitHub (*http://bit.ly/2Gd4v7e*):

```
trainingScores = []
cvScores = []
predictionsBasedOnKFolds = pd.DataFrame(data=[],
                                index=y_train.index,columns=['prediction'])

for train_index, cv_index in k_fold.split(np.zeros(len(X_train)),
                                y_train.ravel()):
    X_train_fold, X_cv_fold = X_train.iloc[train_index,:], \
        X_train.iloc[cv_index,:]
    y_train_fold, y_cv_fold = y_train.iloc[train_index], \
        y_train.iloc[cv_index]
```

```
dtrain = xgb.DMatrix(data=X_train_fold, label=y_train_fold)
dCV = xgb.DMatrix(data=X_cv_fold)

bst = xgb.cv(params_xGB, dtrain, num_boost_round=2000,
             nfold=5, early_stopping_rounds=200, verbose_eval=50)

best_rounds = np.argmin(bst['test-logloss-mean'])
bst = xgb.train(params_xGB, dtrain, best_rounds)

loglossTraining = log_loss(y_train_fold, bst.predict(dtrain))
trainingScores.append(loglossTraining)

predictionsBasedOnKFolds.loc[X_cv_fold.index,'prediction'] = \
    bst.predict(dCV)
loglossCV = log_loss(y_cv_fold, \
    predictionsBasedOnKFolds.loc[X_cv_fold.index,'prediction'])
cvScores.append(loglossCV)

print('Training Log Loss: ', loglossTraining)
print('CV Log Loss: ', loglossCV)

loglossXGBoostGradientBoosting = \
    log_loss(y_train, predictionsBasedOnKFolds.loc[:,'prediction'])
print('XGBoost Gradient Boosting Log Loss: ', loglossXGBoostGradientBoosting)
```

### Evaluate the results

As shown in the following results, the log loss over the entire training set (using the cross-validation predictions) is one-fifth that of the random forests and one-fiftieth that of logistic regression. This is a substantial improvement over the previous two models:

```
XGBoost Gradient Boosting Log Loss: 0.0029566906288156715
```

As shown in Figure 2-8, the average precision is 0.82, just shy of that of random forests (0.79) and considerably better than that of logistic regression (0.73).

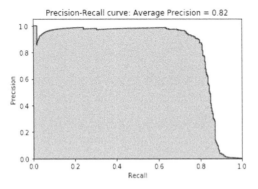

*Figure 2-8. Precision-recall curve of XGBoost gradient boosting*

As shown in Figure 2-9, the auROC curve is 0.97, the same as that of logistic regression (0.97) and an improvement over random forests (0.93). So far, gradient boosting is the best of the three models based on the log loss, the precision-recall curve, and the auROC.

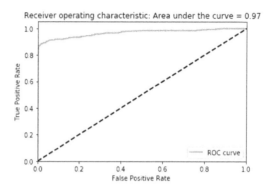

*Figure 2-9. auROC curve of XGBoost gradient boosting*

# Model #4: Gradient Boosting Machine (LightGBM)

Let's now train using another version of gradient boosting known as LightGBM.[9]

### Set the hyperparameters

We will set this up as a binary classification problem and use log loss as the cost function. We will set the max depth of each tree to 4 and use a learning rate of 0.1. For each tree, we will use all the samples and all the features; these are the default settings. We will use the default number of leaves for one tree (31) and set a random state to ensure reproducibility of the results:

```
params_lightGB = {
    'task': 'train',
    'application':'binary',
    'num_class':1,
    'boosting': 'gbdt',
    'objective': 'binary',
    'metric': 'binary_logloss',
    'metric_freq':50,
    'is_training_metric':False,
    'max_depth':4,
    'num_leaves': 31,
    'learning_rate': 0.1,
```

---

9 For more on Microsoft's LightGBM gradient boosting, consult the GitHub repository (*https://github.com/ Microsoft/LightGBM*).

```
    'feature_fraction': 1.0,
    'bagging_fraction': 1.0,
    'bagging_freq': 0,
    'bagging_seed': 2018,
    'verbose': 0,
    'num_threads':16
}
```

## Train the model

As before, we will use *k*-fold cross-validation and cycle through this five times, storing the predictions on the validation sets as we go:

```
trainingScores = []
cvScores = []
predictionsBasedOnKFolds = pd.DataFrame(data=[],
                            index=y_train.index,columns=['prediction'])

for train_index, cv_index in k_fold.split(np.zeros(len(X_train)),
                                y_train.ravel()):
    X_train_fold, X_cv_fold = X_train.iloc[train_index,:], \
        X_train.iloc[cv_index,:]
    y_train_fold, y_cv_fold = y_train.iloc[train_index], \
        y_train.iloc[cv_index]

    lgb_train = lgb.Dataset(X_train_fold, y_train_fold)
    lgb_eval = lgb.Dataset(X_cv_fold, y_cv_fold, reference=lgb_train)
    gbm = lgb.train(params_lightGB, lgb_train, num_boost_round=2000,
                valid_sets=lgb_eval, early_stopping_rounds=200)

    loglossTraining = log_loss(y_train_fold, \
                gbm.predict(X_train_fold, num_iteration=gbm.best_iteration))
    trainingScores.append(loglossTraining)

    predictionsBasedOnKFolds.loc[X_cv_fold.index,'prediction'] = \
        gbm.predict(X_cv_fold, num_iteration=gbm.best_iteration)
    loglossCV = log_loss(y_cv_fold, \
        predictionsBasedOnKFolds.loc[X_cv_fold.index,'prediction'])
    cvScores.append(loglossCV)

    print('Training Log Loss: ', loglossTraining)
    print('CV Log Loss: ', loglossCV)

loglossLightGBMGradientBoosting = \
    log_loss(y_train, predictionsBasedOnKFolds.loc[:,'prediction'])
print('LightGBM gradient boosting Log Loss: ', loglossLightGBMGradientBoosting)
```

For each of the five runs, the gradient boosting model will train for as many as two
thousand rounds, evaluating whether the cross-validation log loss is decreasing as it
goes. If the cross-validation log loss stops improving (over the previous two hundred
rounds), the training process will stop to avoid overfitting. The results of the training

process are verbose, so we will not print them here, but they can be found via the code on GitHub (*http://bit.ly/2Gd4v7e*).

## Evaluate the results

The following results show that the log loss over the entire training set (using the cross-validation predictions) is similar to that of XGBoost, one-fifth that of the random forests and one-fiftieth that of logistic regression. But compared to XGBoost, LightGBM is considerably faster:

```
LightGBM Gradient Boosting Log Loss: 0.0029732268054261826
```

As shown in Figure 2-10, the average precision is 0.82, the same as that of XGboost (0.82), better than that of random forests (0.79), and considerably better than that of logistic regression (0.73).

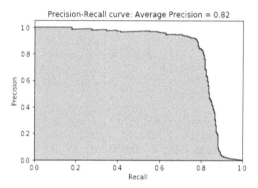

*Figure 2-10. Precision-recall curve of LightGBM gradient boosting*

As shown in Figure 2-11, the auROC curve is 0.98, an improvement over that of XGBoost (0.97), logistic regression (0.97), and random forests (0.93).

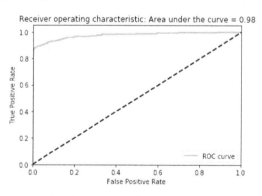

*Figure 2-11. auROC curve of LightGBM gradient boosting*

# Evaluation of the Four Models Using the Test Set

So far in this chapter, we have learned how to:

- Set up the environment for machine learning projects
- Acquire, load, explore, clean, and visualize data
- Split the dataset into training and test sets and set up *k*-fold cross-validation sets
- Choose the appropriate cost function
- Set the hyperparameters and perform training and cross-validation
- Evaluate the results

We have not explored how to adjust the hyperparameters (a process known as hyper-parameter fine-tuning) to improve the results of each machine learning solution and address underfitting/overfitting, but the code on GitHub (*http://bit.ly/2Gd4v7e*) will allow you to conduct these experiments very easily.

Even without such fine-tuning, the results are pretty clear. Based on our training and *k*-fold cross-validation, LightGBM gradient boosting is the best solution, closely followed by XGBoost. Random forests and logistic regression are worse.

Let's use the test set as a final evaluation of each of the four models.

For each model, we will use the trained model to predict the fraud probabilities for the test set transactions. Then, we will calculate the log loss for each model by comparing the fraud probabilities predicted by the model against the true fraud labels:

```
predictionsTestSetLogisticRegression = \
    pd.DataFrame(data=[],index=y_test.index,columns=['prediction'])
predictionsTestSetLogisticRegression.loc[:,'prediction'] = \
    logReg.predict_proba(X_test)[:,1]
logLossTestSetLogisticRegression = \
    log_loss(y_test, predictionsTestSetLogisticRegression)

predictionsTestSetRandomForests = \
    pd.DataFrame(data=[],index=y_test.index,columns=['prediction'])
predictionsTestSetRandomForests.loc[:,'prediction'] = \
    RFC.predict_proba(X_test)[:,1]
logLossTestSetRandomForests = \
    log_loss(y_test, predictionsTestSetRandomForests)

predictionsTestSetXGBoostGradientBoosting = \
    pd.DataFrame(data=[],index=y_test.index,columns=['prediction'])
dtest = xgb.DMatrix(data=X_test)
predictionsTestSetXGBoostGradientBoosting.loc[:,'prediction'] = \
    bst.predict(dtest)
logLossTestSetXGBoostGradientBoosting = \
    log_loss(y_test, predictionsTestSetXGBoostGradientBoosting)
```

```
predictionsTestSetLightGBMGradientBoosting = \
    pd.DataFrame(data=[],index=y_test.index,columns=['prediction'])
predictionsTestSetLightGBMGradientBoosting.loc[:,'prediction'] = \
    gbm.predict(X_test, num_iteration=gbm.best_iteration)
logLossTestSetLightGBMGradientBoosting = \
    log_loss(y_test, predictionsTestSetLightGBMGradientBoosting)
```

There are no surprises in the following log loss block. LightGBM gradient boosting has the lowest log loss on the test set, followed by the rest.

```
Log Loss of Logistic Regression on Test Set: 0.123732961313
Log Loss of Random Forests on Test Set: 0.00918192757674
Log Loss of XGBoost Gradient Boosting on Test Set: 0.00249116807943
Log Loss of LightGBM Gradient Boosting on Test Set: 0.002376320092424
```

Figures 2-12 through 2-19 are the precision-recall curves, average precisions, and auROC curve for all four models, corroborating our findings above.

### Logistic regression

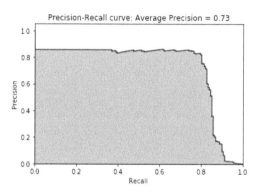

*Figure 2-12. Test set precision-recall curve of logistic regression*

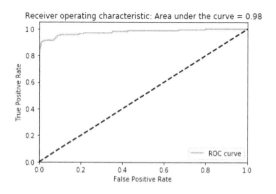

*Figure 2-13. Test set auROC curve of logistic regression*

## Random forests

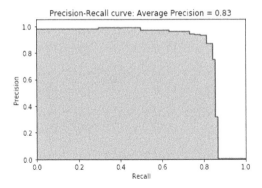

*Figure 2-14. Test set precision-recall curve of random forests*

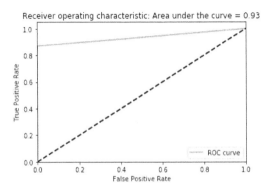

*Figure 2-15. Test set auROC curve of random forests*

## XGBoost gradient boosting

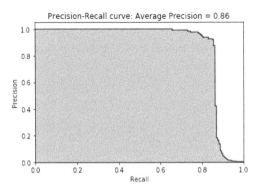

*Figure 2-16. Test set precision-recall curve of XGBoost gradient boosting*

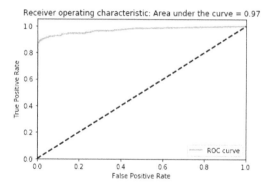

*Figure 2-17. Test set auROC curve of XGBoost gradient boosting*

## LightGBM gradient boosting

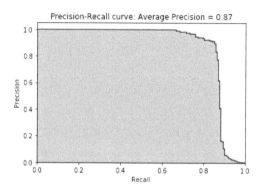

*Figure 2-18. Test set precision-recall curve of LightGBM gradient boosting*

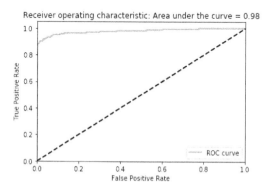

*Figure 2-19. Test set auROC curve of LightGBM gradient boosting*

The results of LightGBM gradient boosting are impressive—we can catch over 80% of the fraudulent transactions with nearly 90% precision (in other words, in catching 80% of the total fraud the LightGBM model gets only 10% of the cases wrong).

Considering how few cases of fraud our dataset has, this is a great accomplishment.

# Ensembles

Instead of picking just one of the machine learning solutions we have developed for use in production, we can evaluate whether an ensemble of the models leads to an improved fraud detection rate.[10]

Generally, if we include similarly strong solutions from different machine learning families (such as one from random forests and one from neural networks), the ensemble of the solutions will lead to a better result than any of the standalone solutions. This is because each of the standalone solutions has different strengths and weaknesses. By including the standalone solutions together in an ensemble, the strengths of some of the models compensate for the weaknesses of the others, and vice versa.

There are important caveats, though. If the standalone solutions are similarly strong, the ensemble will have better performance than any of the standalone solutions. But if one of the solutions is much better than the others, the ensemble's performance will equal the performance of the best standalone solution; the subpar solutions will contribute nothing to the ensemble's performance.

Also, the standalone solutions need to be relatively uncorrelated. If they are very correlated, the strengths of one will mirror those of the rest, and the same will be true with the weaknesses. We will see little benefit from diversifying via an ensemble.

## Stacking

In our problem here, two of the models (LightGBM gradient boosting and XGBoost gradient boosting) are much stronger than the others (random forests and logistic regression). But the two strongest models are from the same family, which means their strengths and weaknesses will be highly correlated.

We can use stacking (which is a form of ensembling) to determine whether we can get an improvement in performance compared to the standalone models from earlier. In stacking, we take the predictions from the *k*-fold cross-validation from each of the four standalone models (known as *layer one predictions*) and append them to the

---

10 For more on ensemble learning, refer to the "Kaggle Ensembling Guide," (*https://mlwave.com/kaggle-ensembling-guide/*) "Introduction to Ensembling/Stacking in Python," (*http://bit.ly/2RYV4iF*) and "A Kaggler's Guide to Model Stacking in Practice" (*http://bit.ly/2Rrs1iI*).

original training dataset. We then train on this original features plus layer one predictions dataset using *k*-fold cross-validation.

This will result in a new set of *k*-fold cross-validation predictions, known as layer two predictions, which we will evaluate to see if we have an improvement in performance over any of the standalone models.

### Combine layer one predictions with the original training dataset

First, let's combine the predictions from each of the four machine learning models that we have built with the original training dataset:

```python
predictionsBasedOnKFoldsFourModels = pd.DataFrame(data=[],index=y_train.index)
predictionsBasedOnKFoldsFourModels = predictionsBasedOnKFoldsFourModels.join(
    predictionsBasedOnKFoldsLogisticRegression['prediction'].astype(float), \
    how='left').join(predictionsBasedOnKFoldsRandomForests['prediction'] \
        .astype(float),how='left',rsuffix="2").join( \
    predictionsBasedOnKFoldsXGBoostGradientBoosting['prediction'] \
        .astype(float), how='left',rsuffix="3").join( \
    predictionsBasedOnKFoldsLightGBMGradientBoosting['prediction'] \
        .astype(float), how='left',rsuffix="4")
predictionsBasedOnKFoldsFourModels.columns = \
    ['predsLR','predsRF','predsXGB','predsLightGBM']

X_trainWithPredictions = \
    X_train.merge(predictionsBasedOnKFoldsFourModels,
                  left_index=True,right_index=True)
```

### Set the hyperparameters

Now we will use LightGBM gradient boosting—the best machine learning algorithm from the earlier exercise—to train on this original features plus layer one predictions dataset. The hyperparameters will remain the same as before:

```python
params_lightGB = {
    'task': 'train',
    'application':'binary',
    'num_class':1,
    'boosting': 'gbdt',
    'objective': 'binary',
    'metric': 'binary_logloss',
    'metric_freq':50,
    'is_training_metric':False,
    'max_depth':4,
    'num_leaves': 31,
    'learning_rate': 0.01,
    'feature_fraction': 1.0,
    'bagging_fraction': 1.0,
    'bagging_freq': 0,
    'bagging_seed': 2018,
    'verbose': 0,
```

```
        'num_threads':16
    }
```

## Train the model

As before, we will use *k*-fold cross-validation and generate fraud probabilities for the five different cross-validation sets:

```
trainingScores = []
cvScores = []
predictionsBasedOnKFoldsEnsemble = \
    pd.DataFrame(data=[],index=y_train.index,columns=['prediction'])

for train_index, cv_index in k_fold.split(np.zeros(len(X_train)), \
                                          y_train.ravel()):
    X_train_fold, X_cv_fold = \
        X_trainWithPredictions.iloc[train_index,:], \
        X_trainWithPredictions.iloc[cv_index,:]
    y_train_fold, y_cv_fold = y_train.iloc[train_index], y_train.iloc[cv_index]

    lgb_train = lgb.Dataset(X_train_fold, y_train_fold)
    lgb_eval = lgb.Dataset(X_cv_fold, y_cv_fold, reference=lgb_train)
    gbm = lgb.train(params_lightGB, lgb_train, num_boost_round=2000,
                    valid_sets=lgb_eval, early_stopping_rounds=200)

    loglossTraining = log_loss(y_train_fold, \
        gbm.predict(X_train_fold, num_iteration=gbm.best_iteration))
    trainingScores.append(loglossTraining)

    predictionsBasedOnKFoldsEnsemble.loc[X_cv_fold.index,'prediction'] = \
        gbm.predict(X_cv_fold, num_iteration=gbm.best_iteration)
    loglossCV = log_loss(y_cv_fold, \
        predictionsBasedOnKFoldsEnsemble.loc[X_cv_fold.index,'prediction'])
    cvScores.append(loglossCV)

    print('Training Log Loss: ', loglossTraining)
    print('CV Log Loss: ', loglossCV)

loglossEnsemble = log_loss(y_train, \
        predictionsBasedOnKFoldsEnsemble.loc[:,'prediction'])
print('Ensemble Log Loss: ', loglossEnsemble)
```

## Evaluate the results

In the following results, we do not see an improvement. The ensemble log loss is very similar to the standalone gradient boosting log loss. Since the best standalone solutions are from the same family (gradient boosting), we do not see an improvement in the results. They have highly correlated strengths and weaknesses in detecting fraud. There is no benefit in diversifying across models:

```
Ensemble Log Loss: 0.002885415974220497
```

As shown in Figures 2-20 and 2-21, the precision-recall curve, the average precision, and the auROC also corroborate the lack of improvement.

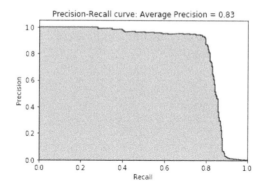

*Figure 2-20. Precision-recall curve of the ensemble*

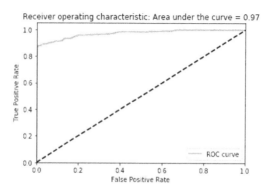

*Figure 2-21. auROC curve of the ensemble*

# Final Model Selection

Since the ensemble does not improve performance, we favor the simplicity of the standalone LightGBM gradient boosting model and will use it in production.

Before we create a pipeline for new, incoming transactions, let's visualize how well the LightGBM model separates the fraudulent transactions from the normal transactions for the test set.

Figure 2-22 displays the predicted probabilities on the x-axis. Based on this plot, the model does a reasonably good job of assigning a high probability of fraud to the transactions that are actually fraudulent. Vice versa, the model generally assigns a low probability to the transactions that are not fraudulent. Occasionally, the model is wrong, and assigns a low probability to a case of actual fraud and a high probability to a case of not fraud.

Overall, the results are pretty impressive.

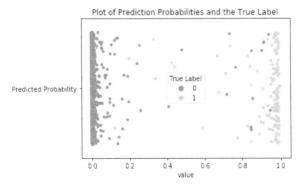

*Figure 2-22. Plot of prediction probabilities and the true label*

# Production Pipeline

Now that we have selected a model for production, let's design a simple pipeline that performs three simple steps on new, incoming data: load the data, scale the features, and generate predictions using the LightGBM model we have already trained and selected for use in production:

```
'''Pipeline for New Data'''
# first, import new data into a dataframe called 'newData'
# second, scale data
# newData.loc[:,featuresToScale] = sX.transform(newData[featuresToScale])
# third, predict using LightGBM
# gbm.predict(newData, num_iteration=gbm.best_iteration)
```

Once these predictions are generated, analysts can act on (i.e., investigate further) the ones with the highest predicted probability of being fraudulent and work through the list. Or, if automation is the goal, analysts can use a system that automatically rejects transactions that have a predicted probability of being fraudulent above a certain threshold.

For example, based on Figure 2-13, if we automatically reject transactions with a predicted probability above 0.90, we will reject cases that are almost certain to be fraudulent without accidentally rejecting a case of not fraud.

# Conclusion

Congratulations! You have built a credit card fraud detection system using supervised learning.

Together, we set up a machine learning environment, acquired and prepared the data, trained and evaluated multiple models, selected the final model for production, and designed a pipeline for new, incoming transactions. You have successfully created an applied machine learning solution.

Now we will use this same hands-on approach to develop applied machine learning solutions using unsupervised learning.

The solution above will need to be retrained over time as the patterns of fraud change. Also, we should find other machine learning algorithms—from different machine learning families—that perform just as well as gradient boosting and include them in an ensemble to improve fraud detection performance overall.

Finally, interpretability is very important for real-world applications of machine learning. Because the features in this credit card transactions dataset are the output of PCA (a form of dimensionality reduction that we will explore in Chapter 3) we cannot explain in plain English why certain transactions are being flagged as potentially fraudulent. For greater interpretability of the results, we need access to the original pre-PCA features, which we do not have for this sample dataset.

# PART II

# Unsupervised Learning Using Scikit-Learn

In the next few chapters, we will introduce two major unsupervised learning concepts —dimensionality reduction and clustering—and use these to perform anomaly detection and group segmentation.

Both anomaly detection and group segmentation have significant real-world applications across many different industries.

Anomaly detection is used to efficiently discover rare events such as fraud; cybersecurity breaches; terrorism; human, arms, and drug trafficking; money laundering; abnormal trading activity; disease outbreaks; and maintenance failures in mission-critical equipment.

Group segmentation allows us to understand user behavior in areas such as marketing, online shopping, music listening, video watching, online dating, and social media activity, among others.

# CHAPTER 3

# Dimensionality Reduction

In this chapter, we will focus on one of the major challenges in building successful applied machine learning solutions: the curse of dimensionality. Unsupervised learning has a great counter—*dimensionality reduction*. In this chapter, we will introduce this concept and build from there so that you can develop an intuition for how it all works.

In Chapter 4, we will build our own unsupervised learning solution based on dimensionality reduction—specifically, an unsupervised learning-based credit card fraud detection system (as opposed to the supervised-based system we built in Chapter 2). This type of unsupervised fraud detection is known as anomaly detection, a rapidly growing area in the field of applied unsupervised learning.

But before we build an anomaly detection system, let's cover dimensionality reduction in this chapter.

## The Motivation for Dimensionality Reduction

As mentioned in Chapter 1, dimensionality reduction helps counteract one of the most commonly occurring problems in machine learning—the curse of dimensionality—in which algorithms cannot effectively and efficiently train on the data because of the sheer size of the feature space.

Dimensionality reduction algorithms project high-dimensional data to a low-dimensional space, retaining as much of the salient information as possible while removing redundant information. Once the data is in the low-dimensional space, machine learning algorithms are able to identify interesting patterns more effectively and efficiently because a lot of the noise has been reduced.

Sometimes, dimensionality reduction is the goal itself—for example, to build anomaly detection systems, as we will show in the next chapter.

Other times, dimensionality reduction is not an end in itself but rather a means to another end. For example, dimensionality reduction is commonly a part of the machine learning pipeline to help solve large-scale, computationally expensive problems involving images, video, speech, and text.

# The MNIST Digits Database

Before we introduce the dimensionality reduction algorithms, let's explore the dataset that we will use in this chapter. We will work with a simple computer vision dataset: the MNIST (Mixed National Institute of Standards and Technology) database of handwritten digits, one of the best known datasets in machine learning. We will use the version of the MNIST dataset publicly available on Yann LeCun's website.[1] To make it easier, we will use the pickled version, courtesy of deeplearning.net.[2]

This dataset has been divided into three sets—a training set with 50,000 examples, a validation set with 10,000 examples, and a test set with 10,000 examples. We have labels for all the examples.

This dataset consists of 28x28 pixel images of handwritten digits. Every single data point (i.e., every image) can be conveyed as an array of numbers, where each number describes how dark each pixel is. In other words, a 28x28 array of numbers corresponds to a 28x28 pixel image.

To make this simpler, we can flatten each array into a 28x28, or 784, dimensional vector. Each component of the vector is a float between zero and one—representing the intensity of each pixel in the image. Zero stands for black; one stands for white. The labels are numbers between zero and nine, and indicate which digit the image represents.

## Data acquisition and exploration

Before we work with the dimensionality reduction algorithms, let's load the libraries we will use:

```
# Import libraries
'''Main'''
import numpy as np
import pandas as pd
import os, time
```

---

1 The MNIST database of handwritten digits (*http://yann.lecun.com/exdb/mnist/*), courtesy of Yann Lecun.

2 The pickled version of the MNIST dataset (*http://deeplearning.net/tutorial/gettingstarted.html*), courtesy of deeplearning.net.

```
import pickle, gzip

'''Data Viz'''
import matplotlib.pyplot as plt
import seaborn as sns
color = sns.color_palette()
import matplotlib as mpl

%matplotlib inline

'''Data Prep and Model Evaluation'''
from sklearn import preprocessing as pp
from scipy.stats import pearsonr
from numpy.testing import assert_array_almost_equal
from sklearn.model_selection import train_test_split
from sklearn.model_selection import StratifiedKFold
from sklearn.metrics import log_loss
from sklearn.metrics import precision_recall_curve, average_precision_score
from sklearn.metrics import roc_curve, auc, roc_auc_score
from sklearn.metrics import confusion_matrix, classification_report

'''Algos'''
from sklearn.linear_model import LogisticRegression
from sklearn.ensemble import RandomForestClassifier
import xgboost as xgb
import lightgbm as lgb
```

## Load the MNIST datasets

Let's now load the MNIST datasets:

```
# Load the datasets
current_path = os.getcwd()
file = '\\datasets\\mnist_data\\mnist.pkl.gz'

f = gzip.open(current_path+file, 'rb')
train_set, validation_set, test_set = pickle.load(f, encoding='latin1')
f.close()

X_train, y_train = train_set[0], train_set[1]
X_validation, y_validation = validation_set[0], validation_set[1]
X_test, y_test = test_set[0], test_set[1]
```

## Verify shape of datasets

Let's verify the shape of the datasets to make sure they loaded properly:

```
# Verify shape of datasets
print("Shape of X_train: ", X_train.shape)
print("Shape of y_train: ", y_train.shape)
print("Shape of X_validation: ", X_validation.shape)
print("Shape of y_validation: ", y_validation.shape)
```

```
print("Shape of X_test: ", X_test.shape)
print("Shape of y_test: ", y_test.shape)
```

The following code confirms the shapes of the datasets are as expected:

```
Shape of X_train:       (50000, 784)
Shape of y_train:       (50000,)
Shape of X_validation:  (10000, 784)
Shape of y_validation:  (10000,)
Shape of X_test:        (10000, 784)
Shape of y_test:        (10000,)
```

### Create Pandas DataFrames from the datasets

Let's convert the numpy arrays into Pandas DataFrames so they are easier to explore and work with:

```
# Create Pandas DataFrames from the datasets
train_index = range(0,len(X_train))
validation_index = range(len(X_train), \
                         len(X_train)+len(X_validation))
test_index = range(len(X_train)+len(X_validation), \
                   len(X_train)+len(X_validation)+len(X_test))

X_train = pd.DataFrame(data=X_train,index=train_index)
y_train = pd.Series(data=y_train,index=train_index)

X_validation = pd.DataFrame(data=X_validation,index=validation_index)
y_validation = pd.Series(data=y_validation,index=validation_index)

X_test = pd.DataFrame(data=X_test,index=test_index)
y_test = pd.Series(data=y_test,index=test_index)
```

### Explore the data

Let's generate a summary view of the data:

```
# Describe the training matrix
X_train.describe()
```

Table 3-1 displays a summary view of the image data. Many of the values are zeros—in other words, most of the pixels in the images are black. This makes sense since the digits are in white and shown in the middle of the image on a black backdrop.

*Table 3-1. Data exploration*

|       | 0       | 1       | 2       | 3       | 4       | 5       | 6       |
|-------|---------|---------|---------|---------|---------|---------|---------|
| count | 50000.0 | 50000.0 | 50000.0 | 50000.0 | 50000.0 | 50000.0 | 50000.0 |
| mean  | 0.0     | 0.0     | 0.0     | 0.0     | 0.0     | 0.0     | 0.0     |
| std   | 0.0     | 0.0     | 0.0     | 0.0     | 0.0     | 0.0     | 0.0     |
| min   | 0.0     | 0.0     | 0.0     | 0.0     | 0.0     | 0.0     | 0.0     |
| 25%   | 0.0     | 0.0     | 0.0     | 0.0     | 0.0     | 0.0     | 0.0     |
| 50%   | 0.0     | 0.0     | 0.0     | 0.0     | 0.0     | 0.0     | 0.0     |
| 75%   | 0.0     | 0.0     | 0.0     | 0.0     | 0.0     | 0.0     | 0.0     |
| max   | 0.0     | 0.0     | 0.0     | 0.0     | 0.0     | 0.0     | 0.0     |

8 rows x 784 columns

The labels data is a one-dimensional vector representing the actual content in the image. Labels for the first few images are as follows:

```
# Show the labels
y_train.head()

0    5
1    0
2    4
3    1
4    9
dtype: int64
```

## Display the images

Let's define a function to view the image along with its label:

```
def view_digit(example):
    label = y_train.loc[example]
    image = X_train.loc[example,:].values.reshape([28,28])
    plt.title('Example: %d  Label: %d' % (example, label))
    plt.imshow(image, cmap=plt.get_cmap('gray'))
    plt.show()
```

A view of the first image—once the 784-dimensional vector is reshaped into a 28 x 28 pixel image—shows the number five (Figure 3-1).

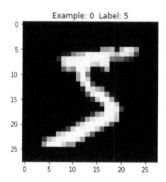

*Figure 3-1. View of the first digit*

# Dimensionality Reduction Algorithms

Now that we've loaded and explored the MNIST digits dataset, let's move to the dimensionality reduction algorithms. For each algorithm, we will introduce the concept first and then build a deeper understanding by applying the algorithm to the MNIST digits dataset.

## Linear Projection vs. Manifold Learning

There are two major branches of dimensionality reduction. The first is known as *linear projection*, which involves linearly projecting data from a high-dimensional space to a low-dimensional space. This includes techniques such as *principal component analysis, singular value decomposition*, and *random projection*.

The second is known as *manifold learning*, which is also referred to as *nonlinear dimensionality reduction*. This involves techniques such as *isomap*, which learns the *curved distance* (also called the *geodesic distance*) between points rather than the *Euclidean distance*. Other techniques include *multidimensional scaling (MDS), locally linear embedding (LLE), t-distributed stochastic neighbor embedding (t-SNE), dictionary learning, random trees embedding*, and *independent component analysis*.

# Principal Component Analysis

We will explore several versions of PCA, including standard PCA, incremental PCA, sparse PCA, and kernel PCA.

## PCA, the Concept

Let's start with standard PCA, one of the most common linear dimensionality reduction techniques. In PCA, the algorithm finds a low-dimensional representation of the data while retaining as much of the variation (i.e., salient information) as possible.

---

PCA does this by addressing the correlation among features. If the correlation is very high among a subset of the features, PCA will attempt to combine the highly correlated features and represent this data with a smaller number of linearly uncorrelated features. The algorithm keeps performing this correlation reduction, finding the directions of maximum variance in the original high-dimensional data and projecting them onto a smaller dimensional space. These newly derived components are known as principal components.

With these components, it is possible to reconstruct the original features—not exactly but generally close enough. The PCA algorithm actively attempts to minimize the reconstruction error during its search for the optimal components.

In our MNIST example, the original feature space has 784 dimensions, known as $d$ dimensions. PCA will project the data onto a smaller subspace of $k$ dimensions (where $k < d$) while retaining as much of the salient information as possible. These $k$ dimensions are known as the principal components.

The number of meaningful principal components we are left with is considerably smaller than the number of dimensions in the original dataset. We lose some of the variance (i.e., information) by moving to this low-dimensional space, but the underlying structure of the data is easier to identify, allowing us to perform tasks like anomaly detection and clustering more effectively and efficiently.

Moreover, by reducing the dimensionality of the data, PCA will reduce the size of the data, improving the performance of machine learning algorithms further along in the machine learning pipeline (for example, for tasks such as image classification).

 It is essential to perform feature scaling before running PCA. PCA is very sensitive to the relative ranges of the original features. Generally we must scale the data to make sure the features are in the same relative range. However, for our MNIST digits dataset, the features are already scaled to a range of zero to one, so we can skip this step.

## PCA in Practice

Now that you have a better grasp of how PCA works, let's apply PCA to the MNIST digits dataset and see how well PCA captures the most salient information about the digits as its projects the data from the original 784-dimensional space to a lower dimensional space.

### Set the hyperparameters

Let's set the hyperparameters for the PCA algorithm:

```python
from sklearn.decomposition import PCA

n_components = 784
whiten = False
random_state = 2018

pca = PCA(n_components=n_components, whiten=whiten, \
          random_state=random_state)
```

### Apply PCA

We will set the number of principal components to the original number of dimensions (i.e., 784). Then, PCA will capture the salient information from the original dimensions and start generating principal components. Once these components are generated, we will determine how many principal components we need to effectively capture most of the variance/information from the original feature set.

Let's fit and transform our training data, generating these principal components:

```python
X_train_PCA = pca.fit_transform(X_train)
X_train_PCA = pd.DataFrame(data=X_train_PCA, index=train_index)
```

### Evaluate PCA

Because we have not reduced the dimensionality at all (we've just transformed the data) the variance/information of the original data captured by the 784 principal components should be 100%:

```python
# Percentage of Variance Captured by 784 principal components
print("Variance Explained by all 784 principal components: ", \
    sum(pca.explained_variance_ratio_))

Variance Explained by all 784 principal components: 0.9999999999999997
```

However, it is important to note that the importance of the 784 principal components varies quite a bit. The importance of the first X principal components are summarized here:

```python
# Percentage of Variance Captured by X principal components
importanceOfPrincipalComponents = \
    pd.DataFrame(data=pca.explained_variance_ratio_)
importanceOfPrincipalComponents = importanceOfPrincipalComponents.T

print('Variance Captured by First 10 Principal Components: ',
    importanceOfPrincipalComponents.loc[:,0:9].sum(axis=1).values)
print('Variance Captured by First 20 Principal Components: ',
    importanceOfPrincipalComponents.loc[:,0:19].sum(axis=1).values)
```

```
print('Variance Captured by First 50 Principal Components: ',
      importanceOfPrincipalComponents.loc[:,0:49].sum(axis=1).values)
print('Variance Captured by First 100 Principal Components: ',
      importanceOfPrincipalComponents.loc[:,0:99].sum(axis=1).values)
print('Variance Captured by First 200 Principal Components: ',
      importanceOfPrincipalComponents.loc[:,0:199].sum(axis=1).values)
print('Variance Captured by First 300 Principal Components: ',
      importanceOfPrincipalComponents.loc[:,0:299].sum(axis=1).values)

Variance Captured by First 10 Principal Components: [0.48876238]
Variance Captured by First 20 Principal Components: [0.64398025]
Variance Captured by First 50 Principal Components: [0.8248609]
Variance Captured by First 100 Principal Components: [0.91465857]
Variance Captured by First 200 Principal Components: [0.96650076]
Variance Captured by First 300 Principal Components: [0.9862489]
```

The first 10 components in total capture approximately 50% of the variance, the first one hundred components over 90%, and the first three hundred components almost 99% of the variance; the information in the rest of the principal components is of negligible value.

The power of PCA should be more apparent now. With just the first two hundred principal components (far fewer than the original 784 dimensions), we capture over 96% of the variance/information.

We can also plot the importance of each principal component, ranked from the first principal component to the last. For the sake of readability, just the first 10 components are displayed in Figure 3-2.

PCA allows us to reduce the dimensionality of the original data substantially while retaining most of the salient information. On the PCA-reduced feature set, other machine learning algorithms—downstream in the machine learning pipeline—will have an easier time separating the data points in space (to perform tasks such as anomaly detection and clustering) and will require fewer computational resources.

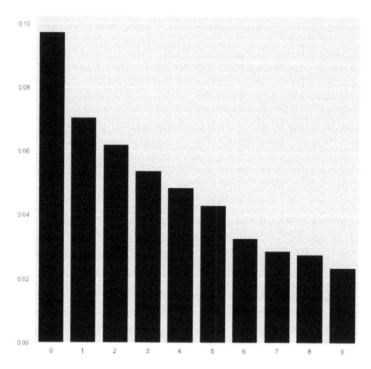

*Figure 3-2. Importance of PCA components*

### Visualize the separation of points in space

To demonstrate the power of PCA to efficiently and compactly capture the variance/
information in data, let's plot the observations in two dimensions. Specifically, we will
display a scatterplot of the first and second principal components and mark the
observations by the true label. Let's create a function for this called `scatterPlot`
because we also need to present visualizations for the other dimensionality algorithms later on:

```
def scatterPlot(xDF, yDF, algoName):
    tempDF = pd.DataFrame(data=xDF.loc[:,0:1], index=xDF.index)
    tempDF = pd.concat((tempDF,yDF), axis=1, join="inner")
    tempDF.columns = ["First Vector", "Second Vector", "Label"]
    sns.lmplot(x="First Vector", y="Second Vector", hue="Label", \
               data=tempDF, fit_reg=False)
    ax = plt.gca()
    ax.set_title("Separation of Observations using "+algoName)

scatterPlot(X_train_PCA, y_train, "PCA")
```

As seen in Figure 3-3, with just the top two principal components, PCA does a good
job of separating the points in space such that similar points are generally closer to

each other than they are to other, less similar points. In other words, images of the same digit are closer to each other than they are to images of other digits.

PCA accomplishes this without using any labels whatsoever. This demonstrates the power of unsupervised learning to capture the underlying structure of data, helping discover hidden patterns in the absence of labels.

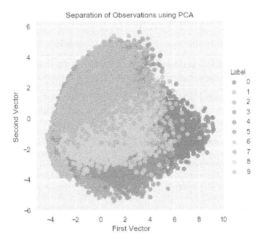

*Figure 3-3. Separation of observations using PCA*

If we run the same two-dimensional scatterplot using two of the most important features from the original 784 feature set—determined by training a supervised learning model—the separation is poor, at best (Figure 3-4).

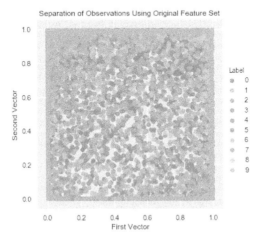

*Figure 3-4. Separation of observations without PCA*

Comparison of Figures 3-3 and 3-4 shows just how powerful PCA is in learning the underlying structure of the dataset without using any labels whatsoever—even with just two dimensions, we can start meaningfully separating the images by the digits they display.

Not only does PCA help separate data so that we can discover hidden patterns more readily, it also helps reduce the size of the feature set, making it less costly—both in time and in computational resources—to train machine learning models.

With the MNIST dataset, the reduction in training time will be modest at best since the dataset is very small—we have only 784 features and 50,000 observations. But if the dataset were millions of features and billions of observations, dimensionality reduction would dramatically reduce the training time of the machine learning algorithms further along in the machine learning pipeline.

Lastly, PCA usually throws away some of the information available in the original feature set but does so wisely, capturing the most important elements and tossing the less valuable ones. A model that is trained on a PCA-reduced feature set may not perform quite as well in terms of accuracy as a model that is trained on the full feature set, but both the training and prediction times will be much faster. This is one of the important trade-offs you must consider when choosing whether to use dimensionality reduction in your machine learning product.

## Incremental PCA

For datasets that are very large and cannot fit in memory, we can perform PCA incrementally in small batches, where each batch is able to fit in memory. The batch size can be either set manually or determined automatically. This batch-based form of PCA is known as *incremental PCA*. The resulting principal components of PCA and incremental PCA are generally pretty similar (Figure 3-5). Here is the code for incremental PCA:

```
# Incremental PCA
from sklearn.decomposition import IncrementalPCA

n_components = 784
batch_size = None

incrementalPCA = IncrementalPCA(n_components=n_components, \
                                batch_size=batch_size)

X_train_incrementalPCA = incrementalPCA.fit_transform(X_train)
X_train_incrementalPCA = \
    pd.DataFrame(data=X_train_incrementalPCA, index=train_index)
```

```
X_validation_incrementalPCA = incrementalPCA.transform(X_validation)
X_validation_incrementalPCA = \
    pd.DataFrame(data=X_validation_incrementalPCA, index=validation_index)

scatterPlot(X_train_incrementalPCA, y_train, "Incremental PCA")
```

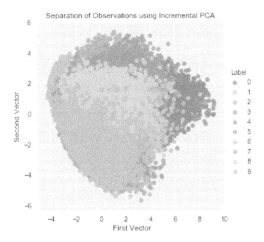

*Figure 3-5. Separation of observations using incremental PCA*

## Sparse PCA

The normal PCA algorithm searches for linear combinations in all the input variables, reducing the original feature space as densely as possible. But for some
machine learning problems, some degree of sparsity may be preferred. A version of
PCA that retains some degree of sparsity—controlled by a hyperparameter called
*alpha*—is known as *sparse PCA*. The sparse PCA algorithm searches for linear combinations in just some of the input variables, reducing the original feature space to
some degree but not as compactly as normal PCA.

Because this algorithm trains a bit more slowly than normal PCA, we will train on
just the first 10,000 examples in our training set (out of the total 50,000 examples).
We will continue this practice of training on fewer than the total number of observations when the algorithm training times are slow.

For our purposes (i.e., developing some intuition of how these dimensionality reduction algorithms work), the reduced training process is fine. For a better solution,
training on the complete training set is advised:

```
# Sparse PCA
from sklearn.decomposition import SparsePCA

n_components = 100
alpha = 0.0001
```

```
random_state = 2018
n_jobs = -1

sparsePCA = SparsePCA(n_components=n_components, \
            alpha=alpha, random_state=random_state, n_jobs=n_jobs)

sparsePCA.fit(X_train.loc[:10000,:])
X_train_sparsePCA = sparsePCA.transform(X_train)
X_train_sparsePCA = pd.DataFrame(data=X_train_sparsePCA, index=train_index)

X_validation_sparsePCA = sparsePCA.transform(X_validation)
X_validation_sparsePCA = \
    pd.DataFrame(data=X_validation_sparsePCA, index=validation_index)

scatterPlot(X_train_sparsePCA, y_train, "Sparse PCA")
```

Figure 3-6 shows a two-dimensional scatterplot using the first two principal components using sparse PCA.

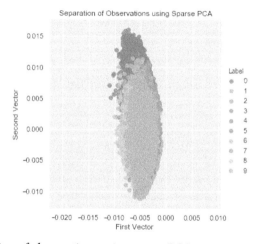

*Figure 3-6. Separation of observations using sparse PCA*

Notice that this scatterplot looks different from that of the normal PCA, as expected.
Normal and sparse PCA generate principal components differently, and the separation of points is somewhat different, too.

## Kernel PCA

Normal PCA, incremental PCA, and sparse PCA linearly project the original data
onto a lower dimensional space, but there is also a nonlinear form of PCA known as
*kernel PCA*, which runs a similarity function over pairs of original data points in
order to perform nonlinear dimensionality reduction.

By using this similarity function (known as the *kernel method*), kernel PCA maps the implicit feature space where the majority of data points lie and creates this implicit feature space in a much smaller number of dimensions than the dimensions in the original feature set. This method is especially effective when the original feature set is not linearly separable.

For the kernel PCA algorithm, we need to set the number of components we desire, the type of kernel, and the kernel coefficient, which is known as the *gamma*. The most popular kernel is the *radial basis function kernel*, more commonly referred to as the *RBF kernel*. This is what we will use here:

```
# Kernel PCA
from sklearn.decomposition import KernelPCA

n_components = 100
kernel = 'rbf'
gamma = None
random_state = 2018
n_jobs = 1

kernelPCA = KernelPCA(n_components=n_components, kernel=kernel, \
                      gamma=gamma, n_jobs=n_jobs, random_state=random_state)

kernelPCA.fit(X_train.loc[:10000,:])
X_train_kernelPCA = kernelPCA.transform(X_train)
X_train_kernelPCA = pd.DataFrame(data=X_train_kernelPCA,index=train_index)

X_validation_kernelPCA = kernelPCA.transform(X_validation)
X_validation_kernelPCA = \
    pd.DataFrame(data=X_validation_kernelPCA, index=validation_index)

scatterPlot(X_train_kernelPCA, y_train, "Kernel PCA")
```

The two-dimensional scatterplot of the kernel PCA is nearly identical to the one of the linear PCA for our MNIST digits dataset (Figure 3-7). Learning the RBF kernel does not improve the dimensionality reduction.

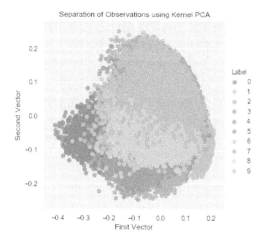

*Figure 3-7. Separation of observations using kernel PCA*

# Singular Value Decomposition

Another approach to learning the underlying structure of the data is to reduce the rank of the original matrix of features to a smaller rank such that the original matrix can be recreated using a linear combination of some of the vectors in the smaller rank matrix. This is known as *singular value decomposition (SVD)*.

To generate the smaller rank matrix, SVD keeps the vectors of the original matrix that have the most information (i.e., the highest singular value). The smaller rank matrix captures the most important elements of the original feature space.

This is very similar to PCA. PCA, which uses the eigen-decomposition of the covariance matrix to perform dimensionality reduction. SVD uses singular value decomposition, as its name implies. In fact, PCA involves the use of SVD in its calculation, but much of this discussion is beyond the scope of this book.

Here is how SVD works:

```
# Singular Value Decomposition
from sklearn.decomposition import TruncatedSVD

n_components = 200
algorithm = 'randomized'
n_iter = 5
random_state = 2018

svd = TruncatedSVD(n_components=n_components, algorithm=algorithm, \
                   n_iter=n_iter, random_state=random_state)

X_train_svd = svd.fit_transform(X_train)
```

```
X_train_svd = pd.DataFrame(data=X_train_svd, index=train_index)

X_validation_svd = svd.transform(X_validation)
X_validation_svd = pd.DataFrame(data=X_validation_svd, index=validation_index)

scatterPlot(X_train_svd, y_train, "Singular Value Decomposition")
```

Figure 3-8 displays the separation of points that we achieve using the two most important vectors from SVD.

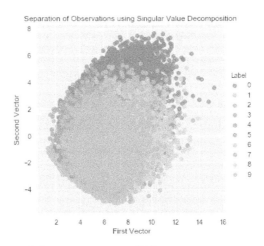

*Figure 3-8. Separation of observations using SVD*

# Random Projection

Another linear dimensionality reduction technique is random projection, which relies on the *Johnson–Lindenstrauss lemma*. According to the Johnson–Lindenstrauss lemma, points in a high-dimensional space can be embedded into a much lower-dimensional space so that distances between the points are nearly preserved. In other words, even as we move from high-dimensional space to low-dimensional space, the relevant structure of the original feature set is preserved.

## Gaussian Random Projection

There are two versions of random projection—the standard version known as *Gaussian random projection* and a sparse version known as *sparse random projection*.

For Gaussian random projection, we can either specify the number of components we would like to have in the reduced feature space, or we can set the hyperparameter *eps*. The eps controls the quality of the embedding according to the Johnson–Lindenstrauss lemma, where smaller values generate a higher number of dimensions. In our case, we will set this hyperparameter:

```
# Gaussian Random Projection
from sklearn.random_projection import GaussianRandomProjection

n_components = 'auto'
eps = 0.5
random_state = 2018

GRP = GaussianRandomProjection(n_components=n_components, eps=eps, \
                               random_state=random_state)

X_train_GRP = GRP.fit_transform(X_train)
X_train_GRP = pd.DataFrame(data=X_train_GRP, index=train_index)

X_validation_GRP = GRP.transform(X_validation)
X_validation_GRP = pd.DataFrame(data=X_validation_GRP, index=validation_index)

scatterPlot(X_train_GRP, y_train, "Gaussian Random Projection")
```

Figure 3-9 shows the two-dimensional scatterplot using Gaussian random projection.

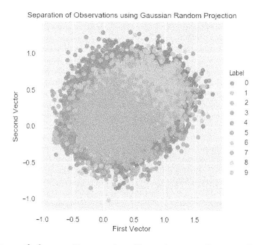

*Figure 3-9. Separation of observations using Gaussian random projection*

Although it is a form of linear projection like PCA, random projection is an entirely different family of dimensionality reduction. Thus the random projection scatterplot looks very different from the scatterplots of normal PCA, incremental PCA, sparse PCA, and kernel PCA.

## Sparse Random Projection

Just as there is a sparse version of PCA, there is a sparse version of random projection known as sparse random projection. It retains some degree of sparsity in the transformed feature set and is generally much more efficient, transforming the original data into the reduced space much faster than normal Gaussian random projection:

---

```
# Sparse Random Projection
from sklearn.random_projection import SparseRandomProjection

n_components = 'auto'
density = 'auto'
eps = 0.5
dense_output = False
random_state = 2018

SRP = SparseRandomProjection(n_components=n_components, \
        density=density, eps=eps, dense_output=dense_output, \
        random_state=random_state)

X_train_SRP = SRP.fit_transform(X_train)
X_train_SRP = pd.DataFrame(data=X_train_SRP, index=train_index)

X_validation_SRP = SRP.transform(X_validation)
X_validation_SRP = pd.DataFrame(data=X_validation_SRP, index=validation_index)

scatterPlot(X_train_SRP, y_train, "Sparse Random Projection")
```

Figure 3-10 shows the two-dimensional scatterplot using sparse random projection.

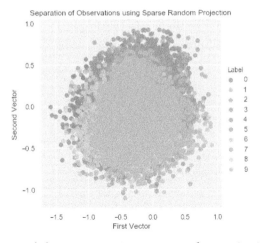

*Figure 3-10. Separation of observations using sparse random projection*

# Isomap

Instead of linearly projecting the data from a high-dimensional space to a low-dimensional space, we can use nonlinear dimensionality reduction methods. These methods are collectively known as manifold learning.

The most vanilla form of manifold learning is known as *isometric mapping*, or *Isomap* for short. Like kernel PCA, Isomap learns a new, low-dimensional embedding of the original feature set by calculating the pairwise distances of all the points, where distance is *curved* or *geodesic distance* rather than *Euclidean distance*. In other words, it learns the intrinsic geometry of the original data based on where each point lies relative to its neighbors on a manifold:

```
# Isomap

from sklearn.manifold import Isomap

n_neighbors = 5
n_components = 10
n_jobs = 4

isomap = Isomap(n_neighbors=n_neighbors, \
                n_components=n_components, n_jobs=n_jobs)

isomap.fit(X_train.loc[0:5000,:])
X_train_isomap = isomap.transform(X_train)
X_train_isomap = pd.DataFrame(data=X_train_isomap, index=train_index)

X_validation_isomap = isomap.transform(X_validation)
X_validation_isomap = pd.DataFrame(data=X_validation_isomap, \
                                   index=validation_index)

scatterPlot(X_train_isomap, y_train, "Isomap")
```

Figure 3-11 shows the two-dimensional scatterplot using Isomap.

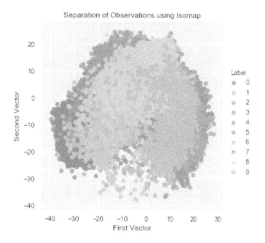

*Figure 3-11. Separation of observations using isomap*

# Multidimensional Scaling

*Multidimensional scaling (MDS)* is a form of nonlinear dimensionality reduction that learns the similarity of points in the original dataset and, using this similarity learning, models this in a lower dimensional space:

```
# Multidimensional Scaling
from sklearn.manifold import MDS

n_components = 2
n_init = 12
max_iter = 1200
metric = True
n_jobs = 4
random_state = 2018

mds = MDS(n_components=n_components, n_init=n_init, max_iter=max_iter, \
          metric=metric, n_jobs=n_jobs, random_state=random_state)

X_train_mds = mds.fit_transform(X_train.loc[0:1000,:])
X_train_mds = pd.DataFrame(data=X_train_mds, index=train_index[0:1001])

scatterPlot(X_train_mds, y_train, "Multidimensional Scaling")
```

Figure 3-12 displays the two-dimensional scatterplot using MDS.

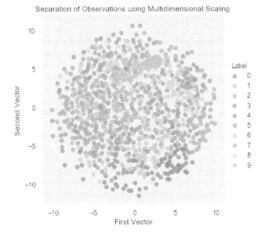

*Figure 3-12. Separation of observations using MDS*

# Locally Linear Embedding

Another popular nonlinear dimensionality reduction method is called *locally linear embedding (LLE)*. This method preserves distances within local neighborhoods as it projects the data from the original feature space to a reduced space. LLE discovers the nonlinear structure in the original, high-dimensional data by segmenting the data into smaller components (i.e., into neighborhoods of points) and modeling each component as a linear embedding.

For this algorithm, we set the number of components we desire and the number of points to consider in a given neighborhood:

```
# Locally Linear Embedding (LLE)
from sklearn.manifold import LocallyLinearEmbedding

n_neighbors = 10
n_components = 2
method = 'modified'
n_jobs = 4
random_state = 2018

lle = LocallyLinearEmbedding(n_neighbors=n_neighbors, \
        n_components=n_components, method=method, \
        random_state=random_state, n_jobs=n_jobs)

lle.fit(X_train.loc[0:5000,:])
X_train_lle = lle.transform(X_train)
X_train_lle = pd.DataFrame(data=X_train_lle, index=train_index)

X_validation_lle = lle.transform(X_validation)
X_validation_lle = pd.DataFrame(data=X_validation_lle, index=validation_index)

scatterPlot(X_train_lle, y_train, "Locally Linear Embedding")
```

Figure 3-13 shows the two-dimensional scatterplot using LLE.

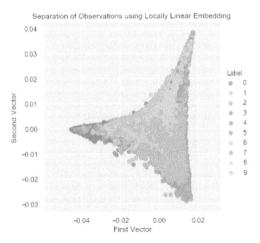

*Figure 3-13. Separation of observations using LLE*

# t-Distributed Stochastic Neighbor Embedding

*t-distributed stochastic neighbor embedding (t-SNE)* is a nonlinear dimensionality reduction technique for visualizing high-dimensional data. t-SNE accomplishes this by modeling each high-dimensional point into a two- or three-dimensional space, where similar points are modeled close to each other and dissimilar points are modeled farther away. It does this by constructing two probability distributions, one over pairs of points in the high-dimensional space and another over pairs of points in the low-dimensional space such that similar points have a high probability and dissimilar points have a lower probability. Specifically, t-SNE minimizes the *Kullback–Leibler divergence* between the two probability distributions.

In real-world applications of t-SNE, it is best to use another dimensionality reduction technique (such as PCA, as we do here) to reduce the number of dimensions before applying t-SNE. By applying another form of dimensionality reduction first, we reduce the noise in the features that are fed into t-SNE and speed up the computation of the algorithm:

```
# t-SNE
from sklearn.manifold import TSNE

n_components = 2
learning_rate = 300
perplexity = 30
early_exaggeration = 12
init = 'random'
random_state = 2018

tSNE = TSNE(n_components=n_components, learning_rate=learning_rate, \
            perplexity=perplexity, early_exaggeration=early_exaggeration, \
```

```
                    init=init, random_state=random_state)

X_train_tSNE = tSNE.fit_transform(X_train_PCA.loc[:5000,:9])
X_train_tSNE = pd.DataFrame(data=X_train_tSNE, index=train_index[:5001])

scatterPlot(X_train_tSNE, y_train, "t-SNE")
```

 t-SNE has a nonconvex cost function, which means that different initializations of the algorithm will generate different results. There is no stable solution.

Figure 3-14 shows the two-dimensional scatterplot of t-SNE.

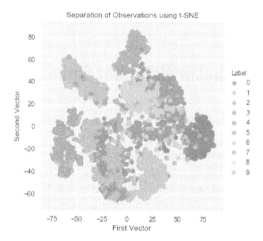

*Figure 3-14. Separation of observations using t-SNE*

# Other Dimensionality Reduction Methods

We have covered both linear and nonlinear forms of dimensionality reduction. Now we will move to methods that do not rely on any sort of geometry or distance metric.

# Dictionary Learning

One such method is *dictionary learning*, which learns the sparse representation of the original data. The resulting matrix is known as the *dictionary*, and the vectors in the dictionary are known as *atoms*.

Assuming there are *d* features in the original data and *n* atoms in the dictionary, we can have a dictionary that is either *undercomplete*, where $n < d$, or *overcomplete*, where $n > d$. The undercomplete dictionary achieves dimensionality reduction, representing the original data with a fewer number of vectors, which is what we will focus on.[3]

There is a mini-batch version of dictionary learning that we will apply to our dataset of digits. As with the other dimensionality reduction methods, we will set the number of components. We will also set the batch size and the number of iterations to perform the training.

Since we want to visualize the images using a two-dimensional scatterplot, we will learn a very dense dictionary, but, in practice, we would use a much sparser version:

```
# Mini-batch dictionary learning

from sklearn.decomposition import MiniBatchDictionaryLearning

n_components = 50
alpha = 1
batch_size = 200
n_iter = 25
random_state = 2018

miniBatchDictLearning = MiniBatchDictionaryLearning( \
                        n_components=n_components, alpha=alpha, \
                        batch_size=batch_size, n_iter=n_iter, \
                        random_state=random_state)

miniBatchDictLearning.fit(X_train.loc[:,:10000])
X_train_miniBatchDictLearning = miniBatchDictLearning.fit_transform(X_train)
X_train_miniBatchDictLearning = pd.DataFrame( \
    data=X_train_miniBatchDictLearning, index=train_index)

X_validation_miniBatchDictLearning = \
    miniBatchDictLearning.transform(X_validation)
X_validation_miniBatchDictLearning = \
    pd.DataFrame(data=X_validation_miniBatchDictLearning, \
    index=validation_index)

scatterPlot(X_train_miniBatchDictLearning, y_train, \
            "Mini-batch Dictionary Learning")
```

Figure 3-15 shows the two-dimensional scatterplot using dictionary learning.

---

3 The overcomplete dictionary serves a different purpose and has applications such as image compression.

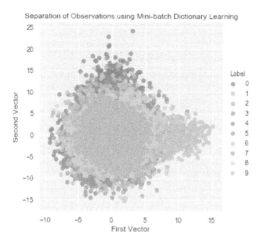

*Figure 3-15. Separation of observations using dictionary learning*

# Independent Component Analysis

One common problem with unlabeled data is that there are many independent signals embedded together into the features we are given. Using *independent component analysis (ICA)*, we can separate these blended signals into their individual components. After the separation is complete, we can reconstruct any of the original features by adding together some combination of the individual components we generate. ICA is commonly used in signal processing tasks (for example, to identify the individual voices in an audio clip of a busy coffeehouse).

The following shows how ICA works:

```
# Independent Component Analysis
from sklearn.decomposition import FastICA

n_components = 25
algorithm = 'parallel'
whiten = True
max_iter = 100
random_state = 2018

fastICA = FastICA(n_components=n_components, algorithm=algorithm, \
                  whiten=whiten, max_iter=max_iter, random_state=random_state)

X_train_fastICA = fastICA.fit_transform(X_train)
X_train_fastICA = pd.DataFrame(data=X_train_fastICA, index=train_index)

X_validation_fastICA = fastICA.transform(X_validation)
X_validation_fastICA = pd.DataFrame(data=X_validation_fastICA, \
                                    index=validation_index)
```

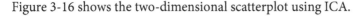

```
scatterPlot(X_train_fastICA, y_train, "Independent Component Analysis")
```

Figure 3-16 shows the two-dimensional scatterplot using ICA.

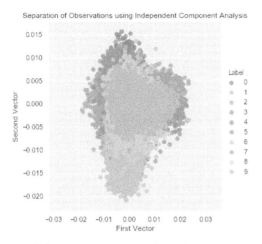

*Figure 3-16. Separation of observations using independent component analysis*

# Conclusion

In this chapter, we introduced and explored a number of dimensionality reduction algorithms starting with linear methods such as PCA and random projection. Then, we switched to nonlinear methods—also known as manifold learning—such as Isomap, multidimensional scaling, LLE, and t-SNE. We also covered nondistance-based methods such as dictionary learning and ICA.

Dimensionality reduction captures the most salient information in a dataset in a small number of dimensions by learning the underlying structure of the data, and it does this without using any labels. By applying these algorithms to the MNIST digits dataset, we were able to meaningfully separate the images based on the digits they represented with just the top two dimensions.

This highlights the power of dimensionality reduction.

In Chapter 4, we will build an applied unsupervised learning solution using these dimensionality reduction algorithms. Specifically, we will revist the fraud detection problem introduced in Chapter 2 and attempt to separate fraudulent transactions from normal ones without using labels.

# CHAPTER 4
# Anomaly Detection

In Chapter 3, we introduced the core dimensionality reduction algorithms and explored their ability to capture the most salient information in the MNIST digits database in significantly fewer dimensions than the original 784 dimensions. Even in just two dimensions, the algorithms meaningfully separated the digits, without using labels. This is the power of unsupervised learning algorithms—they can learn the underlying structure of data and help discover hidden patterns in the absence of labels.

Let's build an applied machine learning solution using these dimensionality reduction methods. We will turn to the problem we introduced in Chapter 2 and build a credit card fraud detection system without using labels.

In the real world, fraud often goes undiscovered, and only the fraud that is caught provides any labels for the datasets. Moreover, fraud patterns change over time, so supervised systems that are built using fraud labels—like the one we built in Chapter 2—become stale, capturing historical patterns of fraud but failing to adapt to newly emerging patterns.

For these reasons (the lack of sufficient labels and the need to adapt to newly emerging patterns of fraud as quickly as possible), unsupervised learning fraud detection systems are in vogue.

In this chapter, we will build such a solution using some of the dimensionality reduction algorithms we explored in the previous chapter.

# Credit Card Fraud Detection

Let's revisit the credit card transactions problem from Chapter 2.

## Prepare the Data

Like we did in Chapter 2, let's load the credit card transactions dataset, generate the features matrix and labels array, and split the data into training and test sets. We will not use the labels to perform anomaly detection, but we will use the labels to help evaluate the fraud detection systems we build.

As a reminder, we have 284,807 credit card transactions in total, of which 492 are fraudulent, with a positive (fraud) label of one. The rest are normal transactions, with a negative (not fraud) label of zero.

We have 30 features to use for anomaly detection—time, amount, and 28 principal components. And, we will split the dataset into a training set (with 190,820 transactions and 330 cases of fraud) and a test set (with the remaining 93,987 transactions and 162 cases of fraud):

```
# Load datasets
current_path = os.getcwd()
file = '\\datasets\\credit_card_data\\credit_card.csv'
data = pd.read_csv(current_path + file)

dataX = data.copy().drop(['Class'],axis=1)
dataY = data['Class'].copy()

featuresToScale = dataX.columns
sX = pp.StandardScaler(copy=True)
dataX.loc[:,featuresToScale] = sX.fit_transform(dataX[featuresToScale])

X_train, X_test, y_train, y_test = \
    train_test_split(dataX, dataY, test_size=0.33, \
                     random_state=2018, stratify=dataY)
```

## Define Anomaly Score Function

Next, we need to define a function that calculates how anomalous each transaction is. The more anomalous the transaction is, the more likely it is to be fraudulent, assuming that fraud is rare and looks somewhat different than the majority of transactions, which are normal.

As we discussed in the previous chapter, dimensionality reduction algorithms reduce the dimensionality of data while attempting to minimize the reconstruction error. In other words, these algorithms try to capture the most salient information of the original features in such a way that they can reconstruct the original feature set from the reduced feature set as well as possible. However, these dimensionality reduction algo-rithms cannot capture all the information of the original features as they move to a lower dimensional space; therefore, there will be some error as these algorithms reconstruct the reduced feature set back to the original number of dimensions.

In the context of our credit card transactions dataset, the algorithms will have the largest reconstruction error on those transactions that are hardest to model—in other words, those that occur the least often and are the most anomalous. Since fraud is rare and presumably different than normal transactions, the fraudulent transactions should exhibit the largest reconstruction error. So let's define the anomaly score as the reconstruction error. The reconstruction error for each transaction is the sum of the squared differences between the original feature matrix and the reconstructed matrix using the dimensionality reduction algorithm. We will scale the sum of the squared differences by the max-min range of the sum of the squared differences for the entire dataset, so that all the reconstruction errors are within a zero to one range.

The transactions that have the largest sum of squared differences will have an error close to one, while those that have the smallest sum of squared differences will have an error close to zero.

This should be familiar. Like the supervised fraud detection solution we built in Chapter 2, the dimensionality reduction algorithm will effectively assign each trans-action an anomaly score between zero and one. Zero is normal and one is anomalous (and most likely to be fraudulent).

Here is the function:

```
def anomalyScores(originalDF, reducedDF):
    loss = np.sum((np.array(originalDF)-np.array(reducedDF))**2, axis=1)
    loss = pd.Series(data=loss,index=originalDF.index)
    loss = (loss-np.min(loss))/(np.max(loss)-np.min(loss))
    return loss
```

## Define Evaluation Metrics

Although we will not use the fraud labels to build the unsupervised fraud detection solutions, we will use the labels to evaluate the unsupervised solutions we develop. The labels will help us understand just how well these solutions are at catching known patterns of fraud.

As we did in Chapter 2, we will use the precision-recall curve, the average precision, and the auROC as our evaluation metrics.

Here is the function that will plot these results:

```
def plotResults(trueLabels, anomalyScores, returnPreds = False):
    preds = pd.concat([trueLabels, anomalyScores], axis=1)
    preds.columns = ['trueLabel', 'anomalyScore']
    precision, recall, thresholds = \
```

```python
    precision_recall_curve(preds['trueLabel'],preds['anomalyScore'])
average_precision = \
    average_precision_score(preds['trueLabel'],preds['anomalyScore'])

plt.step(recall, precision, color='k', alpha=0.7, where='post')
plt.fill_between(recall, precision, step='post', alpha=0.3, color='k')

plt.xlabel('Recall')
plt.ylabel('Precision')
plt.ylim([0.0, 1.05])
plt.xlim([0.0, 1.0])

plt.title('Precision-Recall curve: Average Precision = \
{0:0.2f}'.format(average_precision))

fpr, tpr, thresholds = roc_curve(preds['trueLabel'], \
                                 preds['anomalyScore'])
areaUnderROC = auc(fpr, tpr)

plt.figure()
plt.plot(fpr, tpr, color='r', lw=2, label='ROC curve')
plt.plot([0, 1], [0, 1], color='k', lw=2, linestyle='--')
plt.xlim([0.0, 1.0])
plt.ylim([0.0, 1.05])
plt.xlabel('False Positive Rate')
plt.ylabel('True Positive Rate')
plt.title('Receiver operating characteristic: \
Area under the curve = {0:0.2f}'.format(areaUnderROC))
plt.legend(loc="lower right")
plt.show()

if returnPreds==True:
    return preds
```

The fraud labels and the evaluation metrics will help us assess just how good the unsupervised fraud detection systems are at catching known patterns of fraud—fraud that we have caught in the past and have labels for.

However, we will not be able to assess how good the unsupervised fraud detection systems are at catching unknown patterns of fraud. In other words, there may be fraud in the dataset that is incorrectly labeled as not fraud because the financial company never discovered it.

As you may see already, unsupervised learning systems are much harder to evaluate than supervised learning systems. Often, unsupervised learning systems are judged by their ability to catch known patterns of fraud. This is an incomplete assessment; a better evaluation metric would be to assess them on their ability to identify unknown patterns of fraud, both in the past and in the future.

Since we cannot go back to the financial company and have them evaluate any unknown patterns of fraud we identify, we will have to evaluate these unsupervised systems solely based on how well they detect the known patterns of fraud. It's important to be mindful of this limitation as we proceed in evaluating the results.

## Define Plotting Function

We will reuse the scatterplot function from Chapter 3 to display the separation of points the dimensionality reduction algorithm achieves in just the first two dimensions:

```
def scatterPlot(xDF, yDF, algoName):
    tempDF = pd.DataFrame(data=xDF.loc[:,0:1], index=xDF.index)
    tempDF = pd.concat((tempDF,yDF), axis=1, join="inner")
    tempDF.columns = ["First Vector", "Second Vector", "Label"]
    sns.lmplot(x="First Vector", y="Second Vector", hue="Label", \
               data=tempDF, fit_reg=False)
    ax = plt.gca()
    ax.set_title("Separation of Observations using "+algoName)
```

# Normal PCA Anomaly Detection

In Chapter 3, we demonstrated how PCA captured the majority of information in the MNIST digits dataset in just a few principal components, far fewer in number than the original dimensions. In fact, with just two dimensions, it was possible to visually separate the images into distinct groups based on the digits they displayed.

Building on this concept, we will now use PCA to learn the underlying structure of the credit card transactions dataset. Once we learn this structure, we will use the learned model to reconstruct the credit card transactions and then calculate how different the reconstructed transactions are from the original transactions. Those transactions that PCA does the poorest job of reconstructing are the most anomalous (and most likely to be fraudulent).

 Remember that the features in the credit card transactions dataset we have are already the output of PCA—this is what we were given by the financial company. However, there is nothing unusual about performing PCA for anomaly detection on an already dimensionality-reduced dataset. We just treat the original principal components that we are given as the original features.

Going forward, we will refer to the original principal components that we were given as the original features. Any future mention of principal components will refer to the principal components from the PCA process rather than the original features we were given.

Let's start by developing a deeper understanding of how PCA—and dimensionality reduction in general—helps perform anomaly detection. As we've defined it, anomaly detection relies on reconstruction error. We want the reconstruction error for rare transactions—the ones that are most likely to be fraudulent—to be as high as possible and the reconstruction error for the rest to be as low as possible.

For PCA, the reconstruction error will depend largely on the number of principal components we keep and use to reconstruct the original transactions. The more principal components we keep, the better PCA will be at learning the underlying structure of the original transactions.

However, there is a balance. If we keep too many principal components, PCA may too easily reconstruct the original transactions, so much so that the reconstruction error will be minimal for all of the transactions. If we keep too few principal components, PCA may not be able to reconstruct any of the original transactions well enough— not even the normal, nonfraudulent transactions.

Let's search for the right number of principal components to keep to build a good fraud detection system.

## PCA Components Equal Number of Original Dimensions

First, let's think about something. If we use PCA to generate the same number of principal components as the number of original features, will we be able to perform anomaly detection?

If you think through this, the answer should be obvious. Recall our PCA example from the previous chapter for the MNIST digits dataset.

When the number of principal components equals the number of original dimensions, PCA captures nearly 100% of the variance/information in the data as it generates the principal components. Therefore, when PCA reconstructs the transactions from the principal components, it will have too little reconstruction error for all the transactions, fraudulent or otherwise. We will not be able to differentiate between rare transactions and normal ones—in other words, anomaly detection will be poor.

To highlight this, let's apply PCA to generate the same number of principal components as the number of original features (30 for our credit card transactions dataset). This is accomplished with the `fit_transform` function from Scikit-Learn.

To reconstruct the original transactions from the principal components we generate, we will use the `inverse_transform` function from Scikit-Learn:

```
# 30 principal components
from sklearn.decomposition import PCA

n_components = 30
whiten = False
random_state = 2018

pca = PCA(n_components=n_components, whiten=whiten, \
          random_state=random_state)

X_train_PCA = pca.fit_transform(X_train)
X_train_PCA = pd.DataFrame(data=X_train_PCA, index=X_train.index)

X_train_PCA_inverse = pca.inverse_transform(X_train_PCA)
X_train_PCA_inverse = pd.DataFrame(data=X_train_PCA_inverse, \
                                   index=X_train.index)

scatterPlot(X_train_PCA, y_train, "PCA")
```

Figure 4-1 shows the plot of the separation of transactions using the first two principal components of PCA.

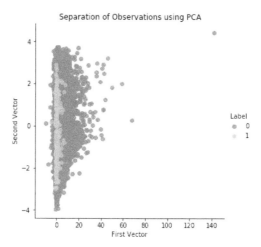

*Figure 4-1. Separation of observations using normal PCA and 30 principal components*

Let's calculate the precision-recall curve and the ROC curve:

```
anomalyScoresPCA = anomalyScores(X_train, X_train_PCA_inverse)
preds = plotResults(y_train, anomalyScoresPCA, True)
```

With an average precision of 0.11, this is a poor fraud detection solution (see Figure 4-2). It catches very little of the fraud.

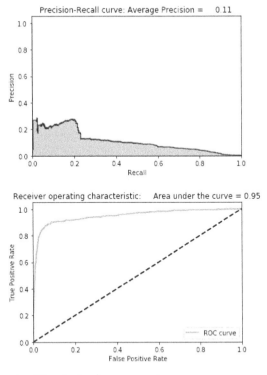

*Figure 4-2. Results using 30 principal components*

## Search for the Optimal Number of Principal Components

Now, let's perform a few experiments by reducing the number of principal components PCA generates and evaluate the fraud detection results. We need the PCA-
based fraud detection solution to have enough error on the rare cases that it can
meaningfully separate fraud cases from the normal ones. But the error cannot be so
low or so high for all the transactions that the rare and normal transactions are virtually indistinguishable.

After some experimentation, which you can perform using the GitHub code (*http://
bit.ly/2Gd4v7e*), we find that 27 principal components is the optimal number for this
credit card transactions dataset.

Figure 4-3 shows the plot of the separation of transactions using the first two principal components of PCA.

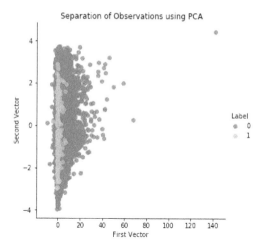

*Figure 4-3. Separation of observations using normal PCA and 27 principal components*

Figure 4-4 shows the precision-recall curve, average precision, and auROC curve.

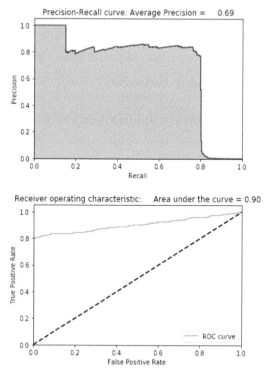

*Figure 4-4. Results using normal PCA and 27 principal components*

As you can see, we are able to catch 80% of the fraud with 75% precision. This is very impressive considering that we did not use any labels. To make these results more tangible, consider that there are 190,820 transactions in the training set and only 330 are fraudulent.

Using PCA, we calculated the reconstruction error for each of these 190,820 transactions. If we sort these transactions by highest reconstruction error (also referred to as anomaly score) in descending order and extract the top 350 transactions from the list, we can see that 264 of these transactions are fraudulent.

That is a precision of 75%. Moreover, the 264 transactions we caught from the 350 we picked represent 80% of the total fraud in the training set (264 out of 330 fraudulent cases). And, remember that we accomplished this without using labels. This is a truly unsupervised fraud detection solution.

Here is the code to highlight this:

```
preds.sort_values(by="anomalyScore",ascending=False,inplace=True)
cutoff = 350
predsTop = preds[:cutoff]
print("Precision: ",np.round(predsTop. \
            anomalyScore[predsTop.trueLabel==1].count()/cutoff,2))
print("Recall: ",np.round(predsTop. \
            anomalyScore[predsTop.trueLabel==1].count()/y_train.sum(),2))
```

The following code summarizes the results:

```
Precision: 0.75
Recall: 0.8
Fraud Caught out of 330 Cases: 264
```

Although this is a pretty good solution already, let's try to develop fraud detection systems using some of the other dimensionality reduction methods.

# Sparse PCA Anomaly Detection

Let's try to use sparse PCA to design a fraud detection solution. Recall that sparse PCA is similar to normal PCA but delivers a less dense version; in other words, sparse PCA provides a sparse representation of the principal components.

We still need to specify the number of principal components we desire, but we must also set the alpha parameter, which controls the degree of sparsity. We will experiment with different values for the principal components and the alpha parameter as we search for the optimal sparse PCA fraud detection solution.

Note that for normal PCA Scikit-Learn used a `fit_transform` function to generate the principal components and an `inverse_transform` function to reconstruct the original dimensions from the principal components. Using these two functions, we were able to calculate the reconstruction error between the original feature set and the reconstructed feature set derived from the PCA.

Unfortunately, Scikit-Learn does not provide an `inverse_transform` function for sparse PCA. Therefore, we must reconstruct the original dimensions after we perform sparse PCA ourselves.

Let's begin by generating the sparse PCA matrix with 27 principal components and the default alpha parameter of 0.0001:

```
# Sparse PCA
from sklearn.decomposition import SparsePCA

n_components = 27
alpha = 0.0001
random_state = 2018
n_jobs = -1

sparsePCA = SparsePCA(n_components=n_components, \
                alpha=alpha, random_state=random_state, n_jobs=n_jobs)

sparsePCA.fit(X_train.loc[:,:])
X_train_sparsePCA = sparsePCA.transform(X_train)
X_train_sparsePCA = pd.DataFrame(data=X_train_sparsePCA, index=X_train.index)

scatterPlot(X_train_sparsePCA, y_train, "Sparse PCA")
```

Figure 4-5 shows the scatterplot for sparse PCA.

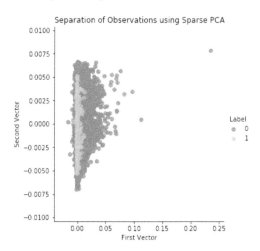

*Figure 4-5. Separation of observations using sparse PCA and 27 principal components*

Now let's generate the original dimensions from the sparse PCA matrix by simple matrix multiplication of the sparse PCA matrix (with 190,820 samples and 27 dimensions) and the sparse PCA components (a 27 x 30 matrix), provided by Scikit-Learn library. This creates a matrix that is the original size (a 190,820 x 30 matrix). We also need to add the mean of each original feature to this new matrix, but then we are done.

From this newly derived inverse matrix, we can calculate the reconstruction errors (anomaly scores) as we did with normal PCA:

```
X_train_sparsePCA_inverse = np.array(X_train_sparsePCA). \
    dot(sparsePCA.components_) + np.array(X_train.mean(axis=0))
X_train_sparsePCA_inverse = \
    pd.DataFrame(data=X_train_sparsePCA_inverse, index=X_train.index)

anomalyScoresSparsePCA = anomalyScores(X_train, X_train_sparsePCA_inverse)
preds = plotResults(y_train, anomalyScoresSparsePCA, True)
```

Now, let's generate the precision-recall curve and ROC curve.

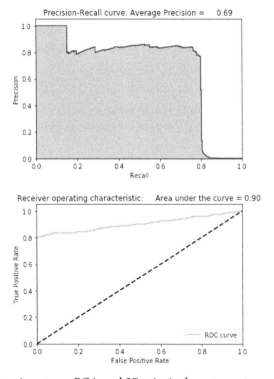

*Figure 4-6. Results using sparse PCA and 27 principal components*

As Figure 4-6 shows, the results are identical to those of normal PCA. This is expected since normal and sparse PCA are very similar—the latter is just a sparse representation of the former.

Using the GitHub code (*http://bit.ly/2Gd4v7e*), you can experiment by changing the number of principal components generated and the alpha parameter, but, based on our experimentation, this is the best sparse PCA-based fraud detection solution.

# Kernel PCA Anomaly Detection

Now let's design a fraud detection solution using kernel PCA, which is a nonlinear form of PCA and is useful if the fraud transactions are not linearly separable from the nonfraud transactions.

We need to specify the number of components we would like to generate, the kernel (we will use the RBF kernel as we did in the previous chapter), and the gamma (which is set to 1/n_features by default, so 1/30 in our case). We also need to set the `fit_inverse_transform` to true to apply the built-in `inverse_transform` function provided by Scikit-Learn.

Finally, because kernel PCA is so expensive to train with, we will train on just the first two thousand samples in the transactions dataset. This is not ideal but it is necessary to perform experiments quickly.

We will use this training to transform the entire training set and generate the principal components. Then, we will use the `inverse_transform` function to recreate the original dimension from the principal components derived by kernel PCA:

```
# Kernel PCA
from sklearn.decomposition import KernelPCA

n_components = 27
kernel = 'rbf'
gamma = None
fit_inverse_transform = True
random_state = 2018
n_jobs = 1

kernelPCA = KernelPCA(n_components=n_components, kernel=kernel, \
                gamma=gamma, fit_inverse_transform= \
                fit_inverse_transform, n_jobs=n_jobs, \
                random_state=random_state)

kernelPCA.fit(X_train.iloc[:2000])
X_train_kernelPCA = kernelPCA.transform(X_train)
X_train_kernelPCA = pd.DataFrame(data=X_train_kernelPCA, \
                            index=X_train.index)

X_train_kernelPCA_inverse = kernelPCA.inverse_transform(X_train_kernelPCA)
X_train_kernelPCA_inverse = pd.DataFrame(data=X_train_kernelPCA_inverse, \
                            index=X_train.index)

scatterPlot(X_train_kernelPCA, y_train, "Kernel PCA")
```

Figure 4-7 shows the scatterplot for kernel PCA.

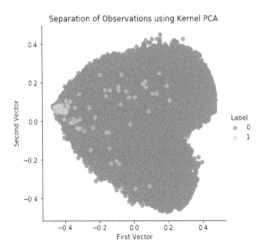

*Figure 4-7. Separation of observations using kernel PCA and 27 principal components*

Now, let's calculate the anomaly scores and print the results.

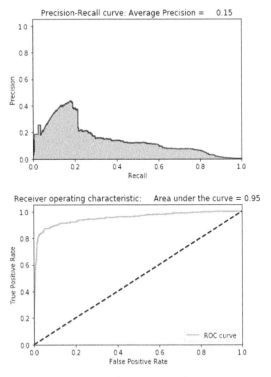

*Figure 4-8. Results using kernel PCA and 27 principal components*

As Figure 4-8 shows, the results are far worse than those for normal PCA and sparse PCA. While it was worth experimenting with kernel PCA, we will not use this solution for fraud detection given that we have better performing solutions from earlier.

We will not build an anomaly detection solution using SVD because the solution is very similar to that of normal PCA. This is expected—PCA and SVD are closely related.

Instead, let's move to random projection-based anomaly detection.

# Gaussian Random Projection Anomaly Detection

Now, let's try to develop a fraud detection solution using Gaussian random projection. Remember that we can set either the number of components we want or the *eps* parameter, which controls the quality of the embedding derived based on the Johnson–Lindenstrauss lemma.

We will choose to explicitly set the number of components. Gaussian random projection trains very quickly, so we can train on the entire training set.

As with sparse PCA, we will need to derive our own `inverse_transform` function because none is provided by Scikit-Learn:

```
# Gaussian Random Projection
from sklearn.random_projection import GaussianRandomProjection

n_components = 27
eps = None
random_state = 2018

GRP = GaussianRandomProjection(n_components=n_components, \
                               eps=eps, random_state=random_state)

X_train_GRP = GRP.fit_transform(X_train)
X_train_GRP = pd.DataFrame(data=X_train_GRP, index=X_train.index)

scatterPlot(X_train_GRP, y_train, "Gaussian Random Projection")
```

Figure 4-9 shows the scatterplot for Gaussian random projection. Figure 4-10 displays the results for Gaussian random projection.

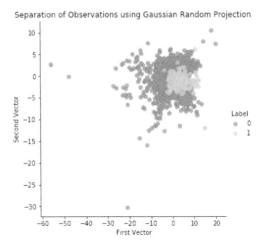

*Figure 4-9. Separation of observations using Gaussian random projection and 27 components*

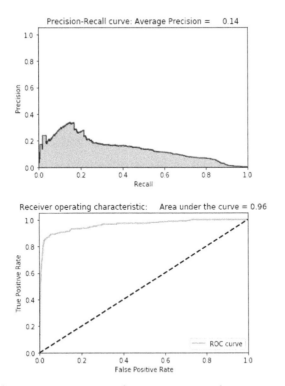

*Figure 4-10. Results using Gaussian random projection and 27 components*

These results are poor, so we won't use Gaussian random projection for fraud detection.

## Sparse Random Projection Anomaly Detection

Let's try to design a fraud detection solution using sparse random projection.

We will designate the number of components we want (instead of setting the *eps* parameter). And, like with Gaussian random projection, we will use our own `inverse_transform` function to create the original dimensions from the sparse random projection-derived components:

```
# Sparse Random Projection

from sklearn.random_projection import SparseRandomProjection

n_components = 27
density = 'auto'
eps = .01
dense_output = True
random_state = 2018

SRP = SparseRandomProjection(n_components=n_components, \
        density=density, eps=eps, dense_output=dense_output, \
                            random_state=random_state)

X_train_SRP = SRP.fit_transform(X_train)
X_train_SRP = pd.DataFrame(data=X_train_SRP, index=X_train.index)

scatterPlot(X_train_SRP, y_train, "Sparse Random Projection")
```

Figure 4-11 shows the scatterplot for sparse random projection. Figure 4-12 displays the results for sparse random projection.

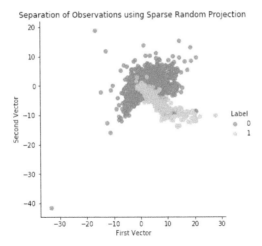

*Figure 4-11. Separation of observations using sparse random projection and 27 components*

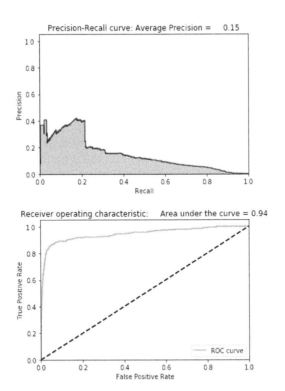

*Figure 4-12. Results using sparse random projection and 27 components*

As with Gaussian random projection, these results are poor. Let's continue to build anomaly detection systems using other dimensionality reduction methods.

# Nonlinear Anomaly Detection

So far, we have developed fraud detection solutions using linear dimensionality reduction methods such as normal PCA, sparse PCA, Gaussian random projection, and sparse random projection. We also developed a solution using the nonlinear version of PCA—kernel PCA.

At this point, PCA is by far the best solution.

We could turn to nonlinear dimensionality reduction algorithms, but the open source versions of these algorithms run very slowly and are not viable for fast fraud detection. Therefore, we will skip this and go directly to nondistance-based dimensionality reduction methods: dictionary learning and independent component analysis.

# Dictionary Learning Anomaly Detection

Let's use dictionary learning to develop a fraud detection solution. Recall that, in dictionary learning, the algorithm learns the sparse representation of the original data. Using the vectors in the learned dictionary, each instance in the original data can be reconstructed as a weighted sum of these learned vectors.

For anomaly detection, we want to learn an undercomplete dictionary so that the vectors in the dictionary are fewer in number than the original dimensions. With this constraint, it will be easier to reconstruct the more frequently occurring normal transactions and much more difficult to construct the rarer fraud transactions.

In our case, we will generate 28 vectors (or components). To learn the dictionary, we will feed in 10 batches, where each batch has 200 samples.

We will need to use our own `inverse_transform` function, too:

```
# Mini-batch dictionary learning
from sklearn.decomposition import MiniBatchDictionaryLearning

n_components = 28
alpha = 1
batch_size = 200
n_iter = 10
random_state = 2018

miniBatchDictLearning = MiniBatchDictionaryLearning( \
    n_components=n_components, alpha=alpha, batch_size=batch_size, \
    n_iter=n_iter, random_state=random_state)

miniBatchDictLearning.fit(X_train)
```

```
X_train_miniBatchDictLearning = \
    miniBatchDictLearning.fit_transform(X_train)
X_train_miniBatchDictLearning = \
    pd.DataFrame(data=X_train_miniBatchDictLearning, index=X_train.index)

scatterPlot(X_train_miniBatchDictLearning, y_train, \
            "Mini-batch Dictionary Learning")
```

Figure 4-13 shows the scatterplot for dictionary learning. Figure 4-14 shows the results for dictionary learning.

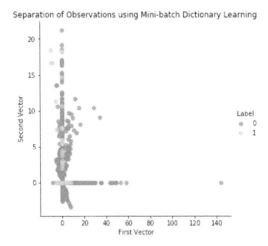

*Figure 4-13. Separation of observations using dictionary learning and 28 components*

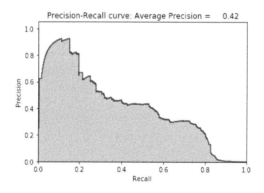

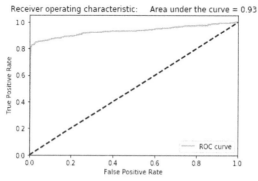

*Figure 4-14. Results using dictionary learning and 28 components*

These results are much better than those for kernal PCA, Gaussian random projection, and sparse random projection but are no match for those of normal PCA.

You can experiment with the code on GitHub to see if you could improve on this solution, but, for now, PCA remains the best fraud detection solution for this credit card transactions dataset.

# ICA Anomaly Detection

Let's use ICA to design our last fraud detection solution.

We need to specify the number of components, which we will set to 27. Scikit-Learn provides an `inverse_transform` function so we do not need to use our own:

```
# Independent Component Analysis

from sklearn.decomposition import FastICA

n_components = 27
algorithm = 'parallel'
whiten = True
```

```
max_iter = 200
random_state = 2018

fastICA = FastICA(n_components=n_components, \
    algorithm=algorithm, whiten=whiten, max_iter=max_iter, \
    random_state=random_state)

X_train_fastICA = fastICA.fit_transform(X_train)
X_train_fastICA = pd.DataFrame(data=X_train_fastICA, index=X_train.index)

X_train_fastICA_inverse = fastICA.inverse_transform(X_train_fastICA)
X_train_fastICA_inverse = pd.DataFrame(data=X_train_fastICA_inverse, \
                                    index=X_train.index)

scatterPlot(X_train_fastICA, y_train, "Independent Component Analysis")
```

Figure 4-15 shows the scatterplot for ICA. Figure 4-16 shows the results for ICA.

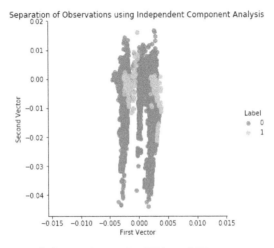

*Figure 4-15. Separation of observations using ICA and 27 components*

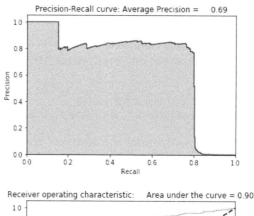

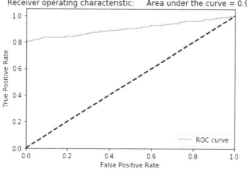

*Figure 4-16. Results using ICA and 27 components*

These results are identical to those of normal PCA. The fraud detection solution using ICA matches the best solution we've developed so far.

# Fraud Detection on the Test Set

Now, to evaluate our fraud detection solutions, let's apply them to the never-before-seen test set. We will do this for the top three solutions we've developed: normal PCA, ICA, and dictionary learning. We will not use sparse PCA because it is very similar to the normal PCA solution.

## Normal PCA Anomaly Detection on the Test Set

Let's start with normal PCA. We will use the PCA embedding that the PCA algorithm learned from the training set and use this to transform the test set. We will then use the Scikit-Learn `inverse_transform` function to recreate the original dimensions from the principal components matrix of the test set.

By comparing the original test set matrix with the newly reconstructed one, we can calculate the anomaly scores (as we've done many times before in this chapter):

```
# PCA on Test Set
X_test_PCA = pca.transform(X_test)
X_test_PCA = pd.DataFrame(data=X_test_PCA, index=X_test.index)

X_test_PCA_inverse = pca.inverse_transform(X_test_PCA)
X_test_PCA_inverse = pd.DataFrame(data=X_test_PCA_inverse, \
                                  index=X_test.index)

scatterPlot(X_test_PCA, y_test, "PCA")
```

Figure 4-17 shows the scatterplot for PCA on the test set. Figure 4-18 displays the results for PCA on the test set.

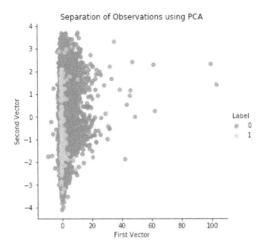

*Figure 4-17. Separation of observations using PCA and 27 components on the test set*

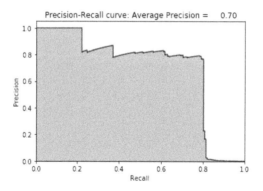

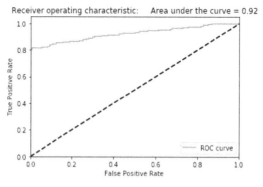

*Figure 4-18. Results using PCA and 27 components on the test set*

These are impressive results. We are able to catch 80% of the known fraud in the test set with an 80% precision—all without using any labels.

## ICA Anomaly Detection on the Test Set

Let's now move to ICA and perform fraud detection on the test set:

```
# Independent Component Analysis on Test Set
X_test_fastICA = fastICA.transform(X_test)
X_test_fastICA = pd.DataFrame(data=X_test_fastICA, index=X_test.index)

X_test_fastICA_inverse = fastICA.inverse_transform(X_test_fastICA)
X_test_fastICA_inverse = pd.DataFrame(data=X_test_fastICA_inverse, \
                                      index=X_test.index)

scatterPlot(X_test_fastICA, y_test, "Independent Component Analysis")
```

Figure 4-19 shows the scatterplot for ICA on the test set. Figure 4-20 shows the results for ICA on the test set.

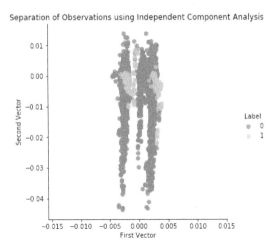

*Figure 4-19. Separation of observations using ICA and 27 components on the test set*

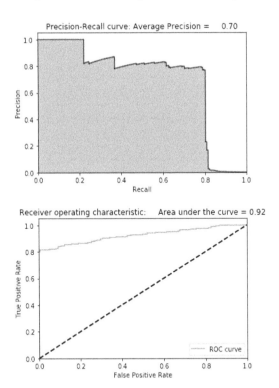

*Figure 4-20. Results using ICA and 27 components on the test set*

The results are identical to normal PCA and thus quite impressive.

# Dictionary Learning Anomaly Detection on the Test Set

Let's now turn to dictionary learning, which did not perform as well as normal PCA and ICA but is worth a final look:

```
X_test_miniBatchDictLearning = miniBatchDictLearning.transform(X_test)
X_test_miniBatchDictLearning = \
    pd.DataFrame(data=X_test_miniBatchDictLearning, index=X_test.index)

scatterPlot(X_test_miniBatchDictLearning, y_test, \
        "Mini-batch Dictionary Learning")
```

Figure 4-21 shows the scatterplot for dictionary learning on the test set. Figure 4-22 displays the results for dictionary learning on the test set.

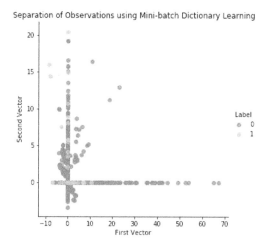

*Figure 4-21. Separation of observations using dictionary learning and 28 components on the test set*

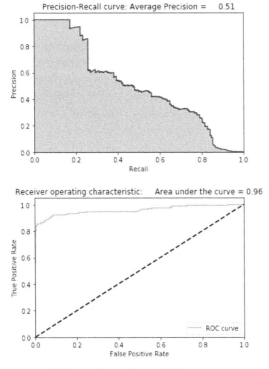

*Figure 4-22. Results using dictionary learning and 28 components on the test set*

While the results are not terrible—we can catch 80% of the fraud with a 20% precision—they fall far short of the results from normal PCA and ICA.

## Conclusion

In this chapter, we used the core dimensionality reduction algorithms from the previous chapter to develop fraud detection solutions for the credit card transactions dataset from Chapter 2.

In Chapter 2 we used labels to build a fraud detection solution, but we did not use any labels during the training process in this chapter. In other words, we built an applied fraud detection system using unsupervised learning.

While not all the dimensionality reduction algorithms performed well on this credit card transactions dataset, two performed remarkably well—normal PCA and ICA.

Normal PCA and ICA caught over 80% of the known fraud with an 80% precision. By comparison, the best-performing supervised learning-based fraud detection system from Chapter 2 caught nearly 90% of the known fraud with an 80% precision. The unsupervised fraud detection system is only marginally worse than the supervised system at catching known patterns of fraud.

Recall that unsupervised fraud detection systems require no labels for training, adapt well to changing fraud patterns, and can catch fraud that had gone previously undiscovered. Given these additional advantages, the unsupervised learning-based solution will generally perform better than the supervised learning-based solution at catching known and unknown or newly emerging patterns of fraud in the future, although using both in tandem is best.

Now that we've covered dimensionality reduction and anomaly detection, let's explore clustering, another major concept in the field of unsupervised learning.

# CHAPTER 5

# Clustering

In Chapter 3, we introduced the most important dimensionality reduction algorithms in unsupervised learning and highlighted their ability to densely capture information. In Chapter 4, we used the dimensionality reduction algorithms to build an anomaly detection system. Specifically, we applied these algorithms to detect credit card fraud without using any labels. These algorithms learned the underlying structure in the credit card transactions. Then, we separated the normal transactions from the rare, potentially fraudulent ones based on the reconstruction error.

In this chapter, we will build on these unsupervised learning concepts by introducing *clustering*, which attempts to group objects together based on similarity. Clustering achieves this without using any labels, comparing how similar the data for one observation is to data for other observations and groups.

Clustering has many applications. For example, in credit card fraud detection, clustering can group fraudulent transactions together, separating them from normal transactions. Or, if we had only a few labels for the observations in our dataset, we could use clustering to group the observations first (without using labels). Then, we could transfer the labels of the few labeled observations to the rest of the observations within the same group. This is a form of *transfer learning*, a rapidly growing field in machine learning.

In areas such as online and retail shopping, marketing, social media, recommender systems for movies, music, books, dating, etc., clustering can group similar people together based on their behavior. Once these groups are established, business users will have better insight into their user base and can craft targeted business strategies for each of the distinct groups.

As we did with dimensionality reduction, let's introduce the concepts first in this chapter, and then we will build an applied unsupervised learning solution in the next chapter.

# MNIST Digits Dataset

To keep things simple, we will continue to work with the MNIST image dataset of digits that we introduced in Chapter 3.

## Data Preparation

Let's first load the necessary libraries:

```
# Import libraries
'''Main'''
import numpy as np
import pandas as pd
import os, time
import pickle, gzip

'''Data Viz'''
import matplotlib.pyplot as plt
import seaborn as sns
color = sns.color_palette()
import matplotlib as mpl

%matplotlib inline

'''Data Prep and Model Evaluation'''
from sklearn import preprocessing as pp
from sklearn.model_selection import train_test_split
from sklearn.metrics import precision_recall_curve, average_precision_score
from sklearn.metrics import roc_curve, auc, roc_auc_score
```

Next, let's load the dataset and create Pandas DataFrames:

```
# Load the datasets
current_path = os.getcwd()
file = '\\datasets\\mnist_data\\mnist.pkl.gz'

f = gzip.open(current_path+file, 'rb')
train_set, validation_set, test_set = pickle.load(f, encoding='latin1')
f.close()

X_train, y_train = train_set[0], train_set[1]
X_validation, y_validation = validation_set[0], validation_set[1]
X_test, y_test = test_set[0], test_set[1]

# Create Pandas DataFrames from the datasets
train_index = range(0,len(X_train))
validation_index = range(len(X_train), \
```

```
                     len(X_train)+len(X_validation))
test_index = range(len(X_train)+len(X_validation), \
                     len(X_train)+len(X_validation)+len(X_test))

X_train = pd.DataFrame(data=X_train,index=train_index)
y_train = pd.Series(data=y_train,index=train_index)

X_validation = pd.DataFrame(data=X_validation,index=validation_index)
y_validation = pd.Series(data=y_validation,index=validation_index)

X_test = pd.DataFrame(data=X_test,index=test_index)
y_test = pd.Series(data=y_test,index=test_index)
```

# Clustering Algorithms

Before we perform clustering, we will reduce the dimensionality of the data using PCA. As shown in Chapter 3, dimensionality reduction algorithms capture the salient information in the original data while reducing the size of the dataset.

As we move from a high number of dimensions to a lower number, the noise in the dataset is minimized because the dimensionality reduction algorithm (PCA, in this case) needs to capture the most important aspects of the original data and cannot devote attention to infrequently occurring elements (such as the noise in the dataset).

Recall that dimensionality reduction algorithms are very powerful in learning the underlying structure in data. In Chapter 3, we showed that it was possible to meaningfully separate the MNIST images based on the digits they displayed using just two dimensions after dimensionality reduction.

Let's apply PCA to the MNIST dataset again:

```
# Principal Component Analysis
from sklearn.decomposition import PCA

n_components = 784
whiten = False
random_state = 2018

pca = PCA(n_components=n_components, whiten=whiten, \
          random_state=random_state)

X_train_PCA = pca.fit_transform(X_train)
X_train_PCA = pd.DataFrame(data=X_train_PCA, index=train_index)
```

Although we did not reduce the dimensionality, we will designate the number of principal components we will use during the clustering stage, effectively reducing the dimensionality.

Now let's move to clustering. The three major clustering algorithms are *k-means*, *hierarchical clustering*, and *DBSCAN*. We will introduce and explore each now.

# k-Means

The objective of clustering is to identify distinct groups in a dataset such that the observations within a group are similar to each other but different from observations in other groups. In *k*-means clustering, we specify the number of desired clusters *k*, and the algorithm will assign each observation to exactly one of these *k* clusters. The algorithm optimizes the groups by minimizing the *within-cluster variation* (also known as *inertia*) such that the sum of the within-cluster variations across all *k* clusters is as small as possible.

Different runs of *k*-means will result in slightly different cluster assignments because *k*-means randomly assigns each observation to one of the *k* clusters to kick off the clustering process. *k*-means does this random initialization to speed up the clustering process. After this random initialization, *k*-means reassigns the observations to different clusters as it attempts to minimize the Euclidean distance between each observation and its cluster's center point, or *centroid*. This random initialization is a source of randomness, resulting in slightly different clustering assignments, from one *k*-means run to another.

Typically, the *k*-means algorithm does several runs and chooses the run that has the best separation, defined as the lowest total sum of within-cluster variations across all *k* clusters.

## k-Means Inertia

Let's introduce the algorithm. We need to set the number of clusters we would like (n_clusters), the number of initializations we would like to perform (n_init), the maximum number of iterations the algorithm will run to reassign observations to minimize inertia (max_iter), and the tolerance to declare convergence (tol).

We will keep the default values for number of initializations (10), maximum number of iterations (300), and tolerance (0.0001). Also, for now, we will use the first 100 principal components from PCA (cutoff). To test how the number of clusters we designate affects the inertia measure, let's run *k*-means for cluster sizes 2 through 20 and record the inertia for each.

Here is the code:

```
# k-means - Inertia as the number of clusters varies
from sklearn.cluster import KMeans

n_clusters = 10
n_init = 10
max_iter = 300
tol = 0.0001
random_state = 2018
n_jobs = 2
```

```
kMeans_inertia = pd.DataFrame(data=[],index=range(2,21), \
                            columns=['inertia'])
for n_clusters in range(2,21):
    kmeans = KMeans(n_clusters=n_clusters, n_init=n_init, \
                    max_iter=max_iter, tol=tol, random_state=random_state, \
                    n_jobs=n_jobs)

    cutoff = 99
    kmeans.fit(X_train_PCA.loc[:,0:cutoff])
    kMeans_inertia.loc[n_clusters] = kmeans.inertia_
```

As Figure 5-1 shows, the inertia decreases as the number of clusters increases. This makes sense. The more clusters we have, the greater the homogeneity among observations within each cluster. However, fewer clusters are easier to work with than more, so finding the right number of clusters to generate is an important consideration when running *k*-means.

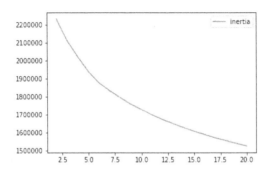

*Figure 5-1. k-means inertia for cluster sizes 2 through 20*

# Evaluating the Clustering Results

To demonstrate how *k*-means works and how increasing the number of clusters results in more homogeneous clusters, let's define a function to analyze the results of each experiment we do. The cluster assignments—generated by the clustering algorithm—will be stored in a Pandas DataFrame called clusterDF.

Let's count the number of observations in each cluster and store these in a Pandas DataFrame called countByCluster:

```
def analyzeCluster(clusterDF, labelsDF):
    countByCluster = \
        pd.DataFrame(data=clusterDF['cluster'].value_counts())
    countByCluster.reset_index(inplace=True,drop=False)
    countByCluster.columns = ['cluster','clusterCount']
```

Next, let's join the clusterDF with the true labels array, which we will call labelsDF:

```
preds = pd.concat([labelsDF,clusterDF], axis=1)
preds.columns = ['trueLabel','cluster']
```

Let's also count the number of observations for each true label in the training set (this won't change but is good for us to know):

```
countByLabel = pd.DataFrame(data=preds.groupby('trueLabel').count())
```

Now, for each cluster, we will count the number of observations for each distinct label within a cluster. For example, if a given cluster has three thousand observations, two thousand may represent the number two, five hundred may represent the number one, three hundred may represent the number zero, and the remaining two hundred may represent the number nine.

Once we calculate these, we will store the count for the most frequently occurring number for each cluster. In the example above, we would store a count of two thousand for this cluster:

```
countMostFreq = \
    pd.DataFrame(data=preds.groupby('cluster').agg( \
                    lambda x:x.value_counts().iloc[0]))
countMostFreq.reset_index(inplace=True,drop=False)
countMostFreq.columns = ['cluster','countMostFrequent']
```

Finally, we will judge the success of each clustering run based on how tightly grouped the observations are within each cluster. For example, in the example above, the cluster has two thousand observations that have the same label out of a total of three thousand observations in the cluster.

This cluster is not great since we ideally want to group similar observations together in the same cluster and exclude dissimilar ones.

Let's define the overall accuracy of the clustering as the sum of the counts of the most frequently occuring observations across all the clusters divided by the total number of observations in the training set (i.e., 50,000):

```
accuracyDF = countMostFreq.merge(countByCluster, \
                    left_on="cluster",right_on="cluster")
overallAccuracy = accuracyDF.countMostFrequent.sum()/ \
                    accuracyDF.clusterCount.sum()
```

We can also assess the accuracy by cluster:

```
accuracyByLabel = accuracyDF.countMostFrequent/ \
                    accuracyDF.clusterCount
```

For the sake of conciseness, we have all this code in a single function, available on GitHub (*http://bit.ly/2Gd4v7e*).

# k-Means Accuracy

Let's now perform the experiments we did earlier, but instead of calculating inertia, we will calculate the overall homogeneity of the clusters based on the accuracy measure we've defined for this MNIST digits dataset:

```
# k-means - Accuracy as the number of clusters varies

n_clusters = 5
n_init = 10
max_iter = 300
tol = 0.0001
random_state = 2018
n_jobs = 2

kMeans_inertia = \
    pd.DataFrame(data=[],index=range(2,21),columns=['inertia'])
overallAccuracy_kMeansDF = \
    pd.DataFrame(data=[],index=range(2,21),columns=['overallAccuracy'])

for n_clusters in range(2,21):
    kmeans = KMeans(n_clusters=n_clusters, n_init=n_init, \
                max_iter=max_iter, tol=tol, random_state=random_state, \
                n_jobs=n_jobs)

    cutoff = 99
    kmeans.fit(X_train_PCA.loc[:,0:cutoff])
    kMeans_inertia.loc[n_clusters] = kmeans.inertia_
    X_train_kmeansClustered = kmeans.predict(X_train_PCA.loc[:,0:cutoff])
    X_train_kmeansClustered = \
        pd.DataFrame(data=X_train_kmeansClustered, index=X_train.index, \
                    columns=['cluster'])

    countByCluster_kMeans, countByLabel_kMeans, countMostFreq_kMeans, \
        accuracyDF_kMeans, overallAccuracy_kMeans, accuracyByLabel_kMeans \
        = analyzeCluster(X_train_kmeansClustered, y_train)

    overallAccuracy_kMeansDF.loc[n_clusters] = overallAccuracy_kMeans
```

Figure 5-2 shows the plot of the overall accuracy for different cluster sizes.

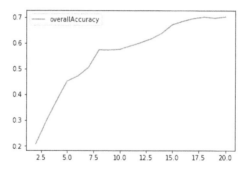

*Figure 5-2. k-means accuracy for cluster sizes 2 through 20*

As Figure 5-2 shows, the accuracy improves as the number of clusters increases. In other words, clusters become more homogeneous as we increase the number of clusters because each cluster becomes smaller and more tightly formed.

Accuracy by cluster varies quite a bit, with some clusters exhibiting a high degree of homogeneity and others exhibiting less. For example, in some clusters, over 90% of the images have the same digit; in other clusters, less than 50% of the images have the same digit:

```
0    0.636506
1    0.928505
2    0.848714
3    0.521805
4    0.714337
5    0.950980
6    0.893103
7    0.919040
8    0.404707
9    0.500522
10   0.381526
11   0.587680
12   0.463382
13   0.958046
14   0.870888
15   0.942325
16   0.791192
17   0.843972
18   0.455679
19   0.926480
dtype:  float64
```

## k-Means and the Number of Principal Components

Let's perform yet another experiment—this time, let's assess how varying the number of principal components we use in the clustering algorithm impacts the homogeneity of the clusters (defined as *accuracy*).

In the experiments earlier, we used one hundred principal components, derived from normal PCA. Recall that the original number of dimensions for the MNIST digits dataset is 784. If PCA does a good job of capturing the underlying structure in the data as compactly as possible, the clustering algorithm will have an easy time grouping similar images together, regardless of whether the clustering happens on just a fraction of the principal components or many more. In other words, clustering should perform just as well using 10 or 50 principal components as it does using one hundred or several hundred principal components.

Let's test this hypothesis. We will pass along 10, 50, 100, 200, 300, 400, 500, 600, 700, and 784 principal components and gauge the accuracy of each clustering experiment. We will then plot these results to see how varying the number of principal components affects the clustering accuracy:

```
# k-means - Accuracy as the number of components varies

n_clusters = 20
n_init = 10
max_iter = 300
tol = 0.0001
random_state = 2018
n_jobs = 2

kMeans_inertia = pd.DataFrame(data=[],index=[9, 49, 99, 199, \
                    299, 399, 499, 599, 699, 784],columns=['inertia'])

overallAccuracy_kMeansDF = pd.DataFrame(data=[],index=[9, 49, \
                    99, 199, 299, 399, 499, 599, 699, 784], \
                    columns=['overallAccuracy'])

for cutoffNumber in [9, 49, 99, 199, 299, 399, 499, 599, 699, 784]:
    kmeans = KMeans(n_clusters=n_clusters, n_init=n_init, \
                max_iter=max_iter, tol=tol, random_state=random_state, \
                n_jobs=n_jobs)

    cutoff = cutoffNumber
    kmeans.fit(X_train_PCA.loc[:,0:cutoff])
    kMeans_inertia.loc[cutoff] = kmeans.inertia_
    X_train_kmeansClustered = kmeans.predict(X_train_PCA.loc[:,0:cutoff])
    X_train_kmeansClustered = pd.DataFrame(data=X_train_kmeansClustered, \
                        index=X_train.index, columns=['cluster'])

    countByCluster_kMeans, countByLabel_kMeans, countMostFreq_kMeans, \
        accuracyDF_kMeans, overallAccuracy_kMeans, accuracyByLabel_kMeans \
        = analyzeCluster(X_train_kmeansClustered, y_train)

    overallAccuracy_kMeansDF.loc[cutoff] = overallAccuracy_kMeans
```

Figure 5-3 shows the plot of the clustering accuracy for the different number of principal components.

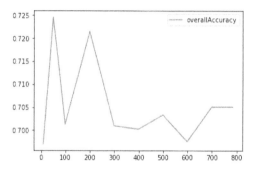

*Figure 5-3. k-means clustering accuracy with varying number of principal components*

This plot supports our hypothesis. As the number of principal components varies from 10 to 784, the clustering accuracy remains stable and consistent around 70%. This is one reason why clustering should be performed on dimensionality-reduced datasets—the clustering algorithms generally perform better, both in terms of time and clustering accuracy, on dimensionality-reduced datasets.

In our case, for the MNIST dataset, the original 784 dimensions are manageable for a clustering algorithm, but imagine if the original dataset were thousands or millions of dimensions large. The case for reducing the dimensionality before performing clustering is even stronger in such a scenario.

## k-Means on the Original Dataset

To make this point clearer, let's perform clustering on the original dataset and measure how varying the number of dimensions we pass into the clustering algorithm affects clustering accuracy.

For the PCA-reduced dataset in the previous section, varying the number of principal components that we passed into the clustering algorithm did not affect the clustering accuracy, which remained stable and consistent at approximately 70%. Is this true for the original dataset, too?

```
# k-means - Accuracy as the number of components varies
# On the original MNIST data (not PCA-reduced)

n_clusters = 20
n_init = 10
max_iter = 300
tol = 0.0001
random_state = 2018
n_jobs = 2

kMeans_inertia = pd.DataFrame(data=[],index=[9, 49, 99, 199, \
                   299, 399, 499, 599, 699, 784],columns=['inertia'])
```

```
overallAccuracy_kMeansDF = pd.DataFrame(data=[],index=[9, 49, \
                99, 199, 299, 399, 499, 599, 699, 784], \
                columns=['overallAccuracy'])

for cutoffNumber in [9, 49, 99, 199, 299, 399, 499, 599, 699, 784]:
    kmeans = KMeans(n_clusters=n_clusters, n_init=n_init, \
                max_iter=max_iter, tol=tol, random_state=random_state, \
                n_jobs=n_jobs)

    cutoff = cutoffNumber
    kmeans.fit(X_train.loc[:,0:cutoff])
    kMeans_inertia.loc[cutoff] = kmeans.inertia_
    X_train_kmeansClustered = kmeans.predict(X_train.loc[:,0:cutoff])
    X_train_kmeansClustered = pd.DataFrame(data=X_train_kmeansClustered, \
                    index=X_train.index, columns=['cluster'])

    countByCluster_kMeans, countByLabel_kMeans, countMostFreq_kMeans, \
        accuracyDF_kMeans, overallAccuracy_kMeans, accuracyByLabel_kMeans \
        = analyzeCluster(X_train_kmeansClustered, y_train)

    overallAccuracy_kMeansDF.loc[cutoff] = overallAccuracy_kMeans
```

Figure 5-4 plots the clustering accuracy at the different original dimensions.

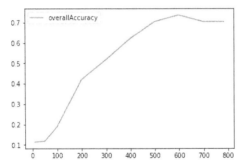

*Figure 5-4. k-means clustering accuracy with varying number of original dimensions*

As the plot shows, clustering accuracy is very poor at lower dimensions but improves to nearly 70% only as the number of dimensions climbs to six hundred dimensions.

In the PCA case, clustering accuracy was approximately 70% even at 10 dimensions, demonstrating the power of dimensionality reduction to densely capture salient information in the original dataset.

# Hierarchical Clustering

Let's move to a second clustering approach called *hierarchical clustering*. This approach does not require us to precommit to a particular number of clusters. Instead, we can choose how many clusters we would like after hierarchical clustering has finished running.

Using the observations in our dataset, the hierarchical clustering algorithm will build a *dendrogram*, which can be depicted as an upside-down tree where the leaves are at the bottom and the tree trunk is at the top.

The leaves at the very bottom are individual instances in the dataset. Hierarchical clustering then joins the leaves together—as we move vertically up the upside-down tree—based on how similar they are to each other. The instances (or groups of instances) that are most similar to each other are joined sooner, while the instances that are not as similar are joined later.

With this iterative process, all the instances are eventually linked together forming the single trunk of the tree.

This vertical depiction is very helpful. Once the hierarchical clustering algorithm has finished running, we can view the dendrogram and determine where we want to cut the tree—the lower we cut, the more individual branches we are left with (i.e., more clusters). If we want fewer clusters, we can cut higher on the dendrogram, closer to the single trunk at the very top of this upside-down tree.

The placement of this horizontal cut is similar to choosing the number of $k$ clusters in the $k$-means clustering algorithm.

## Agglomerative Hierarchical Clustering

The version of hierarchical clustering we will explore is called *agglomerative clustering*. Although Scikit-Learn has a library for this, it performs very slowly. Instead, we will choose to use another version of hierarchical clustering called *fastcluster*. This package is a C++ library with an interface in Python/SciPy.[1]

The main function that we will use in this package is `fastcluster.linkage_vector`. This requires several arguments, including the training matrix $X$, the *method*, and the *metric*. The method—which can be set to `single`, `centroid`, `median`, or `ward`—specifies which clustering scheme to use to determine the distance from a new node in the dendrogram to the other nodes. The metric should be set to `euclidean` in most cases,

---

[1] For more on fastcluster (*https://pypi.org/project/fastcluster/*), check out the project's web page.

and it is required to be euclidean if the method is centroid, median, or ward. For more on these arguments, refer to the fastcluster documentation.

Let's set up the hierarchical clustering algorithm for our data. As before, we will train the algorithm on the first one hundred principal components from the PCA-reduced MNIST image dataset. We will set the method to ward (which performed the best, by far, in the experimentation), and the metric to euclidean.

Ward stands for *Ward's minimum variance method*. You can learn more about this method online (*http://bit.ly/2WwOJK5*). Ward is a good default choice to use in hierarchical clustering, but, as always, it is best to experiment on your specific datasets in practice.

```
import fastcluster
from scipy.cluster.hierarchy import dendrogram, cophenet
from scipy.spatial.distance import pdist

cutoff = 100
Z = fastcluster.linkage_vector(X_train_PCA.loc[:,0:cutoff], \
                               method='ward', metric='euclidean')
Z_dataFrame = pd.DataFrame(data=Z, \
    columns=['clusterOne','clusterTwo','distance','newClusterSize'])
```

The hierarchical clustering algorithm will return a matrix Z. The algorithm treats each observation in our 50,000 MNIST digits dataset as a single-point cluster, and, in each iteration of training, the algorithm will merge the two clusters that have the smallest distance between them.

Initially, the algorithm is just merging single-point clusters together, but as it proceeds, it will merge multipoint clusters with either single-point or multipoint clusters. Eventually, through this iterative process, all the clusters are merged together, forming the trunk in the upside-down tree (dendrogram).

## The Dendrogram

Table 5-1 shows the Z matrix that was generated by the clustering algorithm, showing what the algorithm can accomplish.

*Table 5-1. First few rows of Z matrix of hierarchical clustering*

|    | clusterOne | clusterTwo | distance | newClusterSize |
|----|-----------|-----------|----------|----------------|
| 0  | 42194.0   | 43025.0   | 0.562682 | 2.0 |
| 1  | 28350.0   | 37674.0   | 0.590866 | 2.0 |
| 2  | 26696.0   | 44705.0   | 0.621506 | 2.0 |
| 3  | 12634.0   | 32823.0   | 0.627762 | 2.0 |
| 4  | 24707.0   | 43151.0   | 0.637668 | 2.0 |
| 5  | 20465.0   | 24483.0   | 0.662557 | 2.0 |
| 6  | 466.0     | 42098.0   | 0.664189 | 2.0 |
| 7  | 46542.0   | 49961.0   | 0.665520 | 2.0 |
| 8  | 2301.0    | 5732.0    | 0.671215 | 2.0 |
| 9  | 37564.0   | 47668.0   | 0.675121 | 2.0 |
| 10 | 3375.0    | 26243.0   | 0.685797 | 2.0 |
| 11 | 15722.0   | 30368.0   | 0.686356 | 2.0 |
| 12 | 21247.0   | 21575.0   | 0.694412 | 2.0 |
| 13 | 14900.0   | 42486.0   | 0.696769 | 2.0 |
| 14 | 30100.0   | 41908.0   | 0.699261 | 2.0 |
| 15 | 12040.0   | 13254.0   | 0.701134 | 2.0 |
| 16 | 10508.0   | 25434.0   | 0.708872 | 2.0 |
| 17 | 30695.0   | 30757.0   | 0.710023 | 2.0 |
| 18 | 31019.0   | 31033.0   | 0.712052 | 2.0 |
| 19 | 36264.0   | 37285.0   | 0.713130 | 2.0 |

The first two columns in this table, clusterOne and clusterTwo, list which two clusters—could be single-point clusters (i.e., the original observations) or multipoint clusters—are being merged given their distance relative to each other. The third column, distance, displays this distance, which was determined by the Ward method and euclidean metric that we passed into the clustering algorithm.

As you can see, the distance is monotonically increasing. In other words, the shortest-distance clusters are merged first, and the algorithm iteratively merges the next shortest-distance clusters until all the points have been joined into a single cluster at the top of the dendrogram.

Initially, the algorithm merges single-point clusters together, forming new clusters with a size of two, as shown in the fourth column, newClusterSize. However, as we get much further along, the algorithm joins large multipoint clusters with other large multipoint clusters, as shown in Table 5-2. At the very last iteration (49,998), two large clusters are joined together, forming a single cluster—the top tree trunk—with all 50,000 original observations.

*Table 5-2. Last few rows of Z matrix of hierarchical clustering*

| | clusterOne | clusterTwo | distance | newClusterSize |
|---|---|---|---|---|
| 49980 | 99965.0 | 99972.0 | 161.106998 | 5197.0 |
| 49981 | 99932.0 | 99980.0 | 172.070003 | 6505.0 |
| 49982 | 99945.0 | 99960.0 | 182.840860 | 3245.0 |
| 49983 | 99964.0 | 99976.0 | 184.475761 | 3683.0 |
| 49984 | 99974.0 | 99979.0 | 185.027847 | 7744.0 |
| 49985 | 99940.0 | 99975.0 | 185.345207 | 5596.0 |
| 49986 | 99957.0 | 99967.0 | 211.854714 | 5957.0 |
| 49987 | 99938.0 | 99983.0 | 215.494857 | 4846.0 |
| 49988 | 99978.0 | 99984.0 | 216.760365 | 11072.0 |
| 49989 | 99970.0 | 99973.0 | 217.355871 | 4899.0 |
| 49990 | 99969.0 | 99986.0 | 225.468298 | 8270.0 |
| 49991 | 99981.0 | 99982.0 | 238.845135 | 9750.0 |
| 49992 | 99968.0 | 99977.0 | 266.146782 | 5567.0 |
| 49993 | 99985.0 | 99989.0 | 270.929453 | 10495.0 |
| 49994 | 99990.0 | 99991.0 | 346.840948 | 18020.0 |
| 49995 | 99988.0 | 99993.0 | 394.365194 | 21567.0 |
| 49996 | 99987.0 | 99995.0 | 425.142387 | 26413.0 |
| 49997 | 99992.0 | 99994.0 | 440.148301 | 23587.0 |
| 49998 | 99996.0 | 99997.0 | 494.383855 | 50000.0 |

You may be a bit confused by the clusterOne and clusterTwo entries in this table. For example, in the last row—49,998—cluster 99,996 is joined with cluster 99,997. But as you know, there are only 50,000 observations in the MNIST digits dataset.

clusterOne and clusterTwo refer to the original observations for numbers 0 through 49,999. For numbers above 49,999, the cluster numbers refer to previously clustered points. For example, 50,000 refers to the newly formed cluster in row 0, 50,001 refers to the newly formed cluster in row 1, etc.

In row 49,998, clusterOne, 99,996 refers to the cluster formed in row 49,996, and clusterTwo, 99,997, refers to the cluster formed in row 49,997. You can continue to work your way through this table using this formula to see how the clusters are being joined.

## Evaluating the Clustering Results

Now that we have the dendrogram in place, let's determine where to cut off the dendrogram to make the number of clusters we desire. To more easily compare hierarchical clustering results with those of $k$-means, let's cut the dendrogram to have exactly 20 clusters. We will then use the clustering accuracy metric—defined in the k-means section—to judge how homogenous the hierarchical clustering clusters are.

To create the clusters we desire from the dendrogram, let's pull in the *fcluster* library from SciPy. We need to specify the *distance threshold* of the dendrogram to determine how many distinct clusters we are left with. The larger the distance threshold, the fewer clusters we will have. Data points within the distance threshold we set will belong to the same cluster. A large distance threshold is akin to cutting the upside-down tree at a very high vertical point. Since more and more of the points are grouped together the higher up the tree we go, the fewer clusters we will have.

To get exactly 20 clusters, we need to experiment with the distance threshold, as done here. The *fcluster* library will take our dendrogram and cut it with the distance threshold we specify. Each observation in the 50,000 observations MNIST digits dataset will get a cluster label, and we will store these in a Pandas DataFrame:

```
from scipy.cluster.hierarchy import fcluster

distance_threshold = 160
clusters = fcluster(Z, distance_threshold, criterion='distance')
X_train_hierClustered = \
    pd.DataFrame(data=clusters,index=X_train_PCA.index,columns=['cluster'])
```

Let's verify that there are exactly 20 distinct clusters, given our choice of distance threshold:

```
print("Number of distinct clusters: ", \
      len(X_train_hierClustered['cluster'].unique()))
```

As expected, this confirms the 20 clusters:

```
Number of distinct clusters: 20
```

Now, let's evaluate the results:

```
countByCluster_hierClust, countByLabel_hierClust, \
    countMostFreq_hierClust, accuracyDF_hierClust, \
    overallAccuracy_hierClust, accuracyByLabel_hierClust \
    = analyzeCluster(X_train_hierClustered, y_train)

print("Overall accuracy from hierarchical clustering: ", \
      overallAccuracy_hierClust)
```

We find that the overall accuracy is approximately 77%, even better than the approximately 70% accuracy from *k*-means:

```
Overall accuracy from hierarchical clustering: 0.76882
```

Let's also assess the accuracy by cluster.

As shown here, the accuracy varies quite a bit. For some clusters, the accuracy is remarkably high, nearly 100%. For some, the accuracy is shy of 50%:

---

```
0        0.987962
1        0.983727
2        0.988998
3        0.597356
4        0.678642
5        0.442478
6        0.950033
7        0.829060
8        0.976062
9        0.986141
10       0.990183
11       0.992183
12       0.971033
13       0.554273
14       0.553617
15       0.720183
16       0.538891
17       0.484590
18       0.957732
19       0.977310
dtype:   float64
```

Overall, hierarchical clustering performs well on the MNIST digits dataset. Remember that we accomplished this without using any labels.

This is how it would work on real-world examples: we would apply dimensionality reduction first (such as PCA), then we would perform clustering (such as hierarchical clustering), and finally we would hand-label a few points per cluster. For example, for this MNIST digits dataset, if we did not have any labels, we would look at a few images per cluster and label those images based on the digits they displayed. So long as the clusters were homogeneous enough, the few hand labels we generated could be applied automatically to all the other images in the cluster.

All of a sudden, without much effort, we could have labeled all the images in our 50,000 dataset with a near 77% accuracy. This is impressive and highlights the power of unsupervised learning.

# DBSCAN

Now let's turn to the third and final major clustering algorithm, *DBSCAN*, which stands for *density-based spatial clustering of applications with noise*. As the name implies, this clustering algorithm groups based on the density of points.

DBSCAN will group together closely packed points, where close together is defined as a minimum number of points that must exist within a certain distance. If the point is within a certain distance of multiple clusters, it will be grouped with the cluster to which it is most densely located. Any instance that is not within this certain distance of another cluster is labeled an outlier.

In *k*-means and hierarchical clustering, all points had to be clustered, and outliers were poorly dealt with. In DBSCAN, we can explicitly label points as outliers and avoid having to cluster them. This is powerful. Compared to the other clustering algorithms, DBSCAN is much less prone to the distortion typically caused by outliers in the data. Also, like hierarchical clustering—and unlike *k*-means—we do not need to prespecify the number of clusters.

## DBSCAN Algorithm

Let's first use the DBSCAN library from Scikit-Learn. We need to specify the *maximum distance* (called eps) between two points for them to be considered in the same neighborhood and the *minimum samples* (called min_samples) for a group to be called a cluster. The default value for eps is 0.5, and the default value for min_samples is 5. If eps is set too low, no points may be close enough to other points for them to be considered in the same neighborhood. Hence, all the points would remain unclustered. If eps is set too high, many points may be clustered and only a handful of points would remain unclustered, effectively being labeled as outliers in the dataset.

We need to search for the optimal eps for our MNIST digits dataset. min_samples designates how many points need to be within the eps distance in order for the points to be called a cluster. Once there are min_samples number of closely located points, any other point that is within the eps distance of any of these so-called *core points* is part of that cluster, even if those other points do not have the min_samples number of points within eps distance around them. These other points—if they do not have the *min_samples* number of points within eps distance around them—are called the *border points* of the cluster.

Generally, as the min_samples increases, the number of clusters decreases. As with eps, we need to search for the optimal min_samples for our MNIST digits dataset. As you can see, the clusters have core points and border points, but for all intents and purposes, they belong to the same group. All points that do not get grouped—either as the core or border points of a cluster—are labeled as outliers.

## Applying DBSCAN to Our Dataset

Let's now move to our specific problem. As before, we will apply DBSCAN to the first one hundred principal components of the PCA-reduced MNIST digits dataset:

```
from sklearn.cluster import DBSCAN

eps = 3
min_samples = 5
leaf_size = 30
n_jobs = 4
```

```
db = DBSCAN(eps=eps, min_samples=min_samples, leaf_size=leaf_size,
            n_jobs=n_jobs)

cutoff = 99
X_train_PCA_dbscanClustered = db.fit_predict(X_train_PCA.loc[:,0:cutoff])
X_train_PCA_dbscanClustered = \
    pd.DataFrame(data=X_train_PCA_dbscanClustered, index=X_train.index, \
                 columns=['cluster'])

countByCluster_dbscan, countByLabel_dbscan, countMostFreq_dbscan, \
    accuracyDF_dbscan, overallAccuracy_dbscan, accuracyByLabel_dbscan \
    = analyzeCluster(X_train_PCA_dbscanClustered, y_train)

overallAccuracy_dbscan
```

We will keep the `min_samples` at the default value of five, but we will adjust the `eps` to three to avoid having too few points clustered.

Here is the overall accuracy:

```
Overall accuracy from DBSCAN: 0.242
```

As you can see, the accuracy is very poor compared to *k*-means and hierarchical clustering. We can fidget with the parameters `eps` and `min_samples` to improve the results, but it appears that DBSCAN is poorly suited to cluster the observations for this particular dataset.

To explore why, let's look at the clusters (Table 5-3).

*Table 5-3. Cluster results for DBSCAN*

|   | cluster | clusterCount |
|---|---------|--------------|
| 0 | −1      | 39575        |
| 1 | 0       | 8885         |
| 2 | 8       | 720          |
| 3 | 5       | 92           |
| 4 | 18      | 51           |
| 5 | 38      | 38           |
| 6 | 41      | 22           |
| 7 | 39      | 22           |
| 8 | 4       | 16           |
| 9 | 20      | 16           |

Most of the points are unclustered. You can see this in the plot. 39,651 points—out of the 50,000 observations in the training set—are in cluster -1, which means that they do not belong to any cluster. They are labeled as outliers—noise, in other words.

8,885 points belong in cluster 0. Then, there is a long tail of smaller-sized clusters. It appears that DBSCAN has a hard time finding distinct dense groups of points, and, therefore, does a poor job of clustering the MNIST images based on the digits they display.

## HDBSCAN

Let's try another version of DBSCAN and see if the results improve. This one is known as *HDBSCAN*, or *hierarchical DBSCAN*. The takes the DBSCAN algorithm we introduced and converts it into a hierarchical clustering algorithm. In other words, it groups based on density and then links the density-based clusters based on distance iteratively, like in the hierarchical clustering algorithm we introduced in an earlier section.

The two main parameters for this algorithm are min_cluster_size and min_sam ples, which defaults to min_cluster_size when set to None. Let's use the out-of-the-box parameter selections and gauge if HDBSCAN performs better than DBSCAN did for our MNIST digits dataset:

```
import hdbscan

min_cluster_size = 30
min_samples = None
alpha = 1.0
cluster_selection_method = 'eom'

hdb = hdbscan.HDBSCAN(min_cluster_size=min_cluster_size, \
        min_samples=min_samples, alpha=alpha, \
        cluster_selection_method=cluster_selection_method)

cutoff = 10
X_train_PCA_hdbscanClustered = \
    hdb.fit_predict(X_train_PCA.loc[:,0:cutoff])

X_train_PCA_hdbscanClustered = \
    pd.DataFrame(data=X_train_PCA_hdbscanClustered, \
    index=X_train.index, columns=['cluster'])

countByCluster_hdbscan, countByLabel_hdbscan, \
    countMostFreq_hdbscan, accuracyDF_hdbscan, \
    overallAccuracy_hdbscan, accuracyByLabel_hdbscan \
    = analyzeCluster(X_train_PCA_hdbscanClustered, y_train)
```

Here is the overall accuracy:

```
Overall accuracy from HDBSCAN: 0.24696
```

At 25%, this is only marginally better than that of DBSCAN and well short of the 70%-plus achieved by *k*-means and hierarchical clustering. Table 5-4 displays the cluster count of the various clusters.

*Table 5-4. Cluster results for HDBSCAN*

|   | cluster | clusterCount |
|---|---------|--------------|
| 0 | −1 | 42570 |
| 1 | 4 | 5140 |
| 2 | 7 | 942 |
| 3 | 0 | 605 |
| 4 | 6 | 295 |
| 5 | 3 | 252 |
| 6 | 1 | 119 |
| 7 | 5 | 45 |
| 8 | 2 | 32 |

We see a similar phenomenon as we did for DBSCAN. Most points are unclustered, and then there is a long tail of small-sized clusters. The results do not improve much.

# Conclusion

In this chapter, we introduced three major types of clustering algorithms—$k$-means, hierarchical clustering, and DBSCAN—and applied them to a dimensionality-reduced version of the MNIST digits dataset. The first two clustering algorithms performed very well on the dataset, grouping the images well enough to have a 70%-plus consistency in labels across the clusters.

DBSCAN did not perform quite so well for this dataset but remains a viable clustering algorithm. Now that we've introduced the clustering algorithms, let's build an applied unsupervised learning solution using these algorithms in Chapter 6.

# Group Segmentation

In Chapter 5, we introduced clustering, an unsupervised learning approach to identify the underlying structure in data and grouping points based on similarity. These groups (known as clusters) should be homogeneous and distinct. In other words, the members within a group should be very similar to each other and very distinct from members of any other group.

From an applied perspective, the ability to segment members into groups based on similarity and without any guidance from labels is very powerful. For example, such a technique could be applied to find different consumer groups for online retailers, customizing a marketing strategy for each of the distinct groups (i.e., budget shoppers, fashionistas, sneakerheads, techies, audiophiles, etc.). Group segmentation could improve targeting in online advertising and improve recommendations in recommender systems for movies, music, news, social networking, dating, etc.

In this chapter, we will build an applied unsupervised learning solution using the clustering algorithms from the previous chapter—more specifically, we will perform group segmentation.

## Lending Club Data

For this chapter, we will use loan data from Lending Club, a US peer-to-peer lending company. Borrowers on the platform can borrow between $1,000 to $40,000 in the form of unsecured personal loans, for a term of either three or five years.

Investors can browse the loan applications and choose to finance the loans based on the credit history of the borrower, the amount of the loan, the loan grade, and the purpose of the loan. Investors earn money through interest paid on the loans, and Lending Club makes money from loan origination fees and service charges.

The loan data we will use is from 2007–2011 and is publicly available on the Lending Club website (*http://bit.ly/2FYN2zX*). A data dictionary is also available there.

# Data Preparation

Like in previous chapters, let's prepare the environment to work with the Lending Club data.

## Load libraries

First, let's load the necessary libraries:

```
# Import libraries
'''Main'''
import numpy as np
import pandas as pd
import os, time, re
import pickle, gzip

'''Data Viz'''
import matplotlib.pyplot as plt
import seaborn as sns
color = sns.color_palette()
import matplotlib as mpl

%matplotlib inline

'''Data Prep and Model Evaluation'''
from sklearn import preprocessing as pp
from sklearn.model_selection import train_test_split
from sklearn.metrics import precision_recall_curve, average_precision_score
from sklearn.metrics import roc_curve, auc, roc_auc_score

'''Algorithms'''
from sklearn.decomposition import PCA
from sklearn.cluster import KMeans
import fastcluster
from scipy.cluster.hierarchy import dendrogram, cophenet, fcluster
from scipy.spatial.distance import pdist
```

## Explore the data

Next, let's load the loan data and designate which of the columns to keep:

The original loan data file has 144 columns, but most of these columns are empty and are of little value to us. Therefore, we will designate a subset of the columns that are mostly populated and are worth using in our clustering application. These fields include attributes of the loan such as the amount requested, the amount funded, the term, the interest rate, the loan grade, etc., and attributes of the borrower such as employment length, home ownership status, annual income, address, and purpose for borrowing money.

We will also explore the data a bit:

```
# Load the data
current_path = os.getcwd()
file = '\\datasets\\lending_club_data\\LoanStats3a.csv'
data = pd.read_csv(current_path + file)

# Select columns to keep
columnsToKeep = ['loan_amnt','funded_amnt','funded_amnt_inv','term', \
                 'int_rate','installment','grade','sub_grade', \
                 'emp_length','home_ownership','annual_inc', \
                 'verification_status','pymnt_plan','purpose', \
                 'addr_state','dti','delinq_2yrs','earliest_cr_line', \
                 'mths_since_last_delinq','mths_since_last_record', \
                 'open_acc','pub_rec','revol_bal','revol_util', \
                 'total_acc','initial_list_status','out_prncp', \
                 'out_prncp_inv','total_pymnt','total_pymnt_inv', \
                 'total_rec_prncp','total_rec_int','total_rec_late_fee', \
                 'recoveries','collection_recovery_fee','last_pymnt_d', \
                 'last_pymnt_amnt']

data = data.loc[:,columnsToKeep]

data.shape

data.head()
```

The data has 42,542 loans and 37 features (42,542, 37).

Table 6-1 previews the data.

*Table 6-1. First few rows of the loan data*

|   | loan_amnt | funded_amnt | funded_amnt_inv | term | int_rate | instsallment | grade |
|---|-----------|-------------|-----------------|------|----------|--------------|-------|
| 0 | 5000.0 | 5000.0 | 4975.0 | 36 months | 10.65% | 162.87 | B |
| 1 | 2500.0 | 2500.0 | 2500.0 | 60 months | 15.27% | 59.83 | C |
| 2 | 2400.0 | 2400.0 | 2400.0 | 35 months | 15.96% | 84.33 | C |
| 3 | 10000.0 | 10000.0 | 10000.0 | 36 months | 13.49% | 339.31 | C |
| 4 | 3000.0 | 3000.0 | 3000.0 | 60 months | 12.69% | 67.79 | B |

# Transform String Format to Numerical Format

A few of the features—the term of the loan, the interest rate of the loan, employment length of the borrower, and revolving utilization of the borrower—need to be altered from a string format to a numerical format. Let's perform the transformation:

```
# Transform features from string to numeric
for i in ["term","int_rate","emp_length","revol_util"]:
    data.loc[:,i] = \
        data.loc[:,i].apply(lambda x: re.sub("[^0-9]", "", str(x)))
    data.loc[:,i] = pd.to_numeric(data.loc[:,i])
```

For our clustering application, we will consider just the numerical features and ignore all the categorical features because nonnumerical features cannot be handled by our clustering algorithms in their current form.

# Impute Missing Values

Let's find these numerical features and count the number of NaNs per feature. We will then impute these NaNs with either the mean of the feature or, in some cases, just the number zero, depending on what the feature represents from a business perspective:

```
# Determine which features are numerical
numericalFeats = [x for x in data.columns if data[x].dtype != 'object']

# Display NaNs by feature
nanCounter = np.isnan(data.loc[:,numericalFeats]).sum()
nanCounter
```

The following code shows the number of NaNs by feature:

```
loan_amnt                 7
funded_amnt               7
funded_amnt_inv           7
term                      7
int_rate                  7
installment               7
emp_length             1119
annual_inc               11
dti                       7
delinq_2yrs              36
mths_since_last_delinq 26933
mths_since_last_record 38891
open_acc                 36
pub_rec                  36
revol_bal                 7
revol_util               97
total_acc                36
out_prncp                 7
out_prncp_inv             7
total_pymnt               7
```

```
total_pymnt_inv           7
total_rec_prncp           7
total_rec_int             7
total_rec_late_fee        7
recoveries                7
collection_recovery_fee 7
last_pymnt_amnt           7
dtype: int64
```

Most features have a few NaNs, and some—such as the months since last delinquency and last change in record—have many.

Let's impute these so we do not have to deal with any NaNs during the clustering process:

```
# Impute NaNs with mean
fillWithMean = ['loan_amnt','funded_amnt','funded_amnt_inv','term', \
                'int_rate','installment','emp_length','annual_inc',\
                'dti','open_acc','revol_bal','revol_util','total_acc',\
                'out_prncp','out_prncp_inv','total_pymnt', \
                'total_pymnt_inv','total_rec_prncp','total_rec_int', \
                'last_pymnt_amnt']

# Impute NaNs with zero
fillWithZero = ['delinq_2yrs','mths_since_last_delinq', \
                'mths_since_last_record','pub_rec','total_rec_late_fee', \
                'recoveries','collection_recovery_fee']

# Perform imputation
im = pp.Imputer(strategy='mean')
data.loc[:,fillWithMean] = im.fit_transform(data[fillWithMean])

data.loc[:,fillWithZero] = data.loc[:,fillWithZero].fillna(value=0,axis=1)
```

Let's recalculate the NaNs to make sure no NaNs remain.

We are now safe. All the NaNs have been filled:

```
numericalFeats = [x for x in data.columns if data[x].dtype != 'object']

nanCounter = np.isnan(data.loc[:,numericalFeats]).sum()
nanCounter

loan_amnt                 0
funded_amnt               0
funded_amnt_inv           0
term                      0
int_rate                  0
installment               0
emp_length                0
annual_inc                0
dti                       0
delinq_2yrs               0
mths_since_last_delinq    0
```

```
mths_since_last_record    0
open_acc                  0
pub_rec                   0
revol_bal                 0
revol_util                0
total_acc                 0
out_prncp                 0
out_prncp_inv             0
total_pymnt               0
total_pymnt_inv           0
total_rec_prncp           0
total_rec_int             0
total_rec_late_fee        0
recoveries                0
collection_recovery_fee 0
last_pymnt_amnt           0
dtype: int64
```

## Engineer Features

Let's also engineer a few more features to add to the existing feature set. These new features are mostly ratios between loan amount, revolving balance, payments, and the borrower's annual income:

```
# Feature engineering
data['installmentOverLoanAmnt'] = data.installment/data.loan_amnt
data['loanAmntOverIncome'] = data.loan_amnt/data.annual_inc
data['revol_balOverIncome'] = data.revol_bal/data.annual_inc
data['totalPymntOverIncome'] = data.total_pymnt/data.annual_inc
data['totalPymntInvOverIncome'] = data.total_pymnt_inv/data.annual_inc
data['totalRecPrncpOverIncome'] = data.total_rec_prncp/data.annual_inc
data['totalRecIncOverIncome'] = data.total_rec_int/data.annual_inc

newFeats = ['installmentOverLoanAmnt','loanAmntOverIncome', \
            'revol_balOverIncome','totalPymntOverIncome', \
            'totalPymntInvOverIncome','totalRecPrncpOverIncome', \
            'totalRecIncOverIncome']
```

## Select Final Set of Features and Perform Scaling

Next, we will generate the training dataframe and scale the features for our clustering algorithms:

```
# Select features for training
numericalPlusNewFeats = numericalFeats+newFeats
X_train = data.loc[:,numericalPlusNewFeats]

# Scale data
sX = pp.StandardScaler()
X_train.loc[:,:] = sX.fit_transform(X_train)
```

# Designate Labels for Evaluation

Clustering is an unsupervised learning approach, and, therefore, labels are not used. However, to judge the goodness of our clustering algorithm at finding distinct and homogeneous groups of borrowers in this Lending Club dataset, we will use the loan grade as a proxy label.

The loan grade is currently graded by letters, with loan grade "A" as the most creditworthy and safe and loan grade "G" as the least:

```
labels = data.grade
labels.unique()

array(['B', 'C', 'A', 'E', 'F', 'D', 'G', nan], dtype=object)
```

There are some NaNs in the loan grade. We will fill these with a value of "Z" and then use the LabelEncoder from Scikit-Learn to transform the letter grades to numerical grades. To remain consistent, we will load these labels into a "y_train" Python series:

```
# Fill missing labels
labels = labels.fillna(value="Z")

# Convert labels to numerical values
lbl = pp.LabelEncoder()
lbl.fit(list(labels.values))
labels = pd.Series(data=lbl.transform(labels.values), name="grade")

# Store as y_train
y_train = labels

labelsOriginalVSNew = pd.concat([labels, data.grade],axis=1)
labelsOriginalVSNew
```

*Table 6-2. Numerical versus letter loan grades*

|    | grade | grade |
|----|-------|-------|
| 0  | 1     | B     |
| 1  | 2     | C     |
| 2  | 2     | C     |
| 3  | 2     | C     |
| 4  | 1     | B     |
| 5  | 0     | A     |
| 6  | 2     | C     |
| 7  | 4     | E     |
| 8  | 5     | F     |
| 9  | 1     | B     |
| 10 | 2     | C     |
| 11 | 1     | B     |
| 12 | 2     | C     |
| 13 | 1     | B     |
| 14 | 1     | B     |
| 15 | 3     | D     |
| 16 | 2     | C     |

As you can see from Table 6-2, all the "A" grades have been transformed into 0, the "B" grades into 1, etc.

Let's also check whether grade "A" loans generally have the lowest interest rate charged, since they are the least risky and other loans are charged progressively higher rates of interest:

```
# Compare loan grades with interest rates
interestAndGrade = pd.DataFrame(data=[data.int_rate,labels])
interestAndGrade = interestAndGrade.T

interestAndGrade.groupby("grade").mean()
```

Table 6-3 confirms this. Higher letter grade loans have higher interest rates.[1]

---

1 We can ignore grade "7," which corresponds to loan grade "Z." These are the loans with missing loan grades that we had to fill in.

*Table 6-3. Grade versus interest rate*

| grade | int_rate |
|-------|----------|
| 0.0 | 734.270844 |
| 1.0 | 1101.420857 |
| 2.0 | 1349.988902 |
| 3.0 | 1557.714927 |
| 4.0 | 1737.676783 |
| 5.0 | 1926.530361 |
| 6.0 | 2045.125000 |
| 7.0 | 1216.501563 |

# Goodness of the Clusters

Now the data is ready. We have an X_train with all of our 34 numerical features, and a y_train with the numerical loan grades, which we use only to validate the results, not to train with the algorithm as you would do in a supervised machine learning problem. Before we build our first clustering application, let's introduce a function to analyze the goodness of the clusters we generate using the clustering algorithms. Specifically, we will use the concept of homogeneity to assess the goodness of each cluster.

If the clustering algorithm does a good job separating the borrowers in the Lending Club dataset, each cluster should have borrowers that are very similar to each other and dissimilar to those in other groups. Presumably, borrowers that are similar to each other and grouped together should have similar credit profiles—in other words, their creditworthiness should be similar.

If this is the case (and with real-world problems, a lot of these assumptions are only partially true), borrowers in a given cluster should generally be assigned the same numerical loan grade, which we will validate using the numerical loan grades we set aside in y_train. The higher the percentage of borrowers that have the most frequently occurring numerical loan grade in each and every cluster, the better the clustering application.

As an example, consider a cluster with one hundred borrowers. If 30 borrowers have a numerical loan grade of 0, 25 borrowers have a loan grade of 1, 20 borrowers have a loan grade of 2, and the remaining borrowers have loan grades ranging from 3 to 7, we would say that the cluster has a 30% accuracy, given that the most frequently occuring loan grade for that cluster applies to just 30% of the borrowers in that cluster.

If we did not have a y_train with the numerical loan grades to validate the goodness of the clusters, we could use an alternative approach. We could sample a few borrowers in each cluster, determine the numerical loan grade for them by hand, and determine if we would give roughly the same numerical loan grade to those borrowers. If yes, then the cluster is a good cluster—it is homogeneous enough that we would give roughly the same numerical loan grade to the borrowers we sampled. If not, then the cluster is not good enough—the borrowers are too heterogeneous, and we should try to improve the solution using more data, a different clustering algorithm, etc.

We won't have to sample and manually hand-label the borrowers, though, given that we have the numerical loan grades already, but this is important to keep in mind in case you do not have labels for your particular problem.

Here is the function to analyze the clusters:

```
def analyzeCluster(clusterDF, labelsDF):
    countByCluster = \
        pd.DataFrame(data=clusterDF['cluster'].value_counts())
    countByCluster.reset_index(inplace=True,drop=False)
    countByCluster.columns = ['cluster','clusterCount']

    preds = pd.concat([labelsDF,clusterDF], axis=1)
    preds.columns = ['trueLabel','cluster']

    countByLabel = pd.DataFrame(data=preds.groupby('trueLabel').count())

    countMostFreq = pd.DataFrame(data=preds.groupby('cluster').agg( \
        lambda x:x.value_counts().iloc[0]))
    countMostFreq.reset_index(inplace=True,drop=False)
    countMostFreq.columns = ['cluster','countMostFrequent']

    accuracyDF = countMostFreq.merge(countByCluster, \
        left_on="cluster",right_on="cluster")

    overallAccuracy = accuracyDF.countMostFrequent.sum()/ \
        accuracyDF.clusterCount.sum()

    accuracyByLabel = accuracyDF.countMostFrequent/ \
        accuracyDF.clusterCount

    return countByCluster, countByLabel, countMostFreq, \
        accuracyDF, overallAccuracy, accuracyByLabel
```

# k-Means Application

Our first clustering application using this Lending Club dataset will use *k*-means, which we introduced in Chapter 5. Recall that in *k*-means clustering, we need to specify the desired clusters *k*, and the algorithm will assign each borrower to exactly one of these *k* clusters.

---

The algorithm will accomplish this by minimizing the within-cluster variation, which is also known as inertia, such that the sum of the within-cluster variations across all $k$ clusters is as small as possible.

Instead of specifying just one value of $k$, we will run an experiment where we set $k$ from a range of 10 to 30 and plot the results of the accuracy measure we defined in the previous section.

Based on which $k$ measure performs best, we can build the pipeline for clustering using this best-performing $k$ measure:

```
from sklearn.cluster import KMeans

n_clusters = 10
n_init = 10
max_iter = 300
tol = 0.0001
random_state = 2018
n_jobs = 2

kmeans = KMeans(n_clusters=n_clusters, n_init=n_init, \
                max_iter=max_iter, tol=tol, \
                random_state=random_state, n_jobs=n_jobs)

kMeans_inertia = pd.DataFrame(data=[],index=range(10,31), \
                                columns=['inertia'])

overallAccuracy_kMeansDF = pd.DataFrame(data=[], \
    index=range(10,31),columns=['overallAccuracy'])

for n_clusters in range(10,31):
    kmeans = KMeans(n_clusters=n_clusters, n_init=n_init, \
                    max_iter=max_iter, tol=tol, \
                    random_state=random_state, n_jobs=n_jobs)

    kmeans.fit(X_train)
    kMeans_inertia.loc[n_clusters] = kmeans.inertia_
    X_train_kmeansClustered = kmeans.predict(X_train)
    X_train_kmeansClustered = pd.DataFrame(data= \
        X_train_kmeansClustered, index=X_train.index, \
        columns=['cluster'])

    countByCluster_kMeans, countByLabel_kMeans, \
    countMostFreq_kMeans, accuracyDF_kMeans, \
    overallAccuracy_kMeans, accuracyByLabel_kMeans = \
    analyzeCluster(X_train_kmeansClustered, y_train)

    overallAccuracy_kMeansDF.loc[n_clusters] = \
        overallAccuracy_kMeans

overallAccuracy_kMeansDF.plot()
```

Figure 6-1 displays the plot of the results.

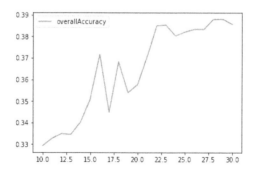

*Figure 6-1. Overall accuracy for different k measures using k-means*

As we can see, the accuracy is best around 30 clusters and levels out there at approximately 39%. In other words, for any given cluster, the most-frequently occurring label for that cluster applies to approximately 39% of the borrowers. The remaining 61% of the borrowers have labels that are not the most-frequently occurring.

The following code displays the accuracy by cluster for $k = 30$:

```
0       0.326633
1       0.258993
2       0.292240
3       0.234242
4       0.388794
5       0.325654
6       0.303797
7       0.762116
8       0.222222
9       0.391381
10      0.292910
11      0.317533
12      0.206897
13      0.312709
14      0.345233
15      0.682208
16      0.327250
17      0.366605
18      0.234783
19      0.288757
20      0.500000
21      0.375466
22      0.332203
23      0.252252
24      0.338509
25      0.232000
26      0.464418
27      0.261583
```

```
28      0.376327
29      0.269129
dtype: float64
```

The accuracy varies quite a bit cluster to cluster. Some clusters are much more homogeneous than others. For example, cluster 7 has an accuracy of 76%, while cluster 12 has an accuracy of just 21%. This is a starting point to build a clustering application to automatically assign new borrowers that apply for a Lending Club loan into a pre-existing group based on how similar they are to other borrowers. Based on this clustering, it is possible to automatically assign a tentative numerical loan grade to the new borrower, which will be correct approximately 39% of the time.

This is not the best possible solution, and we should consider whether acquiring more data, performing more feature engineering and selection, selecting different parameters for the $k$-means algorithm, or changing to a different clustering algorithm will improve the results. It is possible that we do not have enough data to meaningfully separate the borrowers into distinct and homogeneous groups more than we have already; if this is the case, more data and more feature engineering and selection are required. Or, it could be that, for the limited data that we have, $k$-means is not best for performing this separation.

Let's switch to hierarchical clustering to see if our results improve.

# Hierarchical Clustering Application

Recall that in hierarchical clustering we do not need to precommit to a particular number of clusters. Instead, we can choose how many clusters we would like after the hierarchical clustering has finished running. Hierarchical clustering will build a dendrogram, which can be conceptually viewed as an upside-down tree. The leaves at the very bottom are the individual borrowers that apply for loans on Lending Club.

Hierarchical clustering joins the borrowers together as we move vertically up the upside-down tree based on how similar they are to each other. The borrowers that are most similar to each other are joined sooner, while borrowers that are not as similar are joined much later. Eventually, all the borrowers are joined together at the very top —the trunk—of the upside-down tree.

From a business perspective, this clustering process is clearly very powerful. If we are able to find borrowers that are similar to each other and group them together, we can more efficiently assign creditworthiness ratings to them. We can also have specific strategies for distinct groups of borrowers and better manage them from a relationship perspective, providing better overall client service.

Once the hierarchical clustering algorithm finishes running, we can determine where we want to cut the tree. The lower we cut, the more groups of borrowers we are left with.

Let's first train the hierarchical clustering algorithm like we did in Chapter 5:

```
import fastcluster
from scipy.cluster.hierarchy import dendrogram
from scipy.cluster.hierarchy import cophenet
from scipy.spatial.distance import pdist

Z = fastcluster.linkage_vector(X_train, method='ward', \
                               metric='euclidean')

Z_dataFrame = pd.DataFrame(data=Z,columns=['clusterOne', \
                'clusterTwo','distance','newClusterSize'])
```

Table 6-4 shows what the output dataframe looks like. The first few rows are the initial linkages of the bottom-most borrowers.

*Table 6-4. Bottom-most leaves of hierarchical clustering*

|    | clusterOne | clusterTwo | distance | newClusterSize |
|----|-----------|-----------|-----------|----------------|
| 0  | 39786.0 | 39787.0 | 0.000000e+00 | 2.0 |
| 1  | 39788.0 | 42542.0 | 0.000000e+00 | 3.0 |
| 2  | 42538.0 | 42539.0 | 0.000000e+00 | 2.0 |
| 3  | 42540.0 | 42544.0 | 0.000000e+00 | 3.0 |
| 4  | 42541.0 | 42545.0 | 3.399350e-17 | 4.0 |
| 5  | 42543.0 | 42546.0 | 5.139334e-17 | 7.0 |
| 6  | 33251.0 | 33261.0 | 1.561313e-01 | 2.0 |
| 7  | 42512.0 | 42535.0 | 3.342654e-01 | 2.0 |
| 8  | 42219.0 | 42316.0 | 3.368231e-01 | 2.0 |
| 9  | 6112.0 | 21928.0 | 3.384368e-01 | 2.0 |
| 10 | 33248.0 | 33275.0 | 3.583819e-01 | 2.0 |
| 11 | 33253.0 | 33265.0 | 3.595331e-01 | 2.0 |
| 12 | 33258.0 | 42552.0 | 3.719377e-01 | 3.0 |
| 13 | 20430.0 | 23299.0 | 3.757307e-01 | 2.0 |
| 14 | 5455.0 | 32845.0 | 3.828709e-01 | 2.0 |
| 15 | 28615.0 | 30306.0 | 3.900294e-01 | 2.0 |
| 16 | 9056.0 | 9769.0 | 3.967378e-01 | 2.0 |
| 17 | 11162.0 | 13857.0 | 3.991124e-01 | 2.0 |
| 18 | 33270.0 | 42548.0 | 3.995620e-01 | 3.0 |
| 19 | 17422.0 | 17986.0 | 4.061704e-01 | 2.0 |

Recall that the last few rows represent the top of the upside-down tree, and all 42,541 borrowers are combined together eventually (see Table 6-5).

*Table 6-5. Top-most leaves of hierarchical clustering*

|        | clusterOne | clusterTwo | distance   | newClusterSize |
|--------|------------|------------|------------|----------------|
| 42521  | 85038.0    | 85043.0    | 132.715723 | 3969.0         |
| 42522  | 85051.0    | 85052.0    | 141.386569 | 2899.0         |
| 42532  | 85026.0    | 85027.0    | 146.976703 | 2351.0         |
| 42524  | 85048.0    | 85049.0    | 152.660192 | 5691.0         |
| 42525  | 85036.0    | 85059.0    | 153.512281 | 5956.0         |
| 42526  | 85033.0    | 85044.0    | 160.825959 | 2203.0         |
| 42527  | 85055.0    | 85061.0    | 163.701428 | 668.0          |
| 42528  | 85062.0    | 85066.0    | 168.199295 | 6897.0         |
| 42529  | 85054.0    | 85060.0    | 168.924039 | 9414.0         |
| 42530  | 85028.0    | 85064.0    | 185.215769 | 3118.0         |
| 42531  | 85067.0    | 85071.0    | 187.832588 | 15370.0        |
| 42532  | 85056.0    | 85073.0    | 203.212147 | 17995.0        |
| 42533  | 85057.0    | 85063.0    | 205.285993 | 9221.0         |
| 42534  | 85068.0    | 85072.0    | 207.902660 | 5321.0         |
| 42535  | 85069.0    | 85075.0    | 236.754581 | 9889.0         |
| 42536  | 85070.0    | 85077.0    | 298.587755 | 16786.0        |
| 42537  | 85058.0    | 85078.0    | 309.946867 | 16875.0        |
| 42538  | 85074.0    | 85079.0    | 375.698458 | 34870.0        |
| 42539  | 85065.0    | 85080.0    | 400.711547 | 37221.0        |
| 42504  | 85076.0    | 85081.0    | 644.047472 | 42542.0        |

Now, let's cut the dendrogram so that we are left with a manageable number of clusters. This is set based on the `distance_threshold`. Based on trial and error, a `distance_threshold` of 100 results in 32 clusters, which is what we will use for this example.

```
from scipy.cluster.hierarchy import fcluster
distance_threshold = 100
clusters = fcluster(Z, distance_threshold, criterion='distance')
X_train_hierClustered = pd.DataFrame(data=clusters,
  index=X_train_PCA.index,columns=['cluster'])

print("Number of distinct clusters: ",
  len(X_train_hierClustered['cluster'].unique()))
```

The number of distinct clusters given the distance threshold we picked is 32:

```
countByCluster_hierClust, countByLabel_hierClust, countMostFreq_hierClust,
  accuracyDF_hierClust, overallAccuracy_hierClust, accuracyByLabel_hierClust =
  analyzeCluster(X_train_hierClustered, y_train)
print("Overall accuracy from hierarchical clustering: ",
  overallAccuracy_hierClust)
```

The following code shows the overall accuracy of hierarchical clustering:

```
Overall accuracy from hierarchical clustering: 0.3651685393258427
```

The overall accuracy is approximately 37%, a bit worse than with $k$-means clustering. That being said, hierarchical clustering works differently than $k$-means and may group some borrowers more accurately than $k$-means, while $k$-means may group other borrowers more accurately than hierarchical clustering.

In other words, the two clustering algorithms may complement each other, and this is worth exploring by ensembling the two and assessing the ensemble's results compared to the results of either standalone solution.[2] As with $k$-means, the accuracy varies quite a bit across the clusters. Some clusters are much more homogeneous than others:

```
Accuracy by cluster for hierarchical clustering

0       0.304124
1       0.219001
2       0.228311
3       0.379722
4       0.240064
5       0.272011
6       0.314560
7       0.263930
8       0.246138
9       0.318942
10      0.302752
11      0.269772
12      0.335717
13      0.330403
14      0.346320
15      0.440141
16      0.744155
17      0.502227
18      0.294118
19      0.236111
20      0.254727
21      0.241042
22      0.317979
23      0.308771
24      0.284314
25      0.243243
26      0.500000
27      0.289157
28      0.365283
29      0.479693
```

---

2 We explored ensembling in Chapter 2. Refer back to "Ensembles" on page 61 if you need a refresher.

```
30      0.393559
31      0.340875
```

# HDBSCAN Application

Now let's turn to HDBSCAN and apply this clustering algorithm to group similar borrowers in this Lending Club dataset.

Recall that HDBSCAN will group borrowers together based on how closely packed together their attributes are in a high-dimensional space. Unlike $k$-means or hierarchical clustering, not all the borrowers will be grouped. Some borrowers that are very distinct from other groups of borrowers may remain ungrouped. These are outlier borrowers and are worth investigating to see if there is a good business reason they are dissimilar from other borrowers. It may be possible to automatically assign numerical loan grades to some groups of borrowers but other borrowers—those that are dissimilar—may require a more nuanced credit-scoring approach.

Let's see how well HDBSCAN does:

```
import hdbscan

min_cluster_size = 20
min_samples = 20
alpha = 1.0
cluster_selection_method = 'leaf'

hdb = hdbscan.HDBSCAN(min_cluster_size=min_cluster_size, \
    min_samples=min_samples, alpha=alpha, \
    cluster_selection_method=cluster_selection_method)

X_train_hdbscanClustered = hdb.fit_predict(X_train)
X_train_hdbscanClustered = pd.DataFrame(data= \
    X_train_hdbscanClustered, index=X_train.index, \
    columns=['cluster'])

countByCluster_hdbscan, countByLabel_hdbscan, \
    countMostFreq_hdbscan, accuracyDF_hdbscan, \
    overallAccuracy_hdbscan, accuracyByLabel_hdbscan = \
    analyzeCluster(X_train_hdbscanClustered, y_train)
```

The following code shows the overall accuracy for HDBSCAN:

```
Overall accuracy from HDBSCAN: 0.3246203751586667
```

As seen here, the overall accuracy is approximately 32%, worse than that of either $k$-means or hierarchical clustering.

Table 6-6 shows the various clusters and their cluster sizes.

*Table 6-6. Cluster results for HDBSCAN*

| | cluster | clusterCount |
|---|---|---|
| 0 | −1 | 32708 |
| 1 | 7 | 4070 |
| 2 | 2 | 3668 |
| 3 | 1 | 1096 |
| 4 | 4 | 773 |
| 5 | 0 | 120 |
| 6 | 6 | 49 |
| 7 | 3 | 38 |
| 8 | 5 | 20 |

32,708 of the borrowers are in cluster -1, which means they are ungrouped.

The following shows the accuracy by cluster:

```
0      0.284487
1      0.341667
2      0.414234
3      0.332061
4      0.552632
5      0.438551
6      0.400000
7      0.408163
8      0.590663
```

Among these clusters, the accuracy ranges from 28% to 59%.

# Conclusion

In this chapter, we built an unsupervised clustering application based on borrowers that applied for unsecured personal loans on Lending Club from 2007-2011. The applications were based on *k*-means, hierarchical clustering, and hierarchical DBSCAN. *k*-means performed the best, scoring an approximately 39% overall accuracy.

While these applications performed okay, they can be improved quite a bit. You should experiment with these algorithms to improve the solution from here.

This concludes the unsupervised learning using Scikit-Learn portion of the book. Next, we will explore neural network-based forms of unsupervised learning using TensorFlow and Keras. We will start with representation learning and autoencoders in Chapter 7.

# Unsupervised Learning Using TensorFlow and Keras

We just concluded the Scikit-Learn-based unsupervised learning portion of the book. Now we will move to neural network-based unsupervised learning. In the next few chapters, we will introduce neural networks, including the popular frameworks used to apply them, TensorFlow and Keras.

In Chapter 7, we will use an autoencoder—a shallow neural network—to automatically perform feature engineering and feature selection. Moving on from there, in Chapter 8, we will apply autoencoders to a real-world problem. Following that, Chapter 9 explores how to turn unsupervised learning problems into semisupervised ones, leveraging the few labels we have to improve the precision and recall of a purely unsupervised model.

Once we are finished reviewing shallow neural networks, we will look at deep neural networks in the last portion of the book.

# CHAPTER 7

# Autoencoders

The first six chapters of this book explored how to use unsupervised learning to perform dimensionality reduction and clustering, and the concepts we covered helped us build applications to detect anomalies and segment groups based on similarity.

However, unsupervised learning is capable of a lot more. One area that unsupervised learning excels in is *feature extraction*, which is a method used to generate a new feature representation from an original set of features; the new feature representation is called a *learned representation* and is used to improve performance on supervised learning problems. In other words, feature extraction is an unsupervised means to a supervised end.

Autoencoders are one such form of feature extraction. They use a *feedforward, nonrecurrent neural network* to perform *representation learning*. Representation learning is a core part of an entire branch of machine learning involving neural networks.

In autoencoders—which are a form of representation learning—each layer of the neural network learns a representation of the original features, and subsequent layers build on the representation learned by the preceding layers. Layer by layer, the autoencoder learns increasingly complicated representations from simpler ones, building what is known as a hierarchy of concepts that become more and more abstract.

The output layer is the final newly learned representation of the original features. This learned representation can then be used as input into a supervised learning model with the objective of improving the generalization error.

But before we get too far ahead of ourselves, let's begin by introducing neural networks and the Python frameworks TensorFlow and Keras.

# Neural Networks

At their very essence, neural networks perform representation learning, where each layer of the neural network learns a representation from the previous layer. By building more nuanced and detailed representations layer by layer, neural networks can accomplish pretty amazing tasks such as computer vision, speech recognition, and machine translation.

Neural networks come in two forms—shallow and deep. Shallow networks have few layers, and deep networks have many layers. Deep learning gets its name from the deep (many-layered) neural networks it deploys. Shallow neural networks are not particularly powerful since the degree of representation learning is limited by the low number of layers. Deep learning, on the other hand, is incredibly powerful and is currently one of the hottest areas in machine learning.

To be clear, shallow and deep learning using neural networks are just a part of the entire machine learning ecosystem. The major difference between machine learning using neural networks and classical machine learning is that a lot of the feature representation is automatically performed in the neural networks case and is hand-designed in classical machine learning.

Neural networks have an *input layer*, one or many *hidden layers*, and an *output layer*. The number of hidden layers defines just how *deep* the neural network is. You can view these hidden layers as intermediate computations; these hidden layers together allow the entire neural network to perform complex function approximation.

Each layer has a certain number of *nodes* (also known as *neurons* or *units*) that comprise the layer. The nodes of each layer are then connected to the nodes of the next layer. During the training process, the neural network determines the optimal weights to assign to each node.

In addition to adding more layers, we can add more nodes to a neural network to increase the capacity of the neural network to model complex relationships. These nodes are fed into an *activation function*, which determines what value of the current layer is fed into the next layer of the neural network. Common activation functions include *linear*, *sigmoid*, *hyperbolic tangent*, and *rectified linear unit (ReLU)* activation functions. The final activation function is usually the *softmax function*, which outputs a class probability that the input observation falls in. This is pretty typical for classification type problems.

Neural networks may also have *bias nodes*; these nodes are always constant values and, unlike the normal nodes, are not connected to the previous layer. Rather, they allow the input of an activation function to be shifted lower or higher. With the hidden layers—including the nodes, bias nodes, and activation functions—the neural network is trying to learn the right function approximation to use to map the input layer to the output layer.

In the case of supervised learning problems, this is pretty straightforward. The input layer represents the features that are fed into the neural network, and the output layer represents the label assigned to each observation. During the training process, the neural network determines which *weights* across the neural network help minimize the error between its predicted label for each observation and the true label. In unsupervised learning problems, the neural network learns representations of the input layer via the various hidden layers but is not guided by labels.

Neural networks are incredibly powerful and are capable of modeling complex nonlinear relationships to a degree that classical machine learning algorithms struggle with. In general, this is a great characteristic of neural networks, but there is a potential risk. Because neural networks can model such complex nonlinear relationships, they are also much more prone to overfitting, which we should be aware of and address when designing machine learning applications using neural networks.[1]

Although there are multiple types of neural networks such as *recurrent neural networks* in which data can flow in any direction (used for speech recognition and machine translation) and *convolutional neural networks* (used for computer vision), we will focus on the more straightforward feedforward neural network in which data moves in just one direction: forward.

We also must perform a lot more hyperparameter optimization to get neural networks to perform well—including the choice of the cost function, the algorithm to minimize the loss, the type of initialization for the starting weights, the number of iterations to use to train the neural network (i.e., number of epochs), the number of observations to feed in before each weight update (i.e., batch size), and the step size to move the weights in (i.e., learning rate) during the training process.

# TensorFlow

Before we introduce autoencoders, let's explore *TensorFlow*, the primary library we will use to build neural networks. TensorFlow is an open source software library for high-performance numerical computation and was initially developed by the Google Brain team for internal Google use. In November 2015, it was released as open source software.[2]

TensorFlow is available across many operating systems (including Linux, macOS, Windows, Android, and iOS) and can run on multiple CPUs and GPUs, making the

---

1 This process is known as regularization.

2 For more on TensorFlow, consult the website (*https://www.tensorflow.org/*).

software very scalable for fast performance and deployable to most users across desktop, mobile, web, and cloud.

The beauty of TensorFlow is that users can define a neural network—or, more generally, a graph of computations—in Python, and can take the neural network and run it using C++ code, which is much faster than Python.

TensorFlow is also able to *parallelize* the computations, breaking down the entire series of operations into separate chunks and running them in parallel across multiple CPUs and GPUs. Performance like this is a very important consideration for large-scale machine learning applications like those that Google runs for its core operations such as search.

While there are other open source libraries capable of similar feats, TensorFlow has become the most popular, partly due to Google's brand.

### TensorFlow example

Before we move ahead, let's build a TensorFlow graph and run a computation. We will import TensorFlow, define a few variables using the TensorFlow API (which resembles the Scikit-Learn API we've used in previous chapters), and then compute the values for those variables:

```
import tensorflow as tf

b = tf.constant(50)
x = b * 10
y = x + b

with tf.Session() as sess:
    result = y.eval()
    print(result)
```

It is important to realize that there are two phases here. First, we construct the computation graph, defining b, x, and y. Then, we execute the graph by calling `tf.Session()`. Until we call this, no computations are being executed by the CPU and/or GPU. Rather, only the instructions for the computations are being stored. Once you execute this block of code, you will see the result of "550" as expected.

Later on, we will build actual neural networks using TensorFlow.

# Keras

Keras is an open source software library and provides a high-level API that runs on top of TensorFlow. It provides a much more user-friendly interface for TensorFlow, allowing data scientists and researchers to experiment faster and more easily than if they had to work directly with the TensorFlow commands. Keras was also primarily authored by a Google engineer, Francois Chollet.

When we start building models using TensorFlow, we will work hands-on with Keras and explore its advantages.

# Autoencoder: The Encoder and the Decoder

Now that we've introduced neural networks and the popular libraries to work with them in Python—TensorFlow and Keras—let's build an autoencoder, one of the simplest unsupervised learning neural networks.

An autoencoder comprises two parts, an *encoder* and a *decoder*. The encoder converts the input set of features into a different representation—via representation learning—and the decoder converts this newly learned representation to the original format.

The core concept of an autoencoder is similar to the concept of dimensionality reduction we studied in Chapter 3. Similar to dimensionality reduction, an autoencoder does not memorize the original observations and features, which would be what is known as the *identity function*. If it learned the exact identity function, the autoencoder would not be useful. Rather, autoencoders must approximate the original observations as closely as possible—but not exactly—using a newly learned representation; in other words, the autoencoder learns an approximation of the identity function.

Since the autoencoder is constrained, it is forced to learn the most salient properties of the original data, capturing the underlying structure of the data; this is similar to what happens in dimensionality reduction. The constraint is a very important attribute of autoencoders—the constraint forces the autoencoder to intelligently choose which important information to capture and which irrelevant or less important information to discard.

Autoencoders have been around for decades, and, as you may suspect already, they have been used widely for dimensionality reduction and automatic feature engineering/learning. Today, they are often used to build *generative models* such as *generative adversarial networks*.

# Undercomplete Autoencoders

In the autoencoder, we care most about the encoder because this component is the one that learns a new representation of the original data. This new representation is the new set of features derived from the original set of features and observations.

We will refer to the encoder function of the autoencoder as $h = f(x)$, which takes in the original observations $x$ and uses the newly learned representation captured in function $f$ to output $h$. The decoder function that reconstructs the original observations using the output of the encoder function is $r = g(h)$.

As you can see, the decoder function feeds in the encoder's output $h$ and reconstructs the observations, known as $r$, using its reconstruction function $g$. If done correctly, $g(f(x))$ will not be exactly equal to $x$ everywhere but will be close enough.

How do we restrict the encoder function to approximate $x$ so that it is forced to learn only the most salient properties of $x$ without copying it exactly?

We can constrain the encoder function's output, $h$, to have fewer dimensions than $x$. This is known as an *undercomplete* autoencoder since the encoder's dimensions are fewer than the original input dimensions. This is again similar to what happens in dimensionality reduction, where we take in the original input dimensions and reduce them to a much smaller set.

Constrained in this manner, the autoencoder attempts to minimize a *loss function* we define such that the reconstruction error—after the decoder reconstructs the observations approximately using the encoder's output—is as small as possible. It is important to realize that the hidden layers are where the dimensions are constrained. In other words, the output of the encoder has fewer dimensions than the original input. But the output of the decoder is the reconstructed original data and, therefore, has the same number of dimensions as the original input.

When the decoder is linear and the loss function is the mean squared error, an undercomplete autoencoder learns the same sort of new representation as PCA, a form of dimensionality reduction we introduced in Chapter 3. However, if the encoder and decoder functions are nonlinear, the autoencoder can learn much more complex nonlinear representations. This is what we care about most. But be warned—if the autoencoder is given too much capacity and latitude to model complex, nonlinear representations, it will simply memorize/copy the original observations instead of extracting the most salient information from them. Therefore, we must restrict the autoencoder meaningfully enough to prevent this from happening.

## Overcomplete Autoencoders

If the encoder learns a representation in a greater number of dimensions than the original input dimensions, the autoencoder is considered *overcomplete*. Such autoencoders simply copy the original observations and are not forced to efficiently and compactly capture information about the original distribution in a way that undercomplete autoencoders are. That being said, if we employ some form of *regularization*, which penalizes the neural network for learning unnecessarily complex functions, overcomplete autoencoders can be used successfully for dimensionality reduction and automatic feature engineering.

Compared to undercomplete autoencoders, *regularized overcomplete autoencoders* are harder to design successfully but are potentially more powerful because they can learn more complex—but not overly complex—representations that better approximate the original observations without copying them precisely.

In a nutshell, autoencoders that perform well are those that learn new representations that approximate the original obsevations close enough but not exactly. To do this, the autoencoder essentially learns a new probability distribution.

## Dense vs. Sparse Autoencoders

If you recall, in Chapter 3 we had both dense (the normal) and sparse versions of dimensionality reduction algorithms. Autoencoders work similarly. So far, we've discussed just the normal autoencoder that outputs a dense final matrix such that a handful of features have the most salient information that has been captured about the original data. However, we may instead want to output a sparse final matrix such that the information captured is more well-distributed across the features that the autoencoder learns.

To do this, we need to include not just a *reconstruction error* as part of the autoencoder but also a *sparsity penalty* so that the autoencoder must take the sparsity of the final matrix into consideration. Sparse autoencoders are generally overcomplete—the hidden layers have more units than the number of input features with the caveat that only a small fraction of the hidden units are allowed to be active at the same time. When defined in this way, a *sparse autoencoder* will output a final matrix that has many more zeros embedded throughout and the information captured will be better distributed across the features learned.

For certain machine learning applications, sparse autoencoders have better performance and also learn somewhat different representations than the normal (dense) autoencoders would. Later, we will work with real examples to see the difference between these two types of autoencoders.

## Denoising Autoencoder

As you know by now, autoencoders are capable of learning new (and improved) representations from the original input data, capturing the most salient elements but disregarding the noise in the original data.

In some cases, we may want the autoencoder we design to more aggressively ignore the noise in the data, especially if we suspect the original data is corrupted to some degree. Imagine recording a conversation between two people at a noisy coffee shop in the middle of the day. We would want to isolate the conversation (the signal) from the background chatter (the noise). Or, imagine a dataset of images that are grainy or distorted due to low resolution or some blurring effect. We want to isolate the core image (the signal) from the distortion (the noise).

For these problems, we can design a *denoising autoencoder* that receives the corrupted data as input and is trained to output the original, uncorrupted data as best as possible. Of course, while this is not easy to do, this is clearly a very powerful application of autoencoders to solve real-world problems.

# Variational Autoencoder

So far, we have discussed the use of autoencoders to learn new representations of the original input data (via the encoder) to minimize the reconstruction error between the newly reconstructed data (via the decoder) and the original input data.

In these examples, the encoder is of a fixed size, $n$, where $n$ is typically smaller than the number of original dimensions—in other words, we train an undercomplete autoencoder. Or $n$ may be larger than the number of original dimensions—an overcomplete autoencoder—but constrained using a regularization penalty, a sparsity penalty, etc. But in all these cases, the encoder outputs a single vector of a fixed size $n$.

An alternative autoencoder known as the *variational autoencoder* has an encoder that outputs two vectors instead of one: a vector of means, *mu*, and a vector of standard deviations, *sigma*. These two vectors form random variables such that the *ith* element of *mu* and *sigma* corresponds to the *mean* and *standard deviation* of the *ith* random variable. By forming this stochastic output via its encoder, the variational autoencoder is able to sample across a continuous space based on what it has learned from the input data.

The variational autoencoder is not confined to just the examples it has trained on but can generalize and output new examples even if it may have never seen precisely similar ones before. This is incredibly powerful because now the variational autoencoders can generate new synthetic data that appears to belong in the distribution the variational autoencoder has learned from the original input data. Advances like this have led to an entirely new and trending field in unsupervised learning known as generative modeling, which includes *generative adversarial networks*. With these models, it is possible to generate synthetic images, speech, music, art, etc., opening up a world of possibilities for AI-generated data.

# Conclusion

In this chapter, we introduced neural networks and the popular open source libraries, TensorFlow and Keras. We also explored autoencoders and their ability to learn new representations from original input data. Variations include sparse autoencoders, denoising autoencoders, and variational autoencoders, among others.

In Chapter 8, we will build hands-on applications using the techniques we have discussed in this chapter.

Before we proceed, let's revisit why automatic feature extraction is so important. Without the ability to automatically extract features, data scientists and machine learning engineers would have to design by hand features that might be important in solving real-world problems. This is very time-consuming and would dramatically limit progress in the field of AI.

In fact, until Geoffrey Hinton and other researchers developed methods to automatically learn new features using neural networks—launching the deep learning revolution starting in 2006—problems involving computer vision, speech recognition, machine translation, etc., remained largely intractable.

Once autoencoders and other variations of neural networks were used to automatically extract features from input data, a lot of these problems became solvable, leading to some major breakthroughs in machine learning over the past decade.

You will see the power of automatic feature extraction in the hands-on application of autoencoders in Chapter 8.

# Hands-On Autoencoder

In this chapter, we will build applications using various versions of autoencoders, including undercomplete, overcomplete, sparse, denoising, and variational autoencoders.

To start, let's return to the credit card fraud detection problem we introduced in Chapter 3. For this problem, we have 284,807 credit card transactions, of which only 492 are fraudulent. Using a supervised model, we achieved an average precision of 0.82, which is very impressive. We can find well over 80% of the fraud with an over 80% precision. Using an unsupervised model, we achieved an average precision of 0.69, which is very good considering we did not use labels. We can find over 75% of the fraud with an over 75% precision.

Let's see how this same problem can be solved using an autoencoder, which is also an unsupervised algorithm but one that uses a neural network.

## Data Preparation

Let's first load the necessary libaries:

```
'''Main'''
import numpy as np
import pandas as pd
import os, time, re
import pickle, gzip

'''Data Viz'''
import matplotlib.pyplot as plt
import seaborn as sns
color = sns.color_palette()
import matplotlib as mpl
```

```
%matplotlib inline

'''Data Prep and Model Evaluation'''
from sklearn import preprocessing as pp
from sklearn.model_selection import train_test_split
from sklearn.model_selection import StratifiedKFold
from sklearn.metrics import log_loss
from sklearn.metrics import precision_recall_curve, average_precision_score
from sklearn.metrics import roc_curve, auc, roc_auc_score

'''Algos'''
import lightgbm as lgb

'''TensorFlow and Keras'''
import tensorflow as tf
import keras
from keras import backend as K
from keras.models import Sequential, Model
from keras.layers import Activation, Dense, Dropout
from keras.layers import BatchNormalization, Input, Lambda
from keras import regularizers
from keras.losses import mse, binary_crossentropy
```

Next, load the dataset and prepare it for use. We will create a dataX matrix with all the PCA components and the feature Amount, but drop Class and Time. We will store the Class labels in the dataY matrix. We will also scale the features in the dataX matrix so that all the features have a mean of zero and standard deviation of one:

```
data = pd.read_csv('creditcard.csv')
dataX = data.copy().drop(['Class','Time'],axis=1)
dataY = data['Class'].copy()
featuresToScale = dataX.columns
sX = pp.StandardScaler(copy=True, with_mean=True, with_std=True)
dataX.loc[:,featuresToScale] = sX.fit_transform(dataX[featuresToScale])
```

As we did in Chapter 3, we will create a training set with two-thirds of the data and the labels and a test set with one-third of the data and the labels.

Let's store the training set and the test set as *X_train_AE* and *X_test_AE*, respectively. We will use these in the autoencoders soon:

```
X_train, X_test, y_train, y_test = \
    train_test_split(dataX, dataY, test_size=0.33, \
                     random_state=2018, stratify=dataY)

X_train_AE = X_train.copy()
X_test_AE = X_test.copy()
```

Let's also reuse the function we introduced earlier in the book, called anomalyScores, to calculate the reconstruction error between the original feature matrix and the newly reconstructed feature matrix. The function takes the sum of squared errors and normalizes them to a range between zero and one.

This is a crucial function. The transactions with errors close to one are the ones that are most anomalous (i.e., have the highest reconstruction error) and, therefore, are most likely to be fraudulent. The transactions with errors close to zero have the lowest reconstruction error and are most likely to be normal:

```
def anomalyScores(originalDF, reducedDF):
    loss = np.sum((np.array(originalDF) - \
                np.array(reducedDF))**2, axis=1)
    loss = pd.Series(data=loss,index=originalDF.index)
    loss = (loss-np.min(loss))/(np.max(loss)-np.min(loss))
    return loss
```

We will also reuse the function to plot the precision-recall curve, the average precision, and the ROC curve. This function is called plotResults:

```
def plotResults(trueLabels, anomalyScores, returnPreds = False):
    preds = pd.concat([trueLabels, anomalyScores], axis=1)
    preds.columns = ['trueLabel', 'anomalyScore']
    precision, recall, thresholds = \
        precision_recall_curve(preds['trueLabel'], \
                            preds['anomalyScore'])
    average_precision = average_precision_score( \
                    preds['trueLabel'], preds['anomalyScore'])

    plt.step(recall, precision, color='k', alpha=0.7, where='post')
    plt.fill_between(recall, precision, step='post', alpha=0.3, color='k')

    plt.xlabel('Recall')
    plt.ylabel('Precision')
    plt.ylim([0.0, 1.05])
    plt.xlim([0.0, 1.0])

    plt.title('Precision-Recall curve: Average Precision = \
        {0:0.2f}'.format(average_precision))

    fpr, tpr, thresholds = roc_curve(preds['trueLabel'], \
                            preds['anomalyScore'])
    areaUnderROC = auc(fpr, tpr)

    plt.figure()
    plt.plot(fpr, tpr, color='r', lw=2, label='ROC curve')
    plt.plot([0, 1], [0, 1], color='k', lw=2, linestyle='--')
    plt.xlim([0.0, 1.0])
    plt.ylim([0.0, 1.05])
    plt.xlabel('False Positive Rate')
    plt.ylabel('True Positive Rate')
    plt.title('Receiver operating characteristic: Area under the \
        curve = {0:0.2f}'.format(areaUnderROC))
    plt.legend(loc="lower right")
    plt.show()
```

```
if returnPreds==True:
    return preds
```

# The Components of an Autoencoder

First, let's build a very simple autoencoder with the input layer, a single hidden layer, and the output layer. We will feed the original feature matrix $x$ into the autoencoder— this is represented by the input layer. Then, an activation function will be applied to the weighted sum of the input layer, generating the hidden layer. This activation function is called $f$ and represents a part of the *encoder* portion of the autoencoder. The hidden layer is called $h$ (which is equal to $f(x)$) and represents the newly learned representation.

Next, an activation function is applied to the weighted sum of the hidden layer (i.e., the newly learned representation) to reconstruct the original observations. This activation function is called $g$ and represents a part of the *decoder* portion of the autoencoder. The output layer is called $r$ (which is equal to $g(h)$) and represents the newly reconstructed observations. To calculate the reconstruction error, we will compare the newly constructed observations $r$ with the original ones $x$.

# Activation Functions

Before we decide the number of nodes to use in this single hidden layer autoencoder, let's discuss activation functions.

A neural network learns the weights to apply to the nodes at each of the layers but whether the nodes will be activated or not (for use in the next layer) is determined by the activation function. In other words, an activation function is applied to the weighted input (plus bias, if any) at each layer. We will call the weighted input plus bias $Y$.

The activation function takes in $Y$ and either activates (if $Y$ is above a certain threshold) or does not. If activated, the information in a given node is passed to the next layer; otherwise, it is not. However, we do not want simple binary activations. Instead, we want a range of activation values. To do this, we can choose a linear activation function or a nonlinear activation function. The linear activation function is unbounded. It can generate activation values between negative infinity and positive infinity. Common nonlinear activation functions include sigmoid, hyperbolic tangent (or tanh for short), rectified linear unit (or ReLu for short), and softmax:

*Sigmoid function*
> The sigmoid function is bounded and can generate activation values between zero and one.

---

*Tanh function*

The tanh function is also bounded and can generate activation values between negative one and positive one. Its gradient is steeper than that of the sigmoid function.

*ReLu function*

The ReLu function has an interesting property. If $Y$ is positive, ReLu will return $Y$. Otherwise, it will return zero. Therefore, ReLu is unbounded for positive values of $Y$.

*Softmax function*

The softmax function is used as the final activation function in a neural network for classification problems because it normalizes classification probabilities to values that add up to a probability of one.

Of all these functions, the linear activation function is the simplest and least computationally expensive. ReLu is the next least computationally expensive, followed by the others.

# Our First Autoencoder

Let's start with a two-layer autoencoder with a linear activation function for both the encoder and the decoder functions. Note that only the number of hidden layers plus the output layer count toward the *number of layers* in a neural network. Since we have a single hidden layer, this is known as a two-layer neural network.

To build this using TensorFlow and Keras, we must first call the *Sequential model API*. The Sequential model is a linear stack of layers, and we will pass the types of layers we want into the model before we compile the model and train on our data.[1]

```
# Model one
# Two layer complete autoencoder with linear activation

# Call neural network API
model = Sequential()
```

Once we call the Sequential model, we then need to specify the input shape by designating the number of dimensions, which should match the number of dimensions in the original feature matrix, *dataX*. This number is 29.

We also need to specify the activation function (also known as the encoder function) applied to the input layer and the number of nodes we want the hidden layer to have. We will pass *linear* as the activation function.

---

1 Visit the official documentation for more on the Keras Sequential model (*http://bit.ly/2FZbUrq*).

To start, let's use a complete autoencoder, where the number of nodes in the hidden layer equals the number of nodes in the input layer, which is 29. All of this is done using a single line of code:

```
model.add(Dense(units=29, activation='linear',input_dim=29))
```

Similarly, we need to specify the activation function (also known as the decoder function) applied to the hidden layer to reconstruct the observations and the number of dimensions we want the output layer to have. Since we want the final reconstructed matrix to have the same dimensions as the original matrix, the dimension needs to be 29. And, we will use a linear activation function for the decoder, too:

```
model.add(Dense(units=29, activation='linear'))
```

Next, we will need to compile the layers we have designed for the neural network. This requires us to select a *loss function* (also known as the *objective function*) to guide the learning of the weights, an *optimizer* to set the process by which the weights are learned, and a list of *metrics* to output to help us evaluate the goodness of the neural network.

## Loss Function

Let's start with the loss function. Recall that we are evaluating the model based on the reconstruction error between the newly reconstructed matrix of features based on the autoencoder and the original feature matrix that we feed into the autoencoder.

Therefore, we want to use *mean squared error* as the evaluation metric. (For our custom evaluation function, we use sum of squared errors, which is similar.).[2]

## Optimizer

Neural networks train for many rounds (known as *epochs*). In each batch of these epochs, the neural network readjusts its learned weights to reduce its loss from the batches in the previous epoch. The process for learning these weights is set by the optimizer. We want a process that helps the neural network efficiently learn the optimal weights for the various nodes across all the layers that minimizes the loss function we have chosen.

To learn the optimal weights, the neural network needs to adjust its "guess" for the optimal weights in an intelligent way. One approach is to iteratively move the weights in the direction that helps reduce the loss function incrementally. But an even better approach is to move the weights in this direction but with a degree of randomness—in other words, to move the weights stochastically.

---

2 For more on loss functions, refer to the official Keras documentation (*https://keras.io/losses/*).

---

Although there is more to this, this process is known as *stochastic gradient descent* (or SGD for short), the most commonly used optimizer in training neural networks.[3] SGD has a single learning rate, known as *alpha*, for all the weight updates that it makes, and this learning rate does not change during training. However, in most cases, it's better to adjust the learning rate over the course of the training. For example, in the earlier epochs, it makes more sense to adjust the weights by a large degree —in other words, to have a large learning rate or alpha.

In later epochs, when the weights are more optimal, it makes more sense to adjust the weights by a small degree to delicately fine-tune the weights than to take massive steps in one direction or another. Therefore, an even better optimzer than SGD is the *Adam optimization algorithm*, which is derived from adaptive moment estimation. The Adam optimizer dynamically adjusts the learning rate over the course of the training process, unlike SGD, and is the optimizer we will use.[4]

## Training the Model

Finally, we need to choose the evaluation metric, which we will set to `accuracy` to keep things simple:[5]

```
model.compile(optimizer='adam',
              loss='mean_squared_error',
              metrics=['accuracy'])
```

Next, we need to select the number of epochs and the batch size and then begin the training process by calling the method *fit*. The number of epochs determines the number of times the training occurs over the entire dataset we pass into the neural network. We will set this to 10 to start.

The batch sets the number of samples the neural network trains on before making the next gradient update. If the batch is equal to the total number of observations, the neural network will make a gradient update once every epoch. Otherwise, it will make updates multiple times per epoch. We will set this to a generic 32 samples to start.

Into the fit method, we will pass in the initial input matrix, *x*, and the target matrix, *y*. In our case, both *x* and *y* will be the original feature matrix, *X_train_AE*, because we want to compare the output of the autoencoder—the reconstructed feature matrix— with the original feature matrix to calculate the reconstruction error.

---

3  Consult Wikipedia for more on stochastic gradient descent (*http://bit.ly/2G3Ak30*).

4  For more information on optimizers, refer to the documentation (*https://keras.io/optimizers/*).

5  For more on evaluation metrics, refer to the documentation (*https://keras.io/metrics/*).

Remember, this is a purely unsupervised solution so we will not use the $y$ matrix at all. We will also validate our model as we go by testing the reconstruction error on the entire training matrix:

```
num_epochs = 10
batch_size = 32

history = model.fit(x=X_train_AE, y=X_train_AE,
                    epochs=num_epochs,
                    batch_size=batch_size,
                    shuffle=True,
                    validation_data=(X_train_AE, X_train_AE),
                    verbose=1)
```

Since this a complete autoencoder—where the hidden layer has the same number of dimensions as the input layer—the loss is very low, for both the training and validation sets:

```
Training history of complete autoencoder

Train on 190820 samples, validate on 190820 samples
Epoch 1/10
190820/190820 [==============================] - 29s 154us/step - loss: 0.1056
- acc: 0.8728 - val_loss: 0.0013 - val_acc: 0.9903
Epoch 2/10
190820/190820 [==============================] - 27s 140us/step - loss: 0.0012
- acc: 0.9914 - val_loss: 1.0425e-06 - val_acc: 0.9995
Epoch 3/10
190820/190820 [==============================] - 23s 122us/step - loss: 6.6244
e-04 - acc: 0.9949 - val_loss: 5.2491e-04 - val_acc: 0.9913
Epoch 4/10
190820/190820 [==============================] - 23s 119us/step - loss: 0.0016
- acc: 0.9929 - val_loss: 2.2246e-06 - val_acc: 0.9995
Epoch 5/10
190820/190820 [==============================] - 23s 119us/step - loss: 5.7424
e-04 - acc: 0.9943 - val_loss: 9.0811e-05 - val_acc: 0.9970
Epoch 6/10
190820/190820 [==============================] - 22s 118us/step - loss: 5.4950
e-04 - acc: 0.9941 - val_loss: 6.0598e-05 - val_acc: 0.9959
Epoch 7/10
190820/190820 [==============================] - 22s 117us/step - loss: 5.2291
e-04 - acc: 0.9946 - val_loss: 0.0023 - val_acc: 0.9675
Epoch 8/10
190820/190820 [==============================] - 22s 117us/step - loss: 6.5130
e-04 - acc: 0.9932 - val_loss: 4.5059e-04 - val_acc: 0.9945
Epoch 9/10
190820/190820 [==============================] - 23s 122us/step - loss: 4.9077
e-04 - acc: 0.9952 - val_loss: 7.2591e-04 - val_acc: 0.9908
Epoch 10/10
190820/190820 [==============================] - 23s 118us/step - loss: 6.1469
e-04 - acc: 0.9945 - val_loss: 4.4131e-06 - val_acc: 0.9991
```

This is not optimal—the autoencoder has reconstructed the original feature matrix too precisely, memorizing the inputs.

Recall that the autoencoder is meant to learn a new representation that captures the most salient information in the original input matrix while dropping the less relevant information. Simply memorizing the inputs—also known as learning the *identity function*—will not result in new and improved representation learning.

## Evaluating on the Test Set

Let's use the test set to evaluate just how successively this autoencoder can identify fraud in the credit card transactions dataset. We will use the `predict` method to do this:

```
predictions = model.predict(X_test, verbose=1)
anomalyScoresAE = anomalyScores(X_test, predictions)
preds = plotResults(y_test, anomalyScoresAE, True)
```

As seen in Figure 8-1, the average precision is 0.30, which is not very good. The best average precision using unsupervised learning from Chapter 4 was 0.69, and the supervised system had an average precision of 0.82. However, each training process will yield slightly different results for the trained autoencoder, so you may not see the same performance for your run.

To get a better sense of how a two-layer complete autoencoder performs on the test set, let's run this training process ten separate times and store the average precision on the test set for each run. We will assess how good this complete autoencoder is at capturing fraud based on the mean of the average precision from these 10 runs.

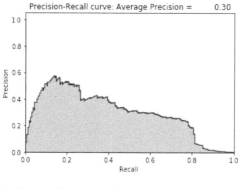

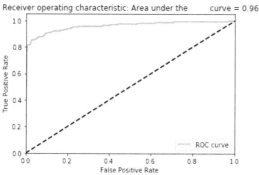

*Figure 8-1. Evaluation metrics of complete autoencoder*

To consolidate our work thus far, here is the code to simulate 10 runs from start to finish:

```
# 10 runs - We will capture mean of average precision
test_scores = []
for i in range(0,10):
    # Call neural network API
    model = Sequential()

    # Apply linear activation function to input layer
    # Generate hidden layer with 29 nodes, the same as the input layer
    model.add(Dense(units=29, activation='linear',input_dim=29))

    # Apply linear activation function to hidden layer
    # Generate output layer with 29 nodes
    model.add(Dense(units=29, activation='linear'))

    # Compile the model
    model.compile(optimizer='adam',
                  loss='mean_squared_error',
                  metrics=['accuracy'])
```

```
# Train the model
num_epochs = 10
batch_size = 32

history = model.fit(x=X_train_AE, y=X_train_AE,
                    epochs=num_epochs,
                    batch_size=batch_size,
                    shuffle=True,
                    validation_data=(X_train_AE, X_train_AE),
                    verbose=1)

# Evaluate on test set
predictions = model.predict(X_test, verbose=1)
anomalyScoresAE = anomalyScores(X_test, predictions)
preds, avgPrecision = plotResults(y_test, anomalyScoresAE, True)
test_scores.append(avgPrecision)

print("Mean average precision over 10 runs: ", np.mean(test_scores))
test_scores
```

Let's summarize the results for the 10 runs. The mean of the average precision is 0.30, but the average precision ranges from a low of 0.02 to .72. The *coefficient of variation* (defined as the standard deviation divided by the mean over 10 runs) is 0.88.

```
Mean average precision over 10 runs: 0.30108318944579776
Coefficient of variation over 10 runs: 0.8755095071789248

[0.25468022666666157,
0.092705950994909,
0.716481644928299,
0.01946589342639965,
0.25623865457838263,
0.33597083510378234,
0.018757053070824415,
0.6188569405068724,
0.6720552647581304,
0.025619070873716072]
```

Let's try to improve our results by building variations of this autoencoder.

# Two-Layer Undercomplete Autoencoder with Linear Activation Function

Let's try an undercomplete autoencoder rather than a complete one.

Compared to the previous autoencoder, the only thing that changes is the number of nodes in the hidden layer. Instead of setting this to the number of original dimensions (29), we will set the nodes to 20. In other words, this autoencoder is a constrained autoencoder. The encoder function is forced to capture the information in the input layer with a fewer number of nodes, and the decoder has to take this new representation to reconstruct the original matrix.

We should expect the loss here to be higher compared to that of the complete autoencoder. Let's run the code. We will perform 10 independent runs to test how well the various undercomplete autoencoders are at catching fraud:

```
# 10 runs - We will capture mean of average precision
test_scores = []
for i in range(0,10):
    # Call neural network API
    model = Sequential()

    # Apply linear activation function to input layer
    # Generate hidden layer with 20 nodes
    model.add(Dense(units=20, activation='linear',input_dim=29))

    # Apply linear activation function to hidden layer
    # Generate output layer with 29 nodes
    model.add(Dense(units=29, activation='linear'))

    # Compile the model
    model.compile(optimizer='adam',
                  loss='mean_squared_error',
                  metrics=['accuracy'])

    # Train the model
    num_epochs = 10
    batch_size = 32

    history = model.fit(x=X_train_AE, y=X_train_AE,
                        epochs=num_epochs,
                        batch_size=batch_size,
                        shuffle=True,
                        validation_data=(X_train_AE, X_train_AE),
                        verbose=1)

    # Evaluate on test set
    predictions = model.predict(X_test, verbose=1)
    anomalyScoresAE = anomalyScores(X_test, predictions)
    preds, avgPrecision = plotResults(y_test, anomalyScoresAE, True)
    test_scores.append(avgPrecision)

print("Mean average precision over 10 runs: ", np.mean(test_scores))
test_scores
```

As the following shows, the losses of the undercomplete autoencoder are considerably higher than those of the complete autoencoder. It is clear that the autoencoder learns a representation that is new and more constrained than the original input matrix—the autoencoder did not simply memorize the inputs:

```
Training history of undercomplete autoencoder with 20 nodes

Train on 190820 samples, validate on 190820 samples
Epoch 1/10
190820/190820 [==============================] - 28s 145us/step - loss: 0.3588
- acc: 0.5672 - val_loss: 0.2789 - val_acc: 0.6078
Epoch 2/10
190820/190820 [==============================] - 29s 153us/step - loss: 0.2817
- acc: 0.6032 - val_loss: 0.2757 - val_acc: 0.6115
Epoch 3/10
190820/190820 [==============================] - 28s 147us/step - loss: 0.2793
- acc: 0.6147 - val_loss: 0.2755 - val_acc: 0.6176
Epoch 4/10
190820/190820 [==============================] - 30s 155us/step - loss: 0.2784
- acc: 0.6164 - val_loss: 0.2750 - val_acc: 0.6167
Epoch 5/10
190820/190820 [==============================] - 29s 152us/step - loss: 0.2786
- acc: 0.6188 - val_loss: 0.2746 - val_acc: 0.6126
Epoch 6/10
190820/190820 [==============================] - 29s 151us/step - loss: 0.2776
- acc: 0.6140 - val_loss: 0.2752 - val_acc: 0.6043
Epoch 7/10
190820/190820 [==============================] - 30s 156us/step - loss: 0.2775
- acc: 0.5947 - val_loss: 0.2745 - val_acc: 0.5946
Epoch 8/10
190820/190820 [==============================] - 29s 149us/step - loss: 0.2770
- acc: 0.5903 - val_loss: 0.2740 - val_acc: 0.5882
Epoch 9/10
190820/190820 [==============================] - 29s 153us/step - loss: 0.2768
- acc: 0.5921 - val_loss: 0.2770 - val_acc: 0.5801
Epoch 10/10
190820/190820 [==============================] - 29s 150us/step - loss: 0.2767
- acc: 0.5803 - val_loss: 0.2744 - val_acc: 0.5743
93987/93987[==============================] - 3s 36us/step
```

This is how an autoencoder should work—it should learn a new representation. Figure 8-2 shows how effective this new representation is at identifying fraud.

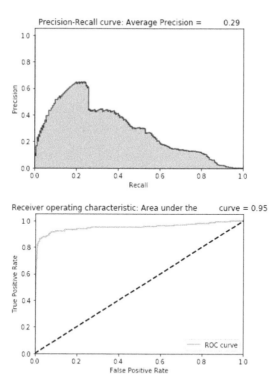

*Figure 8-2. Evaluation metrics of undercomplete autoencoder with 20 nodes*

The average precision is 0.29, similar to that of the complete autoencoder.

The following code shows the distribution of average precisions across the 10 runs. The mean of the average precision is 0.31, but the dispersion is very tight (as the coefficient of variation 0.03 indicates). This is a considerably more stable system than the one designed with a complete autoencoder.

```
Mean average precision over 10 runs: 0.30913783987972737
Coefficient of variation over 10 runs: 0.032251659812254876

[0.2886910204920736,
0.3056142045082387,
0.31658073591381186,
0.30590858583039254,
0.31824197682595556,
0.3136952374067599,
0.30888135217515555,
0.31234000424933206,
0.29695149753706923,
0.3244746838584846]
```

But we are still stuck at a fairly mediocre average precision. Why did the undercomplete autoencoder not perform better? It could be that this undercomplete autoencoder does not have enough nodes. Or, maybe we need to train using more hidden layers. Let's experiment with these two changes, one by one.

## Increasing the Number of Nodes

The following code displays the training losses when using a two-layer undercomplete autocoder with 27 nodes instead of just 20:

```
Training history of undercomplete autoencoder with 27 nodes

Train on 190820 samples, validate on 190820 samples

Epoch 1/10
190820/190820 [==============================] - 29s 150us/step - loss: 0.1169
- acc: 0.8224 - val_loss: 0.0368 - val_acc: 0.8798
Epoch 2/10
190820/190820 [==============================] - 29s 154us/step - loss: 0.0388
- acc: 0.8610 - val_loss: 0.0360 - val_acc: 0.8530
Epoch 3/10
190820/190820 [==============================] - 30s 156us/step - loss: 0.0382
- acc: 0.8680 - val_loss: 0.0359 - val_acc: 0.8745
Epoch 4/10
190820/190820 [==============================] - 30s 156us/step - loss: 0.0371
- acc: 0.8811 - val_loss: 0.0353 - val_acc: 0.9021
Epoch 5/10
190820/190820 [==============================] - 30s 155us/step - loss: 0.0373
- acc: 0.9114 - val_loss: 0.0352 - val_acc: 0.9226
Epoch 6/10
190820/190820 [==============================] - 30s 155us/step - loss: 0.0377
- acc: 0.9361 - val_loss: 0.0370 - val_acc: 0.9416
Epoch 7/10
190820/190820 [==============================] - 30s 156us/step - loss: 0.0361
- acc: 0.9448 - val_loss: 0.0358 - val_acc: 0.9378
Epoch 8/10
190820/190820 [==============================] - 30s 156us/step - loss: 0.0354
- acc: 0.9521 - val_loss: 0.0350 - val_acc: 0.9503
Epoch 9/10
190820/190820 [==============================] - 29s 153us/step - loss: 0.0352
- acc: 0.9613 - val_loss: 0.0349 - val_acc: 0.9263
Epoch 10/10
190820/190820 [==============================] - 29s 153us/step - loss: 0.0353
- acc: 0.9566 - val_loss: 0.0343 - val_acc: 0.9477
93987/93987[==============================] - 4s 39us/step
```

Figure 8-3 displays the average precision, precision-recall curve, and auROC curve.

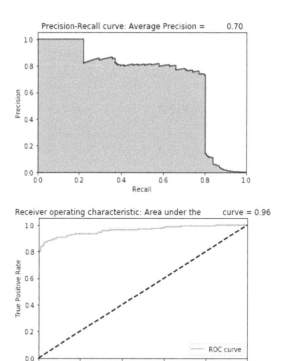

*Figure 8-3. Evaluation metrics of undercomplete autoencoder with 27 nodes*

The average precision improves considerably to 0.70. This is better than the average precision of the complete autoencoder and better than the best unsupervised learning solution from Chapter 4.

The following code summarizes the distribution of average precision across the 10 runs. The mean of the average precision is 0.53, considerably better than the ~0.30 average precision earlier. The dispersion of average precision is reasonably good, with a coefficient of variation of 0.50.

```
Mean average precision over 10 runs: 0.5273341559141779
Coefficient of variation over 10 runs: 0.5006880691999009

[0.689799495450694,
0.7092146840717755,
0.7336692377321005,
0.6154173765950426,
0.7068800243349335,
0.35250757724667586,
0.6904117414832501,
0.02335388808244066,
0.690798140588336,
0.061289393556529626]
```

We have a clear improvement over our previous autoencoder-based anomaly detection system.

## Adding More Hidden Layers

Let's see if we can improve our results by adding an extra hidden layer to the autoencoder. We will continue to use linear activation functions for now.

 Experimentation is a major part of discovering the best neural network architecture for the problem you have to solve. Some changes you make will lead to better results, others to worse. Knowing how to modify the neural network and the hyperparameters as part of your search to improve the solution is very important.

Instead of a single hidden layer with 27 nodes, we will use one hidden layer with 28 nodes and another with 27 nodes. This is only a slight variation from the one we used previously. This is now a three-layer neural network since we have two hidden layers plus the output layer. The input layer does not "count" toward this number.

This additional hidden layer requires just one additional line of code, as shown here:

```
# Model two
# Three layer undercomplete autoencoder with linear activation
# With 28 and 27 nodes in the two hidden layers, respectively

model = Sequential()
model.add(Dense(units=28, activation='linear',input_dim=29))
model.add(Dense(units=27, activation='linear'))
model.add(Dense(units=29, activation='linear'))
```

The following code summarizes the distribution of average precisions across the 10 runs. The mean of the average precision is 0.36, worse than the 0.53 we just achieved. The dispersion of average precision is also worse, with a coefficient of variation of 0.94 (higher is worse):

```
Mean average precision over 10 runs: 0.36075271075596366
Coefficient of variation over 10 runs: 0.9361649046827353

[0.02259626054852924,
 0.6984699403560997,
 0.011035001202665167,
 0.06621450000830197,
 0.0089169866608776182,
 0.705399684020873,
 0.6995233144849828,
 0.008263068338243631,
 0.6904537524978872,
 0.6966545994932775]
```

# Nonlinear Autoencoder

Now let's build an undercomplete autoencoder using a nonlinear activation function. We will use ReLu, but you are welcome to experiment with tanh, sigmoid, and the other nonlinear activation functions.

We will include three hidden layers, with 27, 22, and 27 nodes, respectively. Conceptually, the first two activation functions (applied on the input and first hidden layer) perform the encoding, creating the second hidden layer with 22 nodes. Then, the next two activation functions perform the decoding, reconstructing the 22-node representation to the original number of dimensions, 29:

```
model = Sequential()
model.add(Dense(units=27, activation='relu',input_dim=29))
model.add(Dense(units=22, activation='relu'))
model.add(Dense(units=27, activation='relu'))
model.add(Dense(units=29, activation='relu'))
```

The following code shows the losses from this autoencoder, and Figure 8-4 shows the average precision, the precision-recall curve, and the auROC curve:

```
Training history of undercomplete autoencoder with three hidden layers and ReLu
activation function

Train on 190820 samples, validate on 190820 samples

Epoch 1/10
190820/190820 [==============================] - 32s 169us/step - loss: 0.7010
- acc: 0.5626 - val_loss: 0.6339 - val_acc: 0.6983
Epoch 2/10
190820/190820 [==============================] - 33s 174us/step - loss: 0.6302
- acc: 0.7132 - val_loss: 0.6219 - val_acc: 0.7465
Epoch 3/10
190820/190820 [==============================] - 34s 177us/step - loss: 0.6224
- acc: 0.7367 - val_loss: 0.6198 - val_acc: 0.7528
Epoch 4/10
190820/190820 [==============================] - 34s 179us/step - loss: 0.6227
- acc: 0.7380 - val_loss: 0.6205 - val_acc: 0.7471
Epoch 5/10
190820/190820 [==============================] - 33s 174us/step - loss: 0.6206
- acc: 0.7452 - val_loss: 0.6202 - val_acc: 0.7353
Epoch 6/10
190820/190820 [==============================] - 33s 175us/step - loss: 0.6206
- acc: 0.7458 - val_loss: 0.6192 - val_acc: 0.7485
Epoch 7/10
190820/190820 [==============================] - 33s 174us/step - loss: 0.6199
- acc: 0.7481 - val_loss: 0.6239 - val_acc: 0.7308
Epoch 8/10
190820/190820 [==============================] - 33s 175us/step - loss: 0.6203
- acc: 0.7497 - val_loss: 0.6183 - val_acc: 0.7626
Epoch 9/10
```

```
190820/190820 [==============================] - 34s 177us/step - loss: 0.6197
- acc: 0.7491 - val_loss: 0.6188 - val_acc: 0.7531
Epoch 10/10
190820/190820 [==============================] - 34s 177us/step - loss: 0.6201
- acc: 0.7486 - val_loss: 0.6188 - val_acc: 0.7540
93987/93987 [==============================] - 5s 48 us/step
```

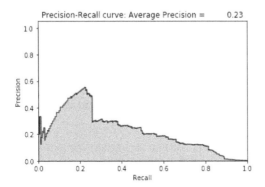

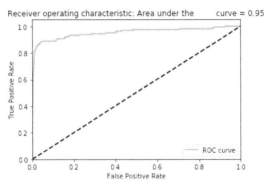

*Figure 8-4. Evaluation metrics of undercomplete autoencoder with three hidden layers and ReLu activation function*

The results are considerably worse.

The following code summarizes the distribution of average precisions across the 10 runs. The mean of the average precision is 0.22, worse than the 0.53 we achieved earlier. The dispersion of average precisions is very tight, with a coefficient of variation of 0.06:

```
Mean average precision over 10 runs:    0.2232934196381843
Coefficient of variation over 10 runs:  0.060779960264380296

[0.22598829389665595,
 0.22616147166925166,
 0.22119489753135715,
 0.2478548473814437,
```

```
0.2251289336369011,
0.2119454446242229,
0.2126914064768752,
0.24581338950742185,
0.20665608837737512,
0.20949942328033827]
```

These results are much worse than those from a simple autoencoder using a linear activation function. It could be that—for this dataset—a linear, undercomplete autoencoder is the best solution.

For other datasets, that may not always be the case. As always, experimentation is required to find the optimal solution. Change the number of nodes, the number of hidden layers, and the mix of activation functions, and see how much better or worse the solutions become.

This type of experimentation is known as *hyperparameter optimization*. You are adjusting the hyperparameters—the number of nodes, the number of layers, and the mix of activation functions—in search of the optimal solution.

# Overcomplete Autoencoder with Linear Activation

Now let's highlight the problem with overcomplete autoencoders. Overcomplete autoencoders have more nodes in the hidden layer than either the input or output layer. Because the *capacity* of the neural network model is so high, the autoencoder simply memorizes the observations it trains on.

In other words, the autoencoder learns the *identity function*, which is exactly what we want to avoid. The autoencoder will overfit the training data and will perform very poorly in separating fraudulent credit card transactions from normal ones.

Recall that we need the autoencoder to learn the salient aspects of the credit card transactions in the training set so that it learns what the normal transactions look like —without memorizing the information in the less normal, rare fraudulent ones.

Only if the autoencoder is able to lose some of the information in the training set will it be able to separate the fraudulent transactions from the normal ones:

```
model = Sequential()
model.add(Dense(units=40, activation='linear',input_dim=29))
model.add(Dense(units=29, activation='linear'))
```

The following code shows the losses from this autoencoder, and Figure 8-5 displays the average precision, the precision-recall curve, and the auROC curve:

```
Training history of overcomplete autoencoder with single hidden layer and
  linear activation function

Train on 190820 samples, validate on 190820 samples
Epoch 1/10
```

```
190820/190820 [==============================] - 31s 161us/step - loss: 0.0498
- acc: 0.9438 - val_loss: 9.2301e-06 - val_acc: 0.9982
Epoch 2/10
190820/190820 [==============================] - 33s 171us/step - loss: 0.0014
- acc: 0.9925 - val_loss: 0.0019 - val_acc: 0.9909
Epoch 3/10
190820/190820 [==============================] - 33s 172us/step - loss: 7.6469
e-04 - acc: 0.9947 - val_loss: 4.5314e-05 - val_acc: 0.9970
Epoch 4/10
190820/190820 [==============================] - 35s 182us/step - loss: 0.0010
- acc: 0.9930 - val_loss: 0.0039 - val_acc: 0.9859
Epoch 5/10
190820/190820 [==============================] - 32s 166us/step - loss: 0.0012
- acc: 0.9924 - val_loss: 8.5141e-04 - val_acc: 0.9886
Epoch 6/10
190820/190820 [==============================] - 31s 163us/step - loss: 5.0655
e-04 - acc: 0.9955 - val_loss: 8.2359e-04 - val_acc: 0.9910
Epoch 7/10
190820/190820 [==============================] - 30s 156us/step - loss: 7.6046
e-04 - acc: 0.9930 - val_loss: 0.0045 - val_acc: 0.9933
Epoch 8/10
190820/190820 [==============================] - 30s 157us/step - loss: 9.1609
e-04 - acc: 0.9930 - val_loss: 7.3662e-04 - val_acc: 0.9872
Epoch 9/10
190820/190820 [==============================] - 30s 158us/step - loss: 7.6287
e-04 - acc: 0.9929 - val_loss: 2.5671e-04 - val_acc: 0.9940
Epoch 10/10
190820/190820 [==============================] - 30s 157us/step - loss: 7.0697
e-04 - acc: 0.9928 - val_loss: 4.5272e-06 - val_acc: 0.9994
93987/93987[==============================] - 4s 48us/step
```

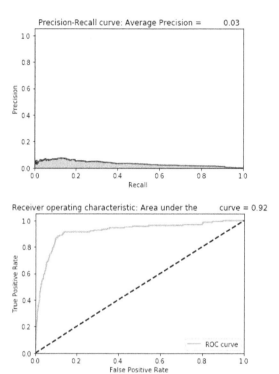

*Figure 8-5. Evaluation metrics of overcomplete autoencoder with single hidden layer and linear activation function*

Dropout helped reduce the overfitting, improving the results modestly. But, overall, the overfit overcomplete autoencoder has poor performance in detecting the fraudulent credit card transactions.

The following code summarizes the distribution of average precision across the 10 runs. The mean of the average precision is 0.31, worse than the 0.53 we achieved earlier. The dispersion of average precision is not very tight, with a coefficient of variation of 0.89:

```
Mean average precision over 10 runs: 0.3061984081568074
Coefficient of variation over 10 runs: 0.8896921668864564

[0.03394897465567298,
0.14322827274920255,
0.03610123178524601,
0.019735235731640446,
0.012571999125881402,
0.6788921569665146,
0.5411349583727725,
0.388474572258503,
```

```
0.7089617645810736,
0.4989349153415674]
```

# Overcomplete Autoencoder with Linear Activation and Dropout

One way to improve the overcomplete autoencoder solution is to use a regularization technique to reduce the overfitting. One such technique is known as *dropout*. With dropout, we force the autoencoder to drop out some defined percentage of units from the layers in the neural network.

With this new constraint, the overcomplete autoencoder cannot simply memorize the credit card transactions in the training set. Instead, the autoencoder has to generalize a bit more. The autoencoder is forced to learn more of the salient features in the dataset and lose some of the less salient information.

We will use a dropout percentage of 10%, which we will apply to the hidden layer. In other words, 10% of the neurons are dropped. The higher the dropout percentage, the stronger the regularization. This is done with just a single additional line of code.

Let's see if this improves the results:

```
model = Sequential()
model.add(Dense(units=40, activation='linear', input_dim=29))
model.add(Dropout(0.10))
model.add(Dense(units=29, activation='linear'))
```

The following code shows the losses from this autoencoder, and Figure 8-6 displays the average precision, the precision-recall curve, and the auROC curve:

```
Training history of overcomplete autoencoder with single hidden layer,
dropout, and linear activation function

Train on 190820 samples, validate on 190820 samples
Epoch 1/10
190820/190820 [==============================] - 27s 141us/step - loss: 0.1358
- acc: 0.7430 - val_loss: 0.0082 - val_acc: 0.9742
Epoch 2/10
190820/190820 [==============================] - 28s 146us/step - loss: 0.0782
- acc: 0.7849 - val_loss: 0.0094 - val_acc: 0.9689
Epoch 3/10
190820/190820 [==============================] - 28s 149us/step - loss: 0.0753
- acc: 0.7858 - val_loss: 0.0102 - val_acc: 0.9672
Epoch 4/10
190820/190820 [==============================] - 28s 148us/step - loss: 0.0772
- acc: 0.7864 - val_loss: 0.0093 - val_acc: 0.9677
Epoch 5/10
190820/190820 [==============================] - 28s 147us/step - loss: 0.0813
- acc: 0.7843 - val_loss: 0.0108 - val_acc: 0.9631
Epoch 6/10
```

```
190820/190820 [==============================] - 28s 149us/step - loss: 0.0756
- acc: 0.7844 - val_loss: 0.0095 - val_acc: 0.9654
Epoch 7/10
190820/190820 [==============================] - 29s 150us/step - loss: 0.0743
- acc: 0.7850 - val_loss: 0.0077 - val_acc: 0.9768
Epoch 8/10
190820/190820 [==============================] - 29s 150us/step - loss: 0.0767
- acc: 0.7840 - val_loss: 0.0070 - val_acc: 0.9759
Epoch 9/10
190820/190820 [==============================] - 29s 150us/step - loss: 0.0762
- acc: 0.7851 - val_loss: 0.0072 - val_acc: 0.9733
Epoch 10/10
190820/190820 [==============================] - 29s 151us/step - loss: 0.0756
- acc: 0.7849 - val_loss: 0.0067 - val_acc: 0.9749
93987/93987 [==============================] - 3s 32us/step
```

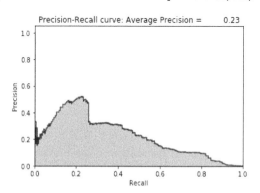

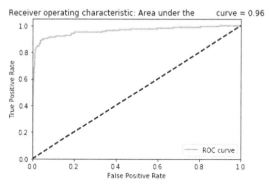

*Figure 8-6. Evaluation metrics of overcomplete autoencoder with single hidden layer, dropout, and linear activation function*

As expected, the losses are very low, and the overfit overcomplete autoencoder has very poor performance in detecting the fraudulent credit card transactions.

The following code summarizes the distribution of average precision across the 10 runs. The mean of the average precision is 0.21, worse than the 0.53 we achieved earlier. The coefficient of variation is 0.40:

```
Mean average precision over 10 runs: 0.21150415381770646
Coefficient of variation over 10 runs: 0.40295807771579256


[0.22549974304927337,
 0.22451178120391296,
 0.17243952488912334,
 0.2533716906936315,
 0.13251890273915556,
 0.1775116247503748,
 0.4343283958332979,
 0.10469065867732033,
 0.19480068075466764,
 0.19537213558630712]
```

# Sparse Overcomplete Autoencoder with Linear Activation

Another regularization technique is *sparsity*. We can force the autoencoder to take the sparsity of the matrix into consideration such that the majority of the autoencoder's neurons are inactive most of the time—in other words, they do not fire. This makes it harder for the autoencoder to memorize the identity function even when the autoencoder is overcomplete because most of the nodes cannot fire and, therefore, cannot overfit the observations as easily.

We will use a single hidden layer overcomplete autoencoder with 40 nodes like before but with just the sparsity penalty, not dropout.

Let's see if the results improve from the 0.21 average precision we had earlier:

```
model = Sequential()
    model.add(Dense(units=40, activation='linear', \
        activity_regularizer=regularizers.l1(10e-5), input_dim=29))
model.add(Dense(units=29, activation='linear'))
```

The following code shows the losses from this autoencoder, and Figure 8-7 displays the average precision, the precision-recall curve, and the auROC curve:

```
Training history of sparse overcomplete autoencoder with single hidden layer
and linear activation function

Train on 190820 samples, validate on 190820 samples
Epoch 1/10
190820/190820 [==============================] - 27s 142us/step - loss: 0.0985
 - acc: 0.9380 - val_loss: 0.0369 - val_acc: 0.9871
Epoch 2/10
190820/190820 [==============================] - 26s 136us/step - loss: 0.0284
 - acc: 0.9829 - val_loss: 0.0261 - val_acc: 0.9698
Epoch 3/10
```

```
190820/190820 [==============================] - 26s 136us/step - loss: 0.0229
- acc: 0.9816 - val_loss: 0.0169 - val_acc: 0.9952
Epoch 4/10
190820/190820 [==============================] - 26s 137us/step - loss: 0.0201
- acc: 0.9821 - val_loss: 0.0147 - val_acc: 0.9943
Epoch 5/10
190820/190820 [==============================] - 26s 137us/step - loss: 0.0183
- acc: 0.9810 - val_loss: 0.0142 - val_acc: 0.9842
Epoch 6/10
190820/190820 [==============================] - 26s 137us/step - loss: 0.0206
- acc: 0.9774 - val_loss: 0.0158 - val_acc: 0.9906
Epoch 7/10
190820/190820 [==============================] - 26s 136us/step - loss: 0.0169
- acc: 0.9816 - val_loss: 0.0124 - val_acc: 0.9866
Epoch 8/10
190820/190820 [==============================] - 26s 137us/step - loss: 0.0165
- acc: 0.9795 - val_loss: 0.0208 - val_acc: 0.9537
Epoch 9/10
190820/190820 [==============================] - 26s 136us/step - loss: 0.0164
- acc: 0.9801 - val_loss: 0.0105 - val_acc: 0.9965
Epoch 10/10
190820/190820 [==============================] - 27s 140us/step - loss: 0.0167
- acc: 0.9779 - val_loss: 0.0102 - val_acc: 0.9955
93987/93987 [==============================] - 3s 32us/step
```

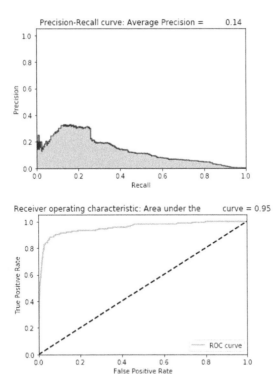

*Figure 8-7. Evaluation metrics of sparse overcomplete autoencoder with single hidden layer and linear activation function*

The following code summarizes the distribution of average precision across the 10 runs. The mean of the average precision is 0.21, worse than the 0.53 we achieved earlier. The coefficient of variation is 0.99:

```
Mean average precision over 10 runs: 0.21373659011504448
Coefficient of variation over 10 runs: 0.9913040763536749

[0.1370972172100049,
0.28328895710699215,
0.6362677613798704,
0.3467265637372019,
0.5197889253491589,
0.01871495737323161,
0.0812609121251577,
0.034749761900336684,
0.04846036143317335,
0.031010483535317393]
```

# Sparse Overcomplete Autoencoder with Linear Activation and Dropout

Of course, we can combine the regularization techniques to improve the solution. Here is a sparse overcomplete autoencoder with linear activation, 40 nodes in the single hidden layer, and dropout of 5%:

```
model = Sequential()
    model.add(Dense(units=40, activation='linear', \
        activity_regularizer=regularizers.l1(10e-5), input_dim=29))
    model.add(Dropout(0.05))
model.add(Dense(units=29, activation='linear'))
```

The following training data shows the losses from this autoencoder, and Figure 8-8 displays the average precision, the precision-recall curve, and the auROC curve:

```
Training history of sparse overcomplete autoencoder with single hidden layer,
dropout, and linear activation function

Train on 190820 samples, validate on 190820 samples
Epoch 1/10
190820/190820 [==============================] - 31s 162us/step - loss: 0.1477
- acc: 0.8150 - val_loss: 0.0506 - val_acc: 0.9727
Epoch 2/10
190820/190820 [==============================] - 29s 154us/step - loss: 0.0756
- acc: 0.8625 - val_loss: 0.0344 - val_acc: 0.9788
Epoch 3/10
190820/190820 [==============================] - 29s 152us/step - loss: 0.0687
- acc: 0.8612 - val_loss: 0.0291 - val_acc: 0.9790
Epoch 4/10
190820/190820 [==============================] - 29s 154us/step - loss: 0.0644
- acc: 0.8606 - val_loss: 0.0274 - val_acc: 0.9734
Epoch 5/10
190820/190820 [==============================] - 31s 163us/step - loss: 0.0630
- acc: 0.8597 - val_loss: 0.0242 - val_acc: 0.9746
Epoch 6/10
190820/190820 [==============================] - 31s 162us/step - loss: 0.0609
- acc: 0.8600 - val_loss: 0.0220 - val_acc: 0.9800
Epoch 7/10
190820/190820 [==============================] - 30s 156us/step - loss: 0.0624
- acc: 0.8581 - val_loss: 0.0289 - val_acc: 0.9633
Epoch 8/10
190820/190820 [==============================] - 29s 154us/step - loss: 0.0589
- acc: 0.8588 - val_loss: 0.0574 - val_acc: 0.9366
Epoch 9/10
190820/190820 [==============================] - 29s 154us/step - loss: 0.0596
- acc: 0.8571 - val_loss: 0.0206 - val_acc: 0.9752
Epoch 10/10
190820/190820 [==============================] - 31s 165us/step - loss: 0.0593
- acc: 0.8590 - val_loss: 0.0204 - val_acc: 0.9808
93987/93987 [==============================] - 4s 38us/step
```

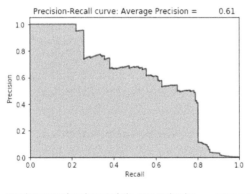

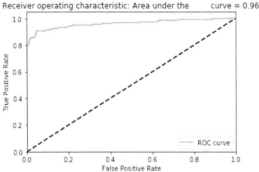

*Figure 8-8. Evaluation metrics of sparse overcomplete autoencoder with single hidden layer, dropout, and linear activation function*

The following code summarizes the distribution of average precision across the 10 runs. The mean of the average precision is 0.24, worse than the 0.53 we achieved earlier. The coefficient of variation is 0.62:

```
Mean average precision over 10 runs: 0.2426994231628755
Coefficient of variation over 10 runs: 0.6153219870606188

[0.6078198313533932,
0.20862366991302814,
0.25854513247057875,
0.08496595007072019,
0.26313491674585093,
0.17001322998258625,
0.15338215561753896,
0.1439107390306835,
0.4073422280287587,
0.1292563784156162]
```

# Working with Noisy Datasets

A common problem with real-world data is noisiness data is often distorted in some way because of data quality issues from data capture, data migration, data transformation, etc. We need autoencoders to be robust enough against such noise so that they are not fooled and can learn from the truly important underlying structure in the data.

To simulate this noise, let's add a Gaussian random matrix of noise to our credit card transactions dataset and then train an autoencoder on this noisy training set. Then, we will see how well the autoencoder does in predicting fraud on the noisy test set:

```
noise_factor = 0.50
X_train_AE_noisy = X_train_AE.copy() + noise_factor * \
 np.random.normal(loc=0.0, scale=1.0, size=X_train_AE.shape)
X_test_AE_noisy = X_test_AE.copy() + noise_factor * \
 np.random.normal(loc=0.0, scale=1.0, size=X_test_AE.shape)
```

# Denoising Autoencoder

Compared to the original, nondistorted dataset, the penalty for overfitting to the noisy dataset of credit card transactions is much higher. There is enough noise in the dataset that an autoencoder that fits too well to the noisy data will have a poor time detecting fraudulent transactions from normal ones.

This should make sense. We need an autoencoder that fits well enough to the data so that it is able to reconstruct most of the observations well enough but not so well enough that it accidentally reconstructs the noise, too. In other words, we want the autoencoder to learn the underlying structure but forget the noise in the data.

Let's try a few options from what has worked well so far. First, we will try a single hidden layer, 27-node undercomplete autoencoder with linear activation. Next, we will try a single hidden layer, 40-node sparse overcomplete autoencoder with dropout. And, finally, we will use an autoencoder with a nonlinear activation function.

## Two-Layer Denoising Undercomplete Autoencoder with Linear Activation

On the clean dataset, the single hidden layer autoencoder with linear activation and 27 nodes had an average precision of 0.69. Let's see how well it does on the noisy dataset. This autoencoder—because it is working with a noisy dataset and trying to denoise it—is known as a *denoising autoencoder*.

The code is similar to what we had before except now we are applying it to the noisy training and test datasets, X_train_AE_noisy and X_test_AE_noisy, respectively:

```
for i in range(0,10):
    # Call neural network API
    model = Sequential()

    # Generate hidden layer with 27 nodes using linear activation
    model.add(Dense(units=27, activation='linear', input_dim=29))

    # Generate output layer with 29 nodes
    model.add(Dense(units=29, activation='linear'))

    # Compile the model
    model.compile(optimizer='adam',
                  loss='mean_squared_error',
                  metrics=['accuracy'])

    # Train the model
    num_epochs = 10
    batch_size = 32

    history = model.fit(x=X_train_AE_noisy, y=X_train_AE_noisy,
                        epochs=num_epochs,
                        batch_size=batch_size,
                        shuffle=True,
                        validation_data=(X_train_AE, X_train_AE),
                        verbose=1)

    # Evaluate on test set
    predictions = model.predict(X_test_AE_noisy, verbose=1)
    anomalyScoresAE = anomalyScores(X_test, predictions)
    preds, avgPrecision = plotResults(y_test, anomalyScoresAE, True)
    test_scores.append(avgPrecision)
    model.reset_states()

print("Mean average precision over 10 runs: ", np.mean(test_scores))
test_scores
```

The following training data shows the losses from this autoencoder, and Figure 8-9 displays the average precision, the precision-recall curve, and the auROC curve:

```
Training history of denoising undercomplete autoencoder with single hidden layer
and linear activation function

Train on 190820 samples, validate on 190820 samples
Epoch 1/10
190820/190820 [==============================] - 25s 133us/step - loss: 0.1733
- acc: 0.7756 - val_loss: 0.0356 - val_acc: 0.9123
Epoch 2/10
190820/190820 [==============================] - 24s 126us/step - loss: 0.0546
- acc: 0.8793 - val_loss: 0.0354 - val_acc: 0.8973
Epoch 3/10
190820/190820 [==============================] - 24s 126us/step - loss: 0.0531
- acc: 0.8764 - val_loss: 0.0350 - val_acc: 0.9399
Epoch 4/10
```

```
190820/190820 [==============================] - 24s 126us/step - loss: 0.0525
- acc: 0.8879 - val_loss: 0.0342 - val_acc: 0.9573
Epoch 5/10
190820/190820 [==============================] - 24s 126us/step - loss: 0.0530
- acc: 0.8910 - val_loss: 0.0347 - val_acc: 0.9503
Epoch 6/10
190820/190820 [==============================] - 24s 126us/step - loss: 0.0524
- acc: 0.8889 - val_loss: 0.0350 - val_acc: 0.9138
Epoch 7/10
190820/190820 [==============================] - 24s 126us/step - loss: 0.0531
- acc: 0.8845 - val_loss: 0.0343 - val_acc: 0.9280
Epoch 8/10
190820/190820 [==============================] - 24s 126us/step - loss: 0.0530
- acc: 0.8798 - val_loss: 0.0339 - val_acc: 0.9507
Epoch 9/10
190820/190820 [==============================] - 24s 126us/step - loss: 0.0526
- acc: 0.8877 - val_loss: 0.0337 - val_acc: 0.9611
Epoch 10/10
190820/190820 [==============================] - 24s 127us/step - loss: 0.0528
- acc: 0.8885 - val_loss: 0.0352 - val_acc: 0.9474
93987/93987 [==============================] - 3s 34us/step
```

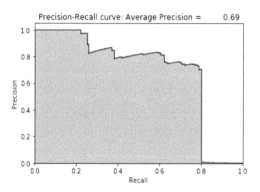

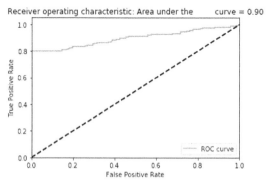

*Figure 8-9. Evaluation metrics of denoising undercomplete autoencoder with single hidden layer and linear activation function*

The mean average precision is now 0.28. You can see just how difficult it is for the linear autoencoder to denoise this noisy dataset:

```
Mean average precision over 10 runs: 0.2825997155005206
Coeficient of variation over 10 runs: 1.1765416185187383


[0.6929639885685303,
 0.008450118408150287,
 0.6970753417267612,
 0.011820311633718597,
 0.0089241248926963773,
 0.010639537507746342,
 0.6884911855668772,
 0.006549332886020607,
 0.6805304226634528,
 0.02055279115125298]
```

It struggles with separating the true underlying structure in the data from the Gaussian noise we added.

## Two-Layer Denoising Overcomplete Autoencoder with Linear Activation

Let's now try a single hidden layer overcomplete autoencoder with 40 nodes, a sparsity regularizer, and dropout of 5%.

This had an average precision of 0.56 on the original dataset:

```
model = Sequential()
model.add(Dense(units=40, activation='linear',
  activity_regularizer=regularizers.l1(10e-5),
                input_dim=29))
model.add(Dropout(0.05))
model.add(Dense(units=29, activation='linear'))
```

The following training data shows the losses from this autoencoder, and Figure 8-10 displays the average precision, the precision-recall curve, and the auROC curve:

```
Training history of denoising overcomplete autoencoder with dropout and linear
activation function

Train on 190820 samples, validate on 190820 samples
Epoch 1/10
190820/190820 [==============================] - 28s 145us/step - loss: 0.1726
- acc: 0.8035 - val_loss: 0.0432 - val_acc: 0.9781
Epoch 2/10
190820/190820 [==============================] - 26s 138us/step - loss: 0.0868
- acc: 0.8490 - val_loss: 0.0307 - val_acc: 0.9775
Epoch 3/10
190820/190820 [==============================] - 26s 138us/step - loss: 0.0809
- acc: 0.8455 - val_loss: 0.0445 - val_acc: 0.9535
Epoch 4/10
```

```
190820/190820 [==============================] - 26s 138us/step - loss: 0.0777
- acc: 0.8438 - val_loss: 0.0257 - val_acc: 0.9709
Epoch 5/10
190820/190820 [==============================] - 27s 139us/step - loss: 0.0748
- acc: 0.8434 - val_loss: 0.0219 - val_acc: 0.9787
Epoch 6/10
190820/190820 [==============================] - 26s 138us/step - loss: 0.0746
- acc: 0.8425 - val_loss: 0.0210 - val_acc: 0.9794
Epoch 7/10
190820/190820 [==============================] - 26s 138us/step - loss: 0.0713
- acc: 0.8437 - val_loss: 0.0294 - val_acc: 0.9503
Epoch 8/10
190820/190820 [==============================] - 26s 138us/step - loss: 0.0708
- acc: 0.8426 - val_loss: 0.0276 - val_acc: 0.9606
Epoch 9/10
190820/190820 [==============================] - 26s 139us/step - loss: 0.0704
- acc: 0.8428 - val_loss: 0.0180 - val_acc: 0.9811
Epoch 10/10
190820/190820 [==============================] - 27s 139us/step - loss: 0.0702
- acc: 0.8424 - val_loss: 0.0185 - val_acc: 0.9710
93987/93987 [==============================] - 4s 38us/step
```

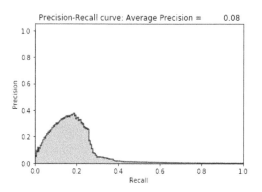

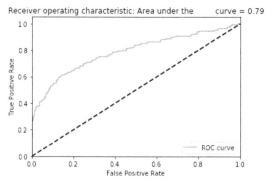

*Figure 8-10. Evaluation metrics of denoising overcomplete autoencoder with dropout and linear activation function*

The following code summarizes the distribution of average precision across the 10 runs. The mean of the average precision is 0.10, worse than the 0.53 we achieved earlier. The coefficient of variation is 0.83:

```
Mean average precision over 10 runs: 0.10112931070692295
Coefficient of variation over 10 runs: 0.8343774832756188

[0.08283546387140524,
 0.043070120657586454,
 0.018901753737287603,
 0.02381040174486509,
 0.16038446580196433,
 0.03461061251209459,
 0.17847771715513427,
 0.2483282420447288,
 0.012981344347664117,
 0.20789298519649893]
```

## Two-Layer Denoising Overcomplete Autoencoder with ReLu Activation

Finally, let's see how the same autoencoder fares using ReLu as the activation function instead of a linear activation function. Recall that the nonlinear activation function autoencoder did not perform quite as well as the one with linear activation on the original dataset:

```
model = Sequential()
    model.add(Dense(units=40, activation='relu', \
        activity_regularizer=regularizers.l1(10e-5), input_dim=29))
    model.add(Dropout(0.05))
model.add(Dense(units=29, activation='relu'))
```

The following training data shows the losses from this autoencoder, and Figure 8-11 displays the average precision, the precision-recall curve, and the auROC curve:

```
Training history of denoising overcomplete autoencoder with dropout and ReLU
activation function"

Train on 190820 samples, validate on 190820 samples
Epoch 1/10
190820/190820 [==============================] - 29s 153us/step - loss: 0.3049
- acc: 0.6454 - val_loss: 0.0841 - val_acc: 0.8873
Epoch 2/10
190820/190820 [==============================] - 27s 143us/step - loss: 0.1806
- acc: 0.7193 - val_loss: 0.0606 - val_acc: 0.9012
Epoch 3/10
190820/190820 [==============================] - 27s 143us/step - loss: 0.1626
- acc: 0.7255 - val_loss: 0.0500 - val_acc: 0.9045
Epoch 4/10
190820/190820 [==============================] - 27s 143us/step - loss: 0.1567
- acc: 0.7294 - val_loss: 0.0445 - val_acc: 0.9116
```

```
Epoch 5/10
190820/190820 [==============================] - 27s 143us/step - loss: 0.1484
- acc: 0.7309 - val_loss: 0.0433 - val_acc: 0.9136
Epoch 6/10
190820/190820 [==============================] - 27s 144us/step - loss: 0.1467
- acc: 0.7311 - val_loss: 0.0375 - val_acc: 0.9101
Epoch 7/10
190820/190820 [==============================] - 27s 143us/step - loss: 0.1427
- acc: 0.7335 - val_loss: 0.0384 - val_acc: 0.9013
Epoch 8/10
190820/190820 [==============================] - 27s 143us/step - loss: 0.1397
- acc: 0.7307 - val_loss: 0.0337 - val_acc: 0.9145
Epoch 9/10
190820/190820 [==============================] - 27s 143us/step - loss: 0.1361
- acc: 0.7322 - val_loss: 0.0343 - val_acc: 0.9066
Epoch 10/10
190820/190820 [==============================] - 27s 144us/step - loss: 0.1349
- acc: 0.7331 - val_loss: 0.0325 - val_acc: 0.9107
93987/93987 [==============================] - 4s 41us/step
```

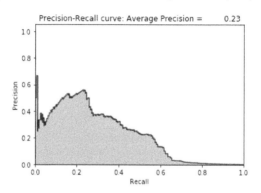

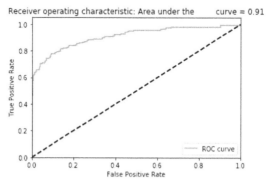

*Figure 8-11. Evaluation metrics of denoising overcomplete autoencoder with dropout and ReLU activation function*

The following code summarizes the distribution of average precision across the 10 runs. The mean of the average precision is 0.20, worse than the 0.53 we achieved earlier. The coefficient of variation is 0.55:

```
Mean average precision over 10 runs: 0.1969608394689088
Coefficient of variation over 10 runs: 0.5566706365802669

[0.22960316854089222,
0.37609633487223315,
0.11429775486529765,
0.10208135698072755,
0.4002384343852861,
0.13317480663248088,
0.15764518571284625,
0.2406315655171392,
0.05080529996343734,
0.1650344872187474]
```

You can experiment with the number of nodes, layers, degree of sparsity, dropout percentage, and the activation functions to see if you can improve the results from here.

# Conclusion

In this chapter, we returned to the credit card fraud problem from earlier in the book to develop a neural network-based unsupervised fraud detection solution.

To find the optimal architecture for our autoencoder, we experimented with a variety of autoencoders. We tried complete, undercomplete, and overcomplete autoencoders with either a single or a few hidden layers. We also used both linear and nonlinear activation functions and employed two major types of regularization, sparsity and dropout.

We found that a pretty simple two-layer undercomplete neural network with linear activation worked best on the original credit card dataset, but we needed a sparse two-layer overcomplete autoencoder with linear activation and dropout to address the noise in the noisy credit card dataset.

A lot of our experiments were based on trial and error—for each experiment, we adjusted several hyperparameters and compared results with previous iterations. It is possible that an even better autoencoder-based fraud detection solution exists, and I encourage you to experiment on your own to see what you find.

So far in this book, we have viewed supervised and unsupervised as separate and distinct approaches, but in Chapter 9, we will explore how to employ both supervised and unsupervised approaches jointly to develop a so-called semisupervised solution that is better than either standalone approach.

# Semisupervised Learning

Until now, we have viewed supervised learning and unsupervised learning as two separate and distinct branches of machine learning. Supervised learning is appropriate when our dataset is labeled, and unsupervised learning is necessary when our dataset is unlabeled.

In the real world, the distinction is not quite so clear. Datasets are usually partially labeled, and we want to efficiently label the unlabeled observations while leveraging the information in the labeled set. With supervised learning, we would have to toss away the majority of the dataset because it is unlabeled. With unsupervised learning, we would have the majority of the data to work with but would not know how to take advantage of the few labels we have.

The field of *semisupervised learning* blends the benefits of both supervised and unsupervised learning, taking advantage of the few labels that are available to uncover structure in a dataset and help label the rest.

We will continue to use the credit card transactions dataset in this chapter to showcase semisupervised learning.

## Data Preparation

As before, let's load in the necessary libraries and prepare the data. This should be pretty familiar by now:

```
'''Main'''
import numpy as np
import pandas as pd
import os, time, re
import pickle, gzip

'''Data Viz'''
```

```
import matplotlib.pyplot as plt
import seaborn as sns
color = sns.color_palette()
import matplotlib as mpl

%matplotlib inline

'''Data Prep and Model Evaluation'''
from sklearn import preprocessing as pp
from sklearn.model_selection import train_test_split
from sklearn.model_selection import StratifiedKFold
from sklearn.metrics import log_loss
from sklearn.metrics import precision_recall_curve, average_precision_score
from sklearn.metrics import roc_curve, auc, roc_auc_score

'''Algos'''
import lightgbm as lgb

'''TensorFlow and Keras'''
import tensorflow as tf
import keras
from keras import backend as K
from keras.models import Sequential, Model
from keras.layers import Activation, Dense, Dropout
from keras.layers import BatchNormalization, Input, Lambda
from keras import regularizers
from keras.losses import mse, binary_crossentropy
```

As before, we will generate a training and test set. But we will drop 90% of the fraudulent credit card transactions from the training set to simulate how to work with *partially labeled* datasets.

While this may seem like a very aggressive move, real-world problems involving payment fraud have similarly low incidences of fraud (as little as 1 fraud per 10,000 cases). By removing 90% of the labels from the training set, we are simulating this type of phenomenon:

```
# Load the data
current_path = os.getcwd()
file = '\\datasets\\credit_card_data\\credit_card.csv'
data = pd.read_csv(current_path + file)

dataX = data.copy().drop(['Class','Time'],axis=1)
dataY = data['Class'].copy()

# Scale data
featuresToScale = dataX.columns
sX = pp.StandardScaler(copy=True, with_mean=True, with_std=True)
dataX.loc[:,featuresToScale] = sX.fit_transform(dataX[featuresToScale])

# Split into train and test
X_train, X_test, y_train, y_test = \
```

```
    train_test_split(dataX, dataY, test_size=0.33, \
                      random_state=2018, stratify=dataY)

# Drop 90% of the labels from the training set
toDrop = y_train[y_train==1].sample(frac=0.90,random_state=2018)
X_train.drop(labels=toDrop.index,inplace=True)
y_train.drop(labels=toDrop.index,inplace=True)
```

We will also reuse the `anomalyScores` and `plotResults` functions:

```
def anomalyScores(originalDF, reducedDF):
    loss = np.sum((np.array(originalDF) - \
                   np.array(reducedDF))**2, axis=1)
    loss = pd.Series(data=loss,index=originalDF.index)
    loss = (loss-np.min(loss))/(np.max(loss)-np.min(loss))
    return loss

def plotResults(trueLabels, anomalyScores, returnPreds = False):
    preds = pd.concat([trueLabels, anomalyScores], axis=1)
    preds.columns = ['trueLabel', 'anomalyScore']
    precision, recall, thresholds = \
        precision_recall_curve(preds['trueLabel'], \
                               preds['anomalyScore'])
    average_precision = average_precision_score( \
                        preds['trueLabel'], preds['anomalyScore'])

    plt.step(recall, precision, color='k', alpha=0.7, where='post')
    plt.fill_between(recall, precision, step='post', alpha=0.3, color='k')

    plt.xlabel('Recall')
    plt.ylabel('Precision')
    plt.ylim([0.0, 1.05])
    plt.xlim([0.0, 1.0])

    plt.title('Precision-Recall curve: Average Precision = \
        {0:0.2f}'.format(average_precision))

    fpr, tpr, thresholds = roc_curve(preds['trueLabel'], \
                                     preds['anomalyScore'])
    areaUnderROC = auc(fpr, tpr)

    plt.figure()
    plt.plot(fpr, tpr, color='r', lw=2, label='ROC curve')
    plt.plot([0, 1], [0, 1], color='k', lw=2, linestyle='--')
    plt.xlim([0.0, 1.0])
    plt.ylim([0.0, 1.05])
    plt.xlabel('False Positive Rate')
    plt.ylabel('True Positive Rate')
    plt.title('Receiver operating characteristic: Area under the \
        curve = {0:0.2f}'.format(areaUnderROC))
    plt.legend(loc="lower right")
    plt.show()
```

```
    if returnPreds==True:
        return preds, average_precision
```

Finally, here's a new function called `precisionAnalysis` to help us assess the precision of our models at a certain level of recall. Specifically, we will determine what the model's precision is to catch 75% of the fraudulent credit card transactions in the test set. The higher the precision, the better the model.

This is a reasonable benchmark. In other words, we want to catch 75% of the fraud with as high of a precision as possible. If we do not achieve a high enough precision, we will unnecessarily reject good credit card transactions, potentially angering our customer base:

```
def precisionAnalysis(df, column, threshold):
    df.sort_values(by=column, ascending=False, inplace=True)
    threshold_value = threshold*df.trueLabel.sum()
    i = 0
    j = 0
    while i < threshold_value+1:
        if df.iloc[j]["trueLabel"]==1:
            i += 1
        j += 1
    return df, i/j
```

# Supervised Model

To benchmark our semisupervised model, let's first see how well a supervised model and a unsupervised model do in isolation.

We will start with a supervised learning solution based on light gradient boosting like the one that performed best in Chapter 2. We will use *k*-fold cross-validation to create five folds:

```
k_fold = StratifiedKFold(n_splits=5,shuffle=True,random_state=2018)
```

Let's next set the parameters for gradient boosting:

```
params_lightGB = {
    'task': 'train',
    'application':'binary',
    'num_class':1,
    'boosting': 'gbdt',
    'objective': 'binary',
    'metric': 'binary_logloss',
    'metric_freq':50,
    'is_training_metric':False,
    'max_depth':4,
    'num_leaves': 31,
    'learning_rate': 0.01,
    'feature_fraction': 1.0,
    'bagging_fraction': 1.0,
```

```
        'bagging_freq': 0,
        'bagging_seed': 2018,
        'verbose': 0,
        'num_threads':16
    }
```

Now, let's train the algorithm:

```
trainingScores = []
cvScores = []
predictionsBasedOnKFolds = pd.DataFrame(data=[], index=y_train.index, \
                                        columns=['prediction'])

for train_index, cv_index in k_fold.split(np.zeros(len(X_train)), \
                                          y_train.ravel()):
    X_train_fold, X_cv_fold = X_train.iloc[train_index,:], \
        X_train.iloc[cv_index,:]
    y_train_fold, y_cv_fold = y_train.iloc[train_index], \
        y_train.iloc[cv_index]

    lgb_train = lgb.Dataset(X_train_fold, y_train_fold)
    lgb_eval = lgb.Dataset(X_cv_fold, y_cv_fold, reference=lgb_train)
    gbm = lgb.train(params_lightGB, lgb_train, num_boost_round=2000,
                    valid_sets=lgb_eval, early_stopping_rounds=200)

    loglossTraining = log_loss(y_train_fold, gbm.predict(X_train_fold, \
                               num_iteration=gbm.best_iteration))
    trainingScores.append(loglossTraining)

    predictionsBasedOnKFolds.loc[X_cv_fold.index,'prediction'] = \
        gbm.predict(X_cv_fold, num_iteration=gbm.best_iteration)
    loglossCV = log_loss(y_cv_fold, \
        predictionsBasedOnKFolds.loc[X_cv_fold.index,'prediction'])
    cvScores.append(loglossCV)

    print('Training Log Loss: ', loglossTraining)
    print('CV Log Loss: ', loglossCV)

loglossLightGBMGradientBoosting = log_loss(y_train, \
        predictionsBasedOnKFolds.loc[:,'prediction'])
print('LightGBM Gradient Boosting Log Loss: ', \
        loglossLightGBMGradientBoosting)
```

We will now use this model to predict the fraud on the test set of credit card transactions.

Figure 9-1 displays the results.

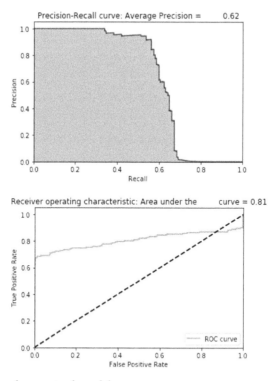

*Figure 9-1. Results of supervised model*

The average precision on the test based on the precision-recall curve is 0.62. To catch 75% of the fraud, we have a precision of just 0.5%.

## Unsupervised Model

Now let's build a fraud detection solution using unsupervised learning. Specifically, we will build a sparse two-layer overcomplete autoencoder with a linear activation function. We will have 40 nodes in the hidden layer and a dropout of 2%.

However, we will adjust our training set by *oversampling* the number of fraudulent cases we have. Oversampling is a technique used to adjust the class distribution in a given dataset. We want to add more fraudulent cases to our dataset so that the autoencoder we train has an easier time separating the normal/nonfraudulent transactions from the abnormal/fraudulent ones.

Recall that after having dropped 90% of the fraudulent cases from the training set, we have just 33 fraudulent cases left. We will take the 33 fraudulent cases, duplicate these 100 times, and then append them to the training set. We will also keep copies of the nonoversampled training set so we can use them for the rest of our machine learning pipeline.

Remember we do not touch the test set—there is no oversampling with the test set, just the training set:

```
oversample_multiplier = 100

X_train_original = X_train.copy()
y_train_original = y_train.copy()
X_test_original = X_test.copy()
y_test_original = y_test.copy()

X_train_oversampled = X_train.copy()
y_train_oversampled = y_train.copy()
X_train_oversampled = X_train_oversampled.append( \
        [X_train_oversampled[y_train==1]]*oversample_multiplier, \
        ignore_index=False)
y_train_oversampled = y_train_oversampled.append( \
        [y_train_oversampled[y_train==1]]*oversample_multiplier, \
        ignore_index=False)

X_train = X_train_oversampled.copy()
y_train = y_train_oversampled.copy()
```

Let's now train our autoencoder:

```
model = Sequential()
model.add(Dense(units=40, activation='linear', \
                activity_regularizer=regularizers.l1(10e-5), \
                input_dim=29,name='hidden_layer'))
model.add(Dropout(0.02))
model.add(Dense(units=29, activation='linear'))

model.compile(optimizer='adam',
              loss='mean_squared_error',
              metrics=['accuracy'])

num_epochs = 5
batch_size = 32

history = model.fit(x=X_train, y=X_train,
                    epochs=num_epochs,
                    batch_size=batch_size,
                    shuffle=True,
                    validation_split=0.20,
                    verbose=1)

predictions = model.predict(X_test, verbose=1)
anomalyScoresAE = anomalyScores(X_test, predictions)
preds, average_precision = plotResults(y_test, anomalyScoresAE, True)
```

Figure 9-2 displays the results.

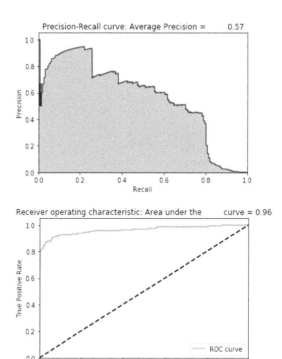

*Figure 9-2. Results of unsupervised model*

The average precision on the test based on the precision-recall curve is 0.57. To catch 75% of the fraud, we have a precision of just 45%. While the average precision of the unsupervised solution is similar to the average precision of the supervised solution, the precision of 45% at 75% recall is better.

However, the unsupervised solution by itself is still not great.

# Semisupervised Model

Now, let's take the representation learned by the autoencoder (the hidden layer), combine it with the original training set, and feed this into the gradient boosting algorithm. This a semisupervised approach, taking advantage of supervised and unsupervised learning.

To get the hidden layer, we call the `Model()` class from the Keras API and use the `get_layer` function:

```
layer_name = 'hidden_layer'

intermediate_layer_model = Model(inputs=model.input, \
```

```
                                    outputs=model.get_layer(layer_name).output)
intermediate_output_train = intermediate_layer_model.predict(X_train_original)
intermediate_output_test = intermediate_layer_model.predict(X_test_original)
```

Let's store these autoencoder representations into DataFrames and then combine them with the original training set:

```
intermediate_output_trainDF = \
    pd.DataFrame(data=intermediate_output_train,index=X_train_original.index)
intermediate_output_testDF = \
    pd.DataFrame(data=intermediate_output_test,index=X_test_original.index)

X_train = X_train_original.merge(intermediate_output_trainDF, \
                                 left_index=True,right_index=True)
X_test = X_test_original.merge(intermediate_output_testDF, \
                                left_index=True,right_index=True)
y_train = y_train_original.copy()
```

We will now train the gradient boosting model on this new training set of 69 features (29 from the original dataset and 40 from the autoencoder's representation):

```
trainingScores = []
cvScores = []
predictionsBasedOnKFolds = pd.DataFrame(data=[],index=y_train.index, \
                                        columns=['prediction'])

for train_index, cv_index in k_fold.split(np.zeros(len(X_train)), \
                                          y_train.ravel()):
    X_train_fold, X_cv_fold = X_train.iloc[train_index,:], \
        X_train.iloc[cv_index,:]
    y_train_fold, y_cv_fold = y_train.iloc[train_index], \
        y_train.iloc[cv_index]

    lgb_train = lgb.Dataset(X_train_fold, y_train_fold)
    lgb_eval = lgb.Dataset(X_cv_fold, y_cv_fold, reference=lgb_train)
    gbm = lgb.train(params_lightGB, lgb_train, num_boost_round=5000,
                    valid_sets=lgb_eval, early_stopping_rounds=200)

    loglossTraining = log_loss(y_train_fold,
                               gbm.predict(X_train_fold, \
                               num_iteration=gbm.best_iteration))
    trainingScores.append(loglossTraining)

    predictionsBasedOnKFolds.loc[X_cv_fold.index,'prediction'] = \
        gbm.predict(X_cv_fold, num_iteration=gbm.best_iteration)
    loglossCV = log_loss(y_cv_fold, \
            predictionsBasedOnKFolds.loc[X_cv_fold.index,'prediction'])
    cvScores.append(loglossCV)

    print('Training Log Loss: ', loglossTraining)
    print('CV Log Loss: ', loglossCV)

loglossLightGBMGradientBoosting = log_loss(y_train, \
```

```
                    predictionsBasedOnKFolds.loc[:,'prediction'])
print('LightGBM Gradient Boosting Log Loss: ', \
                    loglossLightGBMGradientBoosting)
```

Figure 9-3 displays the results.

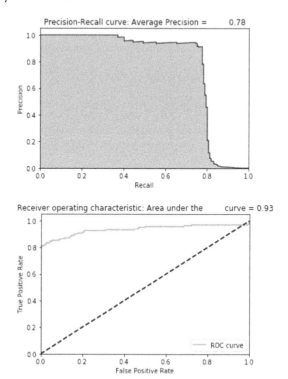

*Figure 9-3. Results of semisupervised model*

The average precision on the test set based on the precision-recall curve is 0.78. This is a good bit higher than both the supervised and the unsupervised models.

To catch 75% of the fraud, we have a precision of 92%. This is a considerable improvement. With this level of precision, the payment processor should feel comfortable rejecting transactions that the model flags as potentially fraudulent. Less than one in ten will be wrong, and we will catch approximately 75% of the fraud.

# The Power of Supervised and Unsupervised

In this semisupervised credit card fraud detection solution, both supervised learning and unsupervised learning have important roles to play. One way to explore this is by analyzing which features the final gradient boosting model found most important.

---

Let's find and store those feature importance values from the model we just trained:

```
featuresImportance = pd.DataFrame(data=list(gbm.feature_importance()), \
                         index=X_train.columns,columns=['featImportance'])
featuresImportance = featuresImportance/featuresImportance.sum()
featuresImportance.sort_values(by='featImportance', \
                         ascending=False,inplace=True)
featuresImportance
```

Table 9-1 shows some of the most important features, sorted in descending order.

*Table 9-1. Feature importance from semisupervised model*

|        | featImportance |
| ------ | -------------- |
| V28    | 0.047843       |
| Amount | 0.037263       |
| 21     | 0.030244       |
| V21    | 0.029624       |
| V26    | 0.029469       |
| V12    | 0.028334       |
| V27    | 0.028024       |
| 6      | 0.027405       |
| 28     | 0.026941       |
| 36     | 0.024050       |
| 5      | 0.022347       |

As you can see here, some of the top features are features the hidden layer learned by the autoencoder (the non "V" features) while others are the principal components from the original dataset (the "V" features) as well as the amount of the transaction.

# Conclusion

The semisupervised model trounces the performance of both the standalone supervised model and the standalone unsupervised model.

We just scratched the surface of what's possible with semisupervised learning, but this should help reframe the conversation from debating between supervised and unsupervised learning to combining supervised and unsupervised learning in the search for an optimal applied solution.

# PART IV

# Deep Unsupervised Learning Using TensorFlow and Keras

Until now, we have worked with only shallow neural networks; in other words, networks with only a few hidden layers. Shallow neural networks are certainly useful in building machine learning systems, but the most powerful advances in machine learning over the past decade have come from neural networks with many hidden layers, known as *deep neural networks*. This subfield of machine learning is known as *deep learning*. Deep learning on large, labeled datasets has led to major commercial successes in areas such as computer vision, object recognition, speech recognition, and machine translation.

We will focus on deep learning on large, unlabeled datsets, which is also commonly referred to as *deep unsupervised learning*. This field is still very new, full of potential but with fewer commerical successes to date compared to the supervised variant. Over the next few chapters, we will build deep unsupervised learning systems, starting with the simplest building blocks.

Chapter 10 covers restricted Boltzmann machines, which we will use to build a recommender system for movies. In Chapter 11, we will stack restricted Boltzmann machines on top of each other, creating deep neural nets known as deep belief networks. In Chapter 12, we will generate synthetic data using generative adversarial networks, one of the hottest areas of deep unsupervised learning today. Then in Chapter 13, we will return to clustering but work with time series data this time.

This is a lot of advanced material, but a lot of deep unsupervised learning draws on the fundamental principles we introduced earlier in the book.

# CHAPTER 10

# Recommender Systems Using Restricted Boltzmann Machines

Earlier in this book, we used unsupervised learning to learn the underlying (hidden) structure in unlabeled data. Specifically, we performed dimensionality reduction, reducing a high-dimensional dataset to one with much fewer dimensions, and built an anomaly detection system. We also performed clustering, grouping objects together based on how similar or dissimilar they were to each other.

Now, we will move into *generative unsupervised models*, which involve learning a probability distribution from an original dataset and using it to make inferences about never-before-seen data. In later chapters, we will use such models to generate seemingly real data, which at times is virtually indistinguishable from the original data.

Until now, we have looked at mostly *discriminative models* that learn to separate observations based on what the algorithms learn from the data; these discriminative models do not learn the probability distribution from the data. Discriminative models include supervised ones such as the logistic regression and decision trees from Chapter 2 as well as clustering methods such as *k*-means and hierarchical clustering from Chapter 5.

Let's start with the simplest of the generative unsupervised models known as the *restricted Boltzmann machine*.

## Boltzmann Machines

*Boltzmann machines* were first invented in 1985 by Geoffrey Hinton (then a professor at Carnegie Mellon University and now one of the fathers of the deep learning movement, a professor at the University of Toronto, and a machine learning researcher at

Google) and Terry Sejnowski (who was a professor at John Hopkins University at the time).

Boltzmann machines—of the unrestricted type—consist of a neural network with an input layer and one or several hidden layers. The neurons or units in the neural network make stochastic decisions about whether to turn on or not based on the data fed in during training and the cost function the Boltzmann machine is trying to minimize. With this training, the Boltzmann machine discovers interesting features about the data, which helps model the complex underlying relationships and patterns present in the data.

However, these unrestricted Boltzmann machines use neural networks with neurons that are connected not only to other neurons in other layers but also to neurons within the same layer. That, coupled with the presence of many hidden layers, makes training an unrestricted Boltzmann machine very inefficient. Unrestricted Boltzmann machines had little commercial success during the 1980s and 1990s as a result.

## Restricted Boltzmann Machines

In the 2000s, Geoffrey Hinton and others began to have commercial success by using a modified version of the original unrestricted Boltzmann machines. These *restricted Boltzmann machines (RBMs)* have an input layer (also referred to as the *visible layer*) and just a single hidden layer, and the connections among neurons are restricted such that neurons are connected only to the neurons in other layers but not to neurons within the same layer. In other words, there are no visible-visible connections and no hidden-hidden connections.[1]

Geoffrey Hinton also demonstrated that such simple RBMs could be stacked on top of each other so that the output of the hidden layer of one RBM can be fed into the input layer of another RBM. This sort of RBM stacking can be repeated many times to learn progressively more nuanced hidden representations of the original data. This network of many RBMs can be viewed as one deep, multilayered neural network model—and thus the field of deep learning took off, starting in 2006.

Note that RBMs use a *stochastic* approach to learning the underlying structure of data, whereas autoencoders, for example, use a *deterministic* approach.

---

1 The most common training algorithm for this class of RBMs is known as the gradient-based contrastive divergence algorithm.

# Recommender Systems

In this chapter, we will use RBMs to build a *recommender system*, one of the most successful applications of machine learning to date and widely used in industry to help predict user preferences for movies, music, books, news, search, shopping, digital advertising, and online dating.

There are two major categories of recommender systems—*collaborative filtering* recommender systems and *content-based filtering* recommender systems. Collaborative filtering involves building a recommender system from a user's past behavior and those of other users to which the user is similar to. This recommender system can then predict items that the user may have an interest in even though the user has never expressed explicit interest. Movie recommendations on Netflix rely on collaborative filtering.

Content-based filtering involves learning the distinct properties of an item to recommend additional items with similar properties. Music recommendations on Pandora rely on content-based filtering.

## Collaborative Filtering

Content-based filtering is not commonly used because it is a rather difficult task to learn the distinct properties of items—this level of understanding is very challenging for artificial machines to achieve currently. It is much easier to collect and analyze a large amount of information on users' behaviors and preferences and make predictions based on this. Therefore, collaborative filtering is much more widely used and is the type of recommender system we will focus on here.

Collaborative filtering requires no knowledge of the underlying items themselves. Rather, collaborative filtering assumes that users that agreed in the past will agree in the future and that user preferences remain stable over time. By modeling how similar users are to other users, collaborative filtering can make pretty powerful recommendations. Moreover, collaborative filtering does not have to rely on *explicit data* (i.e., ratings that users provide). Rather, it can work with *implicit data* such as how long or how often a user views or clicks on a particular item. For example, in the past Netflix asked users to rate movies but now uses implicit user behavior to make inferences about user likes and dislikes.

However, collaborative filtering has its challenges. First, it requires a lot of user data to make good recommendations. Second, it is a very computationally demanding task. Third, the datasets are generally very sparse since users will have exhibited preferences for only a small fraction of all the items in the universe of possible items. Assuming we have enough data, there are techniques we can use to handle the sparsity of the data and efficiently solve the problem, which we will cover in this chapter.

## The Netflix Prize

In 2006, Netflix sponsored a three-year-long competition to improve its movie rec-ommender system. The company offered a grand prize of one million dollars to the team that could improve the accuracy of its existing recommender system by at least 10%. It also released a dataset of over 100 million movie ratings. In September 2009, BellKor's Pramatic Chaos team won the prize, using an ensemble of many different algorithmic approaches.

Such a high-profile competition with a rich dataset and meaningful prize energized the machine learning community and led to substantial progress in recommender system research, which paved the way for better recommender systems in industry over the past several years.

In this chapter, we will use a similar movie rating dataset to build our own recom-mender system using RBMs.

# MovieLens Dataset

Instead of the 100 million ratings Netflix dataset, we will use a smaller movie ratings dataset known as the *MovieLens 20M Dataset*, provided by GroupLens, a research lab in the Department of Computer Science and Engineering at the University of Minne-sota, Twin Cities. The data contains 20,000,263 ratings across 27,278 movies created by 138,493 users from January 9, 1995 to March 31, 2015. Of users who rated at least 20 movies each, we will select a subset at random.

This dataset is more manageable to work with than the 100 million ratings dataset from Netflix. Because the file size exceeds one hundred megabytes, the file is not accessible on GitHub. You will need to download the file directly from the MovieLens website (*http://bit.ly/2G0ZHCn*).

## Data Preparation

As before, let's load in the necessary libraries:

```
'''Main'''
import numpy as np
import pandas as pd
import os, time, re
import pickle, gzip, datetime

'''Data Viz'''
import matplotlib.pyplot as plt
import seaborn as sns
color = sns.color_palette()
import matplotlib as mpl

%matplotlib inline
```

```
'''Data Prep and Model Evaluation'''
from sklearn import preprocessing as pp
from sklearn.model_selection import train_test_split
from sklearn.model_selection import StratifiedKFold
from sklearn.metrics import log_loss
from sklearn.metrics import precision_recall_curve, average_precision_score
from sklearn.metrics import roc_curve, auc, roc_auc_score, mean_squared_error

'''Algos'''
import lightgbm as lgb

'''TensorFlow and Keras'''
import tensorflow as tf
import keras
from keras import backend as K
from keras.models import Sequential, Model
from keras.layers import Activation, Dense, Dropout
from keras.layers import BatchNormalization, Input, Lambda
from keras import regularizers
from keras.losses import mse, binary_crossentropy
```

Next, we will load in the ratings dataset and convert the fields into the appropriate data types. We have just a few fields. The user ID, the movie ID, the rating provided by the user for the movie, and the timestamp of the rating provided:

```
# Load the data
current_path = os.getcwd()
file = '\\datasets\\movielens_data\\ratings.csv'
ratingDF = pd.read_csv(current_path + file)

# Convert fields into appropriate data types
ratingDF.userId = ratingDF.userId.astype(str).astype(int)
ratingDF.movieId = ratingDF.movieId.astype(str).astype(int)
ratingDF.rating = ratingDF.rating.astype(str).astype(float)
ratingDF.timestamp = ratingDF.timestamp.apply(lambda x: \
                datetime.utcfromtimestamp(x).strftime('%Y-%m-%d %H:%M:%S'))
```

Table 10-1 shows a partial view of the data.

*Table 10-1. MovieLens ratings data*

|    | userId | movieId | rating | timestamp |
|----|--------|---------|--------|-----------|
| 0  | 1 | 2   | 3.5 | 2005-04-02 23:53:47 |
| 1  | 1 | 29  | 3.5 | 2005-04-02 23:31:16 |
| 2  | 1 | 32  | 3.5 | 2005-04-02 23:33:39 |
| 3  | 1 | 47  | 3.5 | 2005-04-02 23:32:07 |
| 4  | 1 | 50  | 3.5 | 2005-04-02 23:29:40 |
| 5  | 1 | 112 | 3.5 | 2004-09-10 03:09:00 |
| 6  | 1 | 151 | 4.0 | 2004-09-10 03:08:54 |
| 7  | 1 | 223 | 4.0 | 2005-04-02 23:46:13 |
| 8  | 1 | 253 | 4.0 | 2005-04-02 23:35:40 |
| 9  | 1 | 260 | 4.0 | 2005-04-02 23:33:46 |
| 10 | 1 | 293 | 4.0 | 2005-04-02 23:31:43 |
| 11 | 1 | 296 | 4.0 | 2005-04-02 23:32:47 |
| 12 | 1 | 318 | 4.0 | 2005-04-02 23:33:18 |
| 13 | 1 | 337 | 3.5 | 2004-09-10 03:08:29 |

Let's confirm the number of unique users, unique movies, and total ratings, and we will also calculate the average number of ratings provided by users:

```
n_users = ratingDF.userId.unique().shape[0]
n_movies = ratingDF.movieId.unique().shape[0]
n_ratings = len(ratingDF)
avg_ratings_per_user = n_ratings/n_users

print('Number of unique users: ', n_users)
print('Number of unique movies: ', n_movies)
print('Number of total ratings: ', n_ratings)
print('Average number of ratings per user: ', avg_ratings_per_user)
```

The data is as we expected:

```
Number of unique users: 138493
Number of unique movies: 26744
Number of total ratings: 20000263
Average number of ratings per user: 144.4135299257002
```

To reduce the complexity and size of this dataset, let's focus on the top one thousand most rated movies. This will reduce the number of ratings from about ~20 million to about ~12.8 million.

```
movieIndex = ratingDF.groupby("movieId").count().sort_values(by= \
                "rating",ascending=False)[0:1000].index
ratingDFX2 = ratingDF[ratingDF.movieId.isin(movieIndex)]
ratingDFX2.count()
```

We will also take a sample of one thousand users at random and filter the dataset for just these users. This will reduce the number of ratings from ~12.8 million to just 90,213. This number is sufficient to demonstrate collaborative filtering:

```
userIndex = ratingDFX2.groupby("userId").count().sort_values(by= \
    "rating",ascending=False).sample(n=1000, random_state=2018).index
ratingDFX3 = ratingDFX2[ratingDFX2.userId.isin(userIndex)]
ratingDFX3.count()
```

Let's also reindex `movieID` and `userID` to a range of 1 to 1,000 for our reduced dataset:

```
movies = ratingDFX3.movieId.unique()
moviesDF = pd.DataFrame(data=movies,columns=['originalMovieId'])
moviesDF['newMovieId'] = moviesDF.index+1

users = ratingDFX3.userId.unique()
usersDF = pd.DataFrame(data=users,columns=['originalUserId'])
usersDF['newUserId'] = usersDF.index+1

ratingDFX3 = ratingDFX3.merge(moviesDF,left_on='movieId', \
                              right_on='originalMovieId')
ratingDFX3.drop(labels='originalMovieId', axis=1, inplace=True)

ratingDFX3 = ratingDFX3.merge(usersDF,left_on='userId', \
                              right_on='originalUserId')
ratingDFX3.drop(labels='originalUserId', axis=1, inplace=True)
```

Let's calculate the number of unique users, unique movies, total ratings, and average number of ratings per user for our reduced dataset:

```
n_users = ratingDFX3.userId.unique().shape[0]
n_movies = ratingDFX3.movieId.unique().shape[0]
n_ratings = len(ratingDFX3)
avg_ratings_per_user = n_ratings/n_users

print('Number of unique users: ', n_users)
print('Number of unique movies: ', n_movies)
print('Number of total ratings: ', n_ratings)
print('Average number of ratings per user: ', avg_ratings_per_user)
```

The results are as expected:

```
Number of unique users: 1000
Number of unique movies: 1000
Number of total ratings: 90213
Average number of ratings per user: 90.213
```

Let's generate a test set and a validation set from this reduced dataset so that each holdout set is 5% of the reduced dataset:

```
X_train, X_test = train_test_split(ratingDFX3,
  test_size=0.10, shuffle=True, random_state=2018)
```

```
X_validation, X_test = train_test_split(X_test,
  test_size=0.50, shuffle=True, random_state=2018)
```

The following shows the sizes of the train, validation, and test sets:

```
Size of train set: 81191
Size of validation set: 4511
Size of test set: 4511
```

## Define the Cost Function: Mean Squared Error

Now we are ready to work with the data.

First, let's create a matrix *m* x *n*, where *m* are the users and *n* are the movies. This will be a sparsely populated matrix because users rate only a fraction of the movies. For example, a matrix with one thousand users and one thousand movies will have only 81,191 ratings in the training set. If each of the one thousand users rated each of the one thousand movies, we would have a matrix with one million ratings, but users rate only a small subset of movies on average, so we have only 81,191 ratings on the training set. The rest (nearly 92% of the values in the matrix) will be zeros:

```
# Generate ratings matrix for train
ratings_train = np.zeros((n_users, n_movies))
for row in X_train.itertuples():
    ratings_train[row[6]-1, row[5]-1] = row[3]

# Calculate sparsity of the train ratings matrix
sparsity = float(len(ratings_train.nonzero()[0]))
sparsity /= (ratings_train.shape[0] * ratings_train.shape[1])
sparsity *= 100
print('Sparsity: {:4.2f}%'.format(sparsity))
```

We will generate similar matrices for the validation set and the test set, which will be even sparser, of course:

```
# Generate ratings matrix for validation
ratings_validation = np.zeros((n_users, n_movies))
for row in X_validation.itertuples():
    ratings_validation[row[6]-1, row[5]-1] = row[3]

# Generate ratings matrix for test
ratings_test = np.zeros((n_users, n_movies))
for row in X_test.itertuples():
    ratings_test[row[6]-1, row[5]-1] = row[3]
```

Before we build our recommender systems, let's define the cost function that we will use to judge the goodness of our model. We will use *mean squared error (MSE)*, one of the simplest cost functions in machine learning. MSE measures the averaged squared error between the predicted values and the actual values. To calculate the MSE, we need two vectors of size *[n,1]*, where *n* is the number of ratings we are predicting—4,511 for the validation set. One vector has the actual ratings, and the other vector has the predictions.

Let's first flatten the sparse matrix with the ratings for the validation set. This will be the vector of actual ratings:

```
actual_validation = ratings_validation[ratings_validation.nonzero()].flatten()
```

## Perform Baseline Experiments

As a baseline, let's predict an average rating of 3.5 for the validation set and calculate the MSE:

```
pred_validation = np.zeros((len(X_validation),1))
pred_validation[pred_validation==0] = 3.5
pred_validation

mean_squared_error(pred_validation, actual_validation)
```

The MSE of this very naive prediction is 1.05. This is our baseline:

```
Mean squared error using naive prediction: 1.055420084238528
```

Let's see if we can improve our results by predicting a user's rating for a given movie based on that user's average rating for all other movies:

```
ratings_validation_prediction = np.zeros((n_users, n_movies))
i = 0
for row in ratings_train:
    ratings_validation_prediction[i][ratings_validation_prediction[i]==0] \
        = np.mean(row[row>0])
    i += 1

pred_validation = ratings_validation_prediction \
    [ratings_validation.nonzero()].flatten()
user_average = mean_squared_error(pred_validation, actual_validation)
print('Mean squared error using user average:', user_average)
```

The MSE improves to 0.909:

```
Mean squared error using user average: 0.9090717929472647
```

Now, let's predict a user's rating for a given movie based on the average rating all other users have given that movie:

```
ratings_validation_prediction = np.zeros((n_users, n_movies)).T
i = 0
for row in ratings_train.T:
    ratings_validation_prediction[i][ratings_validation_prediction[i]==0] \
        = np.mean(row[row>0])
    i += 1

ratings_validation_prediction = ratings_validation_prediction.T
pred_validation = ratings_validation_prediction \
```

```
    [ratings_validation.nonzero()].flatten()
movie_average = mean_squared_error(pred_validation, actual_validation)
print('Mean squared error using movie average:', movie_average)
```

The MSE of this approach is 0.914, similar to that found using user average:

```
Mean squared error using movie average: 0.9136057106858655
```

# Matrix Factorization

Before we build a recommender system using RBMs, let's first build one using *matrix factorization*, one of the most successful and popular collaborative filtering algorithms today. Matrix factorization decomposes the user-item matrix into a product of two lower dimensionality matrices. Users are represented in lower dimensional latent space, and so are the items.

Assume our user-item matrix is $R$, with $m$ users and $n$ items. Matrix factorization will create two lower dimensionality matrices, $H$ and $W$. $H$ is an "$m$ users" x "$k$ latent factors" matrix, and $W$ is a "$k$ latent factors" x "$n$ items" matrix.

The ratings are computed by matrix multiplication: $R = H \times W$.

The number of $k$ latent factors determines the capacity of the model. The higher the $k$, the greater the capacity of the model. By increasing $k$, we can improve the personalization of rating predictions for users, but, if $k$ is too high, the model will overfit the data.

All of this should be familiar to you. Matrix factorization learns representations for the users and items in a lower dimensional space and makes predictions based on the newly learned representations.

## One Latent Factor

Let's start with the simplest form of matrix factorization—with just one latent factor. We will use Keras to perform our matrix factorization.

First, we need to define the graph. The input is the one-dimensional vector of users for the user embedding and the one-dimensional vector of movies for the movie embedding. We will embed these input vectors into a latent space of one and then flatten them. To generate the output vector *product*, we will take the dot product of the movie vector and user vector. We will use the *Adam optimizer* to minimize our cost fuction, which is defined as the mean_squared_error:

```
n_latent_factors = 1

user_input = Input(shape=[1], name='user')
user_embedding = Embedding(input_dim=n_users + 1, output_dim=n_latent_factors,
  name='user_embedding')(user_input)
user_vec = Flatten(name='flatten_users')(user_embedding)
```

```
movie_input = Input(shape=[1], name='movie')
movie_embedding = Embedding(input_dim=n_movies + 1, output_dim=n_latent_factors,
  name='movie_embedding')(movie_input)
movie_vec = Flatten(name='flatten_movies')(movie_embedding)

product = dot([movie_vec, user_vec], axes=1)
model = Model(inputs=[user_input, movie_input], outputs=product)
model.compile('adam', 'mean_squared_error')
```

Let's train the model by feeding in the user and movie vectors from the training data-set. We will also evaluate the model on the validation set while we train. The MSE will be calculated against the actual ratings we have.

We will train for one hundred epochs and store the history of the training and validation results. Let's also plot the results:

```
history = model.fit(x=[X_train.newUserId, X_train.newMovieId], \
                    y=X_train.rating, epochs=100, \
                    validation_data=([X_validation.newUserId, \
                    X_validation.newMovieId], X_validation.rating), \
                    verbose=1)

pd.Series(history.history['val_loss'][10:]).plot(logy=False)
plt.xlabel("Epoch")
plt.ylabel("Validation Error")
print('Minimum MSE: ', min(history.history['val_loss']))
```

Figure 10-1 shows the results.

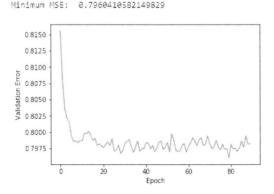

*Figure 10-1. Plot of validation MSE using matrix factorization and one latent factor*

The minimum MSE using matrix factorization and one latent factor is 0.796. This is a better MSE than our user average and movie average approaches from earlier.

Let's see if we can do even better by increasing the number of latent factors (i.e., the capacity of the model).

# Three Latent Factors

Figure 10-2 displays the results of using three latent factors.

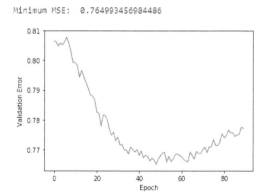

*Figure 10-2. Plot of validation MSE using matrix factorization and three latent factors*

The minimum MSE is 0.765, which is better than the one using one latent factor and the best yet.

# Five Latent Factors

Let's now build a matrix factorization model using five latent factors (see Figure 10-3 for the results).

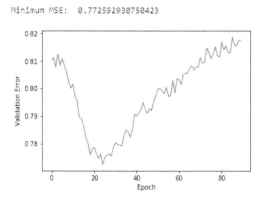

*Figure 10-3. Plot of validation MSE using matrix factorization and five latent factors*

The minimum MSE fails to improve, and there are clear signs of overfitting after the first 25 epochs or so. The validation error troughs and then begins to increase. Adding more capacity to the matrix factorization model will not help much more.

# Collaborative Filtering Using RBMs

Let's turn back to RBMs again. Recall that RBMs have two layers—the input/visible layer and the hidden layer. The neurons in each layer communicate with neurons in the other layer but not with neurons in the same layer. In other words, there is no intralayer communication among the neurons—this is the *restricted* bit of RBMs.

Another important feature of RBMs is that the communication between layers happens in both directions—not just in one direction. For example, with autoencoders, the neurons communicate with the next layer, passing information only in a feedforward way.

With RBMs, the neurons in the visible layer communicate with the hidden layer, and then the hidden layer passes back information to the visibile layer, going back and forth several times. RBMs perform this communication—the passes back and forth between the visible and hidden layer—to develop a generative model such that the reconstructions from the outputs of the hidden layer are similar to the original inputs.

In other words, the RBMs are trying to create a generative model that will help predict whether a user will like a movie that the user has never seen based on how similar the movie is to other movies the user has rated and based on how similar the user is to the other users that have rated that movie.

The visible layer will have X neurons, where X is the number of movies in the dataset. Each neuron will have a normalized rating value from zero to one, where zero means the user has not seen the movie. The closer the normalized rating value is to one, the more the user likes the movie represented by the neuron.

The neurons in the visible layer will communicate with the neurons in the hidden layer, which will try to learn the underlying, latent features that characterize the user-movie preferences.

Note that RBMs are also referred to as *symmetrical bipartite, bidirectional graphs*—symmetrical because each visible node is connected to each hidden node, bipartite because there are two layers of nodes, and bidirectional because the communication happens in both directions.

## RBM Neural Network Architecture

For our movie-recommender system, we have an $m$ x $n$ matrix with $m$ users and $n$ movies. To train the RBM, we pass along a batch of $k$ users with their $n$ movie ratings into the neural network and train for a certain number of *epochs*.

Each input $x$ that is passed into the neural network represents a single user's rating preferences for all $n$ movies, where $n$ is one thousand in our example. Therefore, the visible layer has $n$ nodes, one for each movie.

We can specify the number of nodes in the hidden layer, which will generally be fewer than the nodes in the visible layer to force the hidden layer to learn the most salient aspects of the original input as efficiently as possible.

Each input $v0$ is multiplied by its respective weight $W$. The weights are learned by the connections from the visible layer to the hidden layer. Then we add a bias vector at the hidden layer called $hb$. The bias ensures that at least some of the neurons fire. This $W \times v0 + hb$ result is passed through an activation function.

After this, we will take a sample of the outputs generated via a process known as *Gibbs sampling*. In other words, the activation of the hidden layer results in final outputs that are generated stochastically. This level of randomness helps build a better-performing and more robust generative model.

Next, the output after Gibbs sampling—known as $h0$—is passed back through the neural network in the opposite direction in what is called a *backward pass*. In the backward pass, the activations in the *forward pass* after Gibbs sampling are fed into the hidden layer and multiplied by the same weights $W$ as before. We then add a new bias vector at the visible layer called $vb$.

This $W \times h0 + vb$ is passed through an activation function, and then we perform Gibbs sampling. The output of this is $v1$, which is then passed as the new input into the visible layer and through the neural network as another forward pass.

The RBM goes through a series of forward and backward passes like this to learn the optimal weights as it attempts to build a robust generative model. RBMs are the first type of *generative learning* model that we have explored. By performing Gibbs sampling and retraining weights via forward and backward passes, RBMs are trying to learn the *probability distribution* of the original input. Specifically, RBMs minimize the *Kullback–Leibler divergence*, which measures how one probability distribution is different from another; in this case, RBMs are minimizing the divergence between the probability distribution of the original input and the probability distribution of the reconstructed data.

By iteratively readjusting the weights in the neural net, the RBM learns to approximate the original data as best as possible.

With this newly learned probability distribution, RBMs are able to make predictions about never-before-seen data. In this case, the RBM we design will attempt to predict ratings for movies that the user has never seen based on the user's similarity to other users and the ratings those movies have received by the other users.

# Build the Components of the RBM Class

First, we will initialize the class with a few parameters; these are the input size of the RBM, the output size, the learning rate, the number of epochs to train for, and the batch size during the training process.

We will also create zero matrices for the weight matrix, the hidden bias vector, and the visible bias vector:

```
# Define RBM class
class RBM(object):

    def __init__(self, input_size, output_size,
                 learning_rate, epochs, batchsize):
        # Define hyperparameters
        self._input_size = input_size
        self._output_size = output_size
        self.learning_rate = learning_rate
        self.epochs = epochs
        self.batchsize = batchsize

        # Initialize weights and biases using zero matrices
        self.w = np.zeros([input_size, output_size], "float")
        self.hb = np.zeros([output_size], "float")
        self.vb = np.zeros([input_size], "float")
```

Next, let's define functions for the forward pass, the backward pass, and the sampling of data during each of these passes back and forth.

Here is the forward pass, where $h$ is the hidden layer and $v$ is the visible layer:

```
def prob_h_given_v(self, visible, w, hb):
    return tf.nn.sigmoid(tf.matmul(visible, w) + hb)
```

Here is the backward pass:

```
def prob_v_given_h(self, hidden, w, vb):
    return tf.nn.sigmoid(tf.matmul(hidden, tf.transpose(w)) + vb)
```

Here is the sampling function:

```
def sample_prob(self, probs):
    return tf.nn.relu(tf.sign(probs - tf.random_uniform(tf.shape(probs))))
```

Now we need a function that performs that training. Since we are using TensorFlow, we first need to create placeholders for the TensorFlow graph, which we will use when we feed data into the TensorFlow session.

We will have placeholders for the weights matrix, the hidden bias vector, and the visible bias vector. We will also need to initialize the values for these three using zeros. And, we will need one set to hold the current values and one set to hold the previous values:

```
_w = tf.placeholder("float", [self._input_size, self._output_size])
_hb = tf.placeholder("float", [self._output_size])
_vb = tf.placeholder("float", [self._input_size])

prv_w = np.zeros([self._input_size, self._output_size], "float")
prv_hb = np.zeros([self._output_size], "float")
prv_vb = np.zeros([self._input_size], "float")

cur_w = np.zeros([self._input_size, self._output_size], "float")
cur_hb = np.zeros([self._output_size], "float")
cur_vb = np.zeros([self._input_size], "float")
```

Likewise, we need a placeholder for the visible layer. The hidden layer is derived from matrix multiplication of the visible layer and the weights matrix and the matrix addition of the hidden bias vector:

```
v0 = tf.placeholder("float", [None, self._input_size])
h0 = self.sample_prob(self.prob_h_given_v(v0, _w, _hb))
```

During the backward pass, we take the hidden layer output, multiply it with the transpose of the weights matrix used during the forward pass, and add the visible bias vector. Note that the weights matrix is the same during both the forward and the backward pass. Then, we perform the forward pass again:

```
v1 = self.sample_prob(self.prob_v_given_h(h0, _w, _vb))
h1 = self.prob_h_given_v(v1, _w, _hb)
```

To update the weights, we perform constrastive divergence.[2]

We also define the error as MSE.

```
positive_grad = tf.matmul(tf.transpose(v0), h0)
negative_grad = tf.matmul(tf.transpose(v1), h1)

update_w = _w + self.learning_rate * \
    (positive_grad - negative_grad) / tf.to_float(tf.shape(v0)[0])
update_vb = _vb +  self.learning_rate * tf.reduce_mean(v0 - v1, 0)
update_hb = _hb +  self.learning_rate * tf.reduce_mean(h0 - h1, 0)

err = tf.reduce_mean(tf.square(v0 - v1))
```

With this, we are ready to initialize the TensorFlow session with the variables we have just defined.

Once we call *sess.run*, we can feed in batches of data to begin the training. During the training, forward and backward passes will be made, and the RBM will update weights based on how the generated data compares to the original input. We will print the reconstruction error from each epoch.

---

2 For more on this topic, see the paper "On Constrastive Divergence Learning" (*http://bit.ly/2RukFuX*).

```
with tf.Session() as sess:
 sess.run(tf.global_variables_initializer())

 for epoch in range(self.epochs):
     for start, end in zip(range(0, len(X),
      self.batchsize),range(self.batchsize,len(X), self.batchsize)):
         batch = X[start:end]
         cur_w = sess.run(update_w, feed_dict={v0: batch,
          _w: prv_w, _hb: prv_hb, _vb: prv_vb})
         cur_hb = sess.run(update_hb, feed_dict={v0: batch,
          _w: prv_w, _hb: prv_hb, _vb: prv_vb})
         cur_vb = sess.run(update_vb, feed_dict={v0: batch,
          _w: prv_w, _hb: prv_hb, _vb: prv_vb})
         prv_w = cur_w
         prv_hb = cur_hb
         prv_vb = cur_vb
     error = sess.run(err, feed_dict={v0: X,
      _w: cur_w, _vb: cur_vb, _hb: cur_hb})
     print ('Epoch: %d' % epoch,'reconstruction error: %f' % error)
 self.w = prv_w
 self.hb = prv_hb
 self.vb = prv_vb
```

## Train RBM Recommender System

To train the RBM, let's create a NumPy array called `inputX` from `ratings_train` and convert these values to float32. We will also define the RBM to take in a one thousand-dimensional input, output a one thousand-dimensional output, use a learning rate of 0.3, train for five hundred epochs, and use a batch size of two hundred. These parameters are just preliminary parameter choices; you should be able to find more optimal parameters with experimentation, which is encouraged:

```
# Begin the training cycle

# Convert inputX into float32
inputX = ratings_train
inputX = inputX.astype(np.float32)

# Define the parameters of the RBMs we will train
rbm=RBM(1000,1000,0.3,500,200)
```

Let's begin training:

```
rbm.train(inputX)
outputX, reconstructedX, hiddenX = rbm.rbm_output(inputX)
```

Figure 10-4 displays the plot of the reconstruction errors.

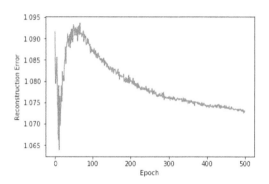

*Figure 10-4. Plot of RBM errors*

The error terms generally decrease the longer we train.

Now let's take the RBM model we developed to predict the ratings for users in the validation set (which has the same users as the training set):

```
# Predict ratings for validation set
inputValidation = ratings_validation
inputValidation = inputValidation.astype(np.float32)

finalOutput_validation, reconstructedOutput_validation, _ = \
    rbm.rbm_output(inputValidation)
```

Next, let's convert the predictions into an array and calculate the MSE against the true validation ratings:

```
predictionsArray = reconstructedOutput_validation
pred_validation = \
    predictionsArray[ratings_validation.nonzero()].flatten()
actual_validation = \
    ratings_validation[ratings_validation.nonzero()].flatten()

rbm_prediction = mean_squared_error(pred_validation, actual_validation)
print('Mean squared error using RBM prediction:', rbm_prediction)
```

The following code displays the MSE on the validation set:

```
Mean squared error using RBM prediction: 9.331135003325205
```

This MSE is a starting point and will likely improve with greater experimentation.

# Conclusion

In this chapter, we explored restricted Boltzmann machines and used them to build a recommender system for movie ratings. The RBM recommender we built learned the probability distribution of ratings of movies for users given their previous ratings and the ratings of users to which they were most similar to. We then used the learned probability distribution to predict ratings on never-before-seen movies.

In Chapter 11, we will stack RBMs together to build deep belief networks and use them to perform even more powerful unsupervised learning tasks.

# Feature Detection Using Deep Belief Networks

In Chapter 10, we explored restricted Boltzmann machines and used them to build a recommender system for movie ratings. In this chapter, we will stack RBMs together to build *deep belief networks (DBNs)*. DBNs were first introduced by Geoff Hinton at the University of Toronto in 2006.

RBMs have just two layers, a visible layer and a hidden layer; in other words, RBMs are just shallow neural networks. DBNs are made up of multiple RBMs—the hidden layer of one RBM serves as the visible layer of the next RBM. Because they involve many layers, DBNs are deep neural networks. In fact, they are the first type of deep unsupervised neural network we've introduced so far.

Shallow unsupervised neural networks, such as RBMs, cannot capture structure in complex data such as images, sound, and text, but DBNs can. DBNs have been used to recognize and cluster images, video capture, sound, and text, although other deep learning methods have surpassed DBNs in performance over the past decade.

## Deep Belief Networks in Detail

Like RBMs, DBNs can learn the underlying structure of input and probabilistically reconstruct it. In other words, DBNs—like RBMs—are generative models. And, as with RBMs, the layers in DBNs have connections only between layers but not between units within each layer.

In the DBN, one layer is trained at a time, starting with the very first hidden layer, which, along with the input layer, makes up the first RBM. Once this first RBM is trained, the hidden layer of the first RBM serves as the visible layer of the next RBM and is used to train the second hidden layer of the DBN.

This process continues until all the layers of the DBN are trained. Except for the first and final layers of the DBN, each layer in the DBN serves as both a hidden layer and a visible layer of an RBM.

The DBN is a hierarchy of representations and, like all neural networks, is a form of representation learning. Note that the DBN does not use any labels. Instead, the DBN is learning the underlying structure in the input data one layer at a time.

Labels can be used to fine-tune the last few layers of the DBN but only after the initial unsupervised learning has been completed. For example, if we want the DBN to be a classifier, we would perform unsupervised learning first (a process known as *pre-training*) and then use labels to fine-tune the DBN (a process called *fine-tuning*).

## MNIST Image Classification

Let's build an image classifier using DBNs. We will turn to the MNIST dataset once again.

First, let's load the necessary libraries:

```
'''Main'''
import numpy as np
import pandas as pd
import os, time, re
import pickle, gzip, datetime

'''Data Viz'''
import matplotlib.pyplot as plt
import seaborn as sns
color = sns.color_palette()
import matplotlib as mpl

%matplotlib inline

'''Data Prep and Model Evaluation'''
from sklearn import preprocessing as pp
from sklearn.model_selection import train_test_split
from sklearn.model_selection import StratifiedKFold
from sklearn.metrics import log_loss, accuracy_score
from sklearn.metrics import precision_recall_curve, average_precision_score
from sklearn.metrics import roc_curve, auc, roc_auc_score, mean_squared_error

'''Algos'''
import lightgbm as lgb

'''TensorFlow and Keras'''
import tensorflow as tf
import keras
from keras import backend as K
from keras.models import Sequential, Model
```

```
from keras.layers import Activation, Dense, Dropout
from keras.layers import BatchNormalization, Input, Lambda
from keras.layers import Embedding, Flatten, dot
from keras import regularizers
from keras.losses import mse, binary_crossentropy
```

We will then load the data and store it in Pandas DataFrames. We will also encode the labels as one-hot vectors. This is all similar to what we did when we first introduced the MNIST dataset earlier in the book:

```
# Load the datasets
current_path = os.getcwd()
file = '\\datasets\\mnist_data\\mnist.pkl.gz'
f = gzip.open(current_path+file, 'rb')
train_set, validation_set, test_set = pickle.load(f, encoding='latin1')
f.close()

X_train, y_train = train_set[0], train_set[1]
X_validation, y_validation = validation_set[0], validation_set[1]
X_test, y_test = test_set[0], test_set[1]

# Create Pandas DataFrames from the datasets
train_index = range(0,len(X_train))
validation_index = range(len(X_train),len(X_train)+len(X_validation))
test_index = range(len(X_train)+len(X_validation), \
                   len(X_train)+len(X_validation)+len(X_test))

X_train = pd.DataFrame(data=X_train,index=train_index)
y_train = pd.Series(data=y_train,index=train_index)

X_validation = pd.DataFrame(data=X_validation,index=validation_index)
y_validation = pd.Series(data=y_validation,index=validation_index)

X_test = pd.DataFrame(data=X_test,index=test_index)
y_test = pd.Series(data=y_test,index=test_index)

def view_digit(X, y, example):
    label = y.loc[example]
    image = X.loc[example,:].values.reshape([28,28])
    plt.title('Example: %d  Label: %d' % (example, label))
    plt.imshow(image, cmap=plt.get_cmap('gray'))
    plt.show()

def one_hot(series):
    label_binarizer = pp.LabelBinarizer()
    label_binarizer.fit(range(max(series)+1))
    return label_binarizer.transform(series)

# Create one-hot vectors for the labels
y_train_oneHot = one_hot(y_train)
y_validation_oneHot = one_hot(y_validation)
y_test_oneHot = one_hot(y_test)
```

# Restricted Boltzmann Machines

Next, let's define an RBM class so we can train several RBMs (which are the building blocks for DBNs) in quick succession.

Remember that RBMs have an input layer (also referred to as the visible layer) and a single hidden layer, and the connections among neurons are restricted such that neurons are connected only to the neurons in other layers but not to neurons within the same layer. Also, recall that communication between layers happens in both directions—not just in one direction or a feedforward way, as in the case of autoencoders.

In an RBM, the neurons in the visible layer communicate with the hidden layer, the hidden layer generates data from the probabilistic model the RBM has learned, and then the hidden layer passes this generated information back to the visible layer. The visible layer takes the generated data from the hidden layer, samples it, compares it to the original data, and, based on the reconstruction error between the generated data sample and the original data, sends new information to the hidden layer to repeat the process once again.

By communicating in this bidirectional way, the RBM develops a generative model such that the reconstructions from the output of the hidden layer are similar to the original input.

## Build the Components of the RBM Class

Like we did in Chapter 10, let's walk through the various components of the RBM class.

First, we will initialize the class with a few parameters; these are the input size of the RBM, the output size, the learning rate, the number of epochs to train for, and the batch size during the training process. We will also create zero matrices for the weight matrix, the hidden bias vector, and the visible bias vector:

```
# Define RBM class
class RBM(object):

    def __init__(self, input_size, output_size,
                 learning_rate, epochs, batchsize):
        # Define hyperparameters
        self._input_size = input_size
        self._output_size = output_size
        self.learning_rate = learning_rate
        self.epochs = epochs
        self.batchsize = batchsize

        # Initialize weights and biases using zero matrices
        self.w = np.zeros([input_size, output_size], "float")
        self.hb = np.zeros([output_size], "float")
        self.vb = np.zeros([input_size], "float")
```

Next, let's define functions for the forward pass, the backward pass, and the sampling of data during each of these passes back and forth.

Here is the forward pass, where $h$ is the hidden layer and $v$ is the visible layer:

```
def prob_h_given_v(self, visible, w, hb):
    return tf.nn.sigmoid(tf.matmul(visible, w) + hb)
```

Here is the backward pass:

```
def prob_v_given_h(self, hidden, w, vb):
    return tf.nn.sigmoid(tf.matmul(hidden, tf.transpose(w)) + vb)
```

Here is the sampling function:

```
def sample_prob(self, probs):
    return tf.nn.relu(tf.sign(probs - tf.random_uniform(tf.shape(probs))))
```

Now we need a function that performs that training. Since we are using TensorFlow, we first need to create placeholders for the TensorFlow graph, which we will use when we feed data into the TensorFlow session.

We will have placeholders for the weights matrix, the hidden bias vector, and the visible bias vector. We will also need to initialize the values for these three using zeros. And, we will need one set to hold the current values and one set to hold the previous values:

```
_w = tf.placeholder("float", [self._input_size, self._output_size])
_hb = tf.placeholder("float", [self._output_size])
_vb = tf.placeholder("float", [self._input_size])

prv_w = np.zeros([self._input_size, self._output_size], "float")
prv_hb = np.zeros([self._output_size], "float")
prv_vb = np.zeros([self._input_size], "float")

cur_w = np.zeros([self._input_size, self._output_size], "float")
cur_hb = np.zeros([self._output_size], "float")
cur_vb = np.zeros([self._input_size], "float")
```

Likewise, we need a placeholder for the visible layer. The hidden layer is derived from matrix multiplication of the visible layer and the weights matrix and the matrix addition of the hidden bias vector:

```
v0 = tf.placeholder("float", [None, self._input_size])
h0 = self.sample_prob(self.prob_h_given_v(v0, _w, _hb))
```

During the backward pass, we take the hidden layer output, multiply it with the transpose of the weights matrix used during the forward pass, and add the visible bias vector. Note that the weights matrix is the same weights matrix during both the forward and the backward pass.

Then we perform the forward pass again:

```
v1 = self.sample_prob(self.prob_v_given_h(h0, _w, _vb))
h1 = self.prob_h_given_v(v1, _w, _hb)
```

To update the weights, we perform constrastive divergence, which we introduced in Chapter 10. We also define the error as the MSE:

```
positive_grad = tf.matmul(tf.transpose(v0), h0)
negative_grad = tf.matmul(tf.transpose(v1), h1)

update_w = _w + self.learning_rate * \
    (positive_grad - negative_grad) / tf.to_float(tf.shape(v0)[0])
update_vb = _vb +  self.learning_rate * tf.reduce_mean(v0 - v1, 0)
update_hb = _hb +  self.learning_rate * tf.reduce_mean(h0 - h1, 0)

err = tf.reduce_mean(tf.square(v0 - v1))
```

With this, we are ready to initialize the TensorFlow session with the variables we have just defined.

Once we call sess.run, we can feed in batches of data to begin the training. During the training, forward and backward passes will be made, and the RBM will update weights based on how the generated data compares to the original input. We will print the reconstruction error from each epoch:

```
with tf.Session() as sess:
    sess.run(tf.global_variables_initializer())

    for epoch in range(self.epochs):
        for start, end in zip(range(0, len(X), self.batchsize), \
                range(self.batchsize,len(X), self.batchsize)):
            batch = X[start:end]
            cur_w = sess.run(update_w, \
                feed_dict={v0: batch, _w: prv_w, \
                        _hb: prv_hb, _vb: prv_vb})
            cur_hb = sess.run(update_hb, \
                feed_dict={v0: batch, _w: prv_w, \
                        _hb: prv_hb, _vb: prv_vb})
            cur_vb = sess.run(update_vb, \
                feed_dict={v0: batch, _w: prv_w, \
                        _hb: prv_hb, _vb: prv_vb})
            prv_w = cur_w
            prv_hb = cur_hb
            prv_vb = cur_vb
        error = sess.run(err, feed_dict={v0: X, _w: cur_w, \
                                    _vb: cur_vb, _hb: cur_hb})
        print ('Epoch: %d' % epoch,'reconstruction error: %f' % error)
    self.w = prv_w
    self.hb = prv_hb
    self.vb = prv_vb
```

## Generate Images Using the RBM Model

Let's also define a function to generate new images from the generative model that the RBM has learned:

```
def rbm_output(self, X):

    input_X = tf.constant(X)
    _w = tf.constant(self.w)
    _hb = tf.constant(self.hb)
    _vb = tf.constant(self.vb)
    out = tf.nn.sigmoid(tf.matmul(input_X, _w) + _hb)
    hiddenGen = self.sample_prob(self.prob_h_given_v(input_X, _w, _hb))
    visibleGen = self.sample_prob(self.prob_v_given_h(hiddenGen, _w, _vb))
    with tf.Session() as sess:
        sess.run(tf.global_variables_initializer())
        return sess.run(out), sess.run(visibleGen), sess.run(hiddenGen)
```

We feed the original matrix of images, called *X*, into the function. We create Tensor-Flow placeholders for the original matrix of images, the weights matrix, the hidden bias vector, and the visible bias vector. Then, we push the input matrix to produce the output of a forward pass (out), a sample of the hidden layer (hiddenGen), and a sample of the reconstructed images generated by the model (visibleGen).

## View the Intermediate Feature Detectors

Finally, let's define a function to show the feature detectors of the hidden layer:

```
def show_features(self, shape, suptitle, count=-1):
    maxw = np.amax(self.w.T)
    minw = np.amin(self.w.T)
    count = self._output_size if count == -1 or count > \
            self._output_size else count
    ncols = count if count < 14 else 14
    nrows = count//ncols
    nrows = nrows if nrows > 2 else 3
    fig = plt.figure(figsize=(ncols, nrows), dpi=100)
    grid = Grid(fig, rect=111, nrows_ncols=(nrows, ncols), axes_pad=0.01)

    for i, ax in enumerate(grid):
        x = self.w.T[i] if i<self._input_size else np.zeros(shape)
        x = (x.reshape(1, -1) - minw)/maxw
        ax.imshow(x.reshape(*shape), cmap=mpl.cm.Greys)
        ax.set_axis_off()

    fig.text(0.5,1, suptitle, fontsize=20, horizontalalignment='center')
    fig.tight_layout()
    plt.show()
    return
```

We will use this and the other functions on the MNIST dataset now.

# Train the Three RBMs for the DBN

We will now use the MNIST data to train three RBMs, one at a time, such that the hidden layer of one RBM is used as the visible layer of the next RBM. These three RBMs will make up the DBN that we are building to perform image classification.

First, let's take the training data and store it as a NumPy array. Next, we will create a list to hold the RBMs we train called rbm_list. Then, we will define the hyperparameters for the three RBMs, including the input size, the output size, the learning rate, the number of epochs to train for, and the batch size for training.

All of these can be built using the RBM class we defined earlier.

For our DBN, we will use the following RBMs: the first will take the original 784-dimension input and output a 700-dimension matrix. The next RBM will use the 700-dimension matrix output of the first RBM and output a 600-dimension matrix. Finally, the last RBM we train will take the 600-dimension matrix and output a 500-dimension matrix.

We will train all three RBMs using a learning rate of 1.0, train for 100 epochs each, and use a batch size of two hundred:

```
# Since we are training, set input as training data
inputX = np.array(X_train)

# Create list to hold our RBMs
rbm_list = []

# Define the parameters of the RBMs we will train
rbm_list.append(RBM(784,700,1.0,100,200))
rbm_list.append(RBM(700,600,1.0,100,200))
rbm_list.append(RBM(600,500,1.0,100,200))
```

Now let's train the RBMs. We will store the trained RBMs in a list called outputList.

Note that we use the rbm_output function we defined earlier to produce the output matrix—in other words, the hidden layer—for use as the input/visible layer of the subsequent RBM we train:

```
outputList = []
error_list = []
#For each RBM in our list
for i in range(0,len(rbm_list)):
    print('RBM', i+1)
    #Train a new one
    rbm = rbm_list[i]
    err = rbm.train(inputX)
    error_list.append(err)
    #Return the output layer
    outputX, reconstructedX, hiddenX = rbm.rbm_output(inputX)
```

---

```
outputList.append(outputX)
inputX = hiddenX
```

The errors of each RBM decline the longer we train (see Figures 11-1, 11-2, and 11-3). Note that the RBM error reflects how similar the reconstructed data of a given RBM is to the data fed into the visible layer of that very RBM.

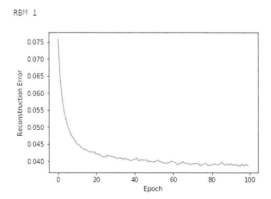

*Figure 11-1. Reconstruction errors of first RBM*

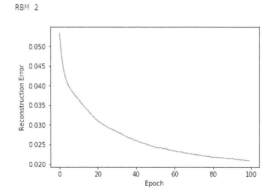

*Figure 11-2. Reconstruction errors of second RBM*

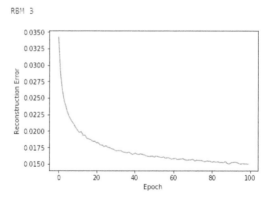

*Figure 11-3. Reconstruction errors of third RBM*

## Examine Feature Detectors

Now let's view the learned features from each of the RBMs using the `rbm.show_fea` `tures` function we defined earlier:

```
rbm_shapes = [(28,28),(25,24),(25,20)]
for i in range(0,len(rbm_list)):
    rbm = rbm_list[i]
    print(rbm.show_features(rbm_shapes[i],
      "RBM learned features from MNIST", 56))
```

Figure 11-4 displays the learned features for the various RBMs.

As you can see, each RBM learns increasingly abstract features from the MNIST data. The features of the first RBM vaguely resemble digits, and the features of the second and the third RBMs are increasingly nuanced and less discernible. This is pretty typical of how feature detectors work on image data; the deeper layers of the neural network recognize increasingly abstract elements from the original images.

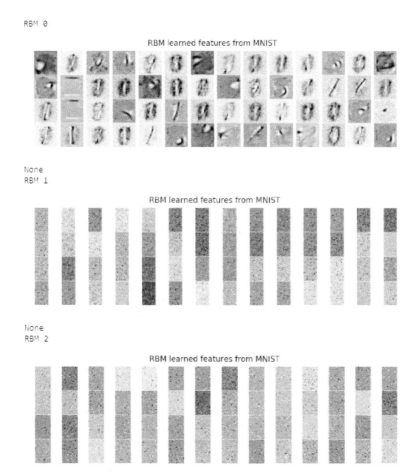

RBM 0

RBM learned features from MNIST

None
RBM 1

RBM learned features from MNIST

None
RBM 2

RBM learned features from MNIST

None

*Figure 11-4. Learned features of the RBMs*

## View Generated Images

Before we build the full DBN, let's view some of the generated images from one of the RBMs we just trained.

To keep things simple, we will feed the original MNIST training matrix into the first RBM we trained, which performs a forward pass and a backward pass, then will produce the generated images we need. We will compare the first ten images of the MNIST dataset with the newly generated images:

```
inputX = np.array(X_train)
rbmOne = rbm_list[0]
```

```
print('RBM 1')
outputX_rbmOne, reconstructedX_rbmOne, hiddenX_rbmOne =
 rbmOne.rbm_output(inputX)
reconstructedX_rbmOne = pd.DataFrame(data=reconstructedX_rbmOne,
 index=X_train.index)
for j in range(0,10):
    example = j
    view_digit(reconstructedX, y_train, example)
    view_digit(X_train, y_train, example)
```

Figure 11-5 shows the first image produced by the RBM compared to the first original image.

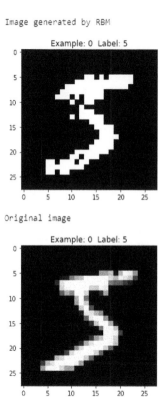

Figure 11-5. First generated image of the first RBM

As you can see, the generated image is similar to the original image — both display the digit five.

Let's view a few more images like this to compare the RBM-generated images with the original ones (see Figures 11-6 through 11-9).

Image generated by RBM

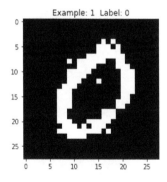

Original image

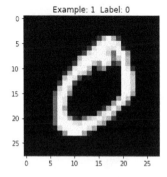

*Figure 11-6. Second generated image of the first RBM*

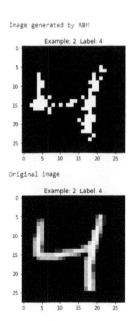

*Figure 11-7. Third generated image of the first RBM*

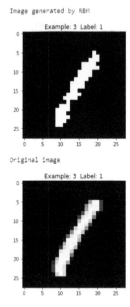

*Figure 11-8. Fourth generated image of the first RBM*

Image generated by RBM

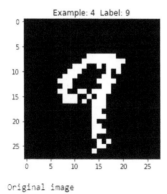

Original image

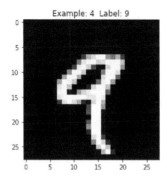

*Figure 11-9. Fifth generated image of the first RBM*

These digits are zero, four, one, and nine, respectively, and the generated images look reasonably similar to the original images.

# The Full DBN

Now, let's define the DBN class, which will take in the three RBMs we just trained and add a fourth RBM that performs forward and backward passes to refine the overall DBN-based generative model.

First, let's define the instance variables of the class. These include the original input size, the output size of the third RBM we just trained, the final output size we would like to have from the DBN, the learning rate, the number of epochs we wish to train for, the batch size for training, and the three RBMs we just trained. Like before, we will need to generate zero matrices for the weights, hidden bias, and visible bias:

```
class DBN(object):
    def __init__(self, original_input_size, input_size, output_size,
                 learning_rate, epochs, batchsize, rbmOne, rbmTwo, rbmThree):
        # Define hyperparameters
```

```
        self._original_input_size = original_input_size
        self._input_size = input_size
        self._output_size = output_size
        self.learning_rate = learning_rate
        self.epochs = epochs
        self.batchsize = batchsize
        self.rbmOne = rbmOne
        self.rbmTwo = rbmTwo
        self.rbmThree = rbmThree

        self.w = np.zeros([input_size, output_size], "float")
        self.hb = np.zeros([output_size], "float")
        self.vb = np.zeros([input_size], "float")
```

Similar to before, we will define functions to perform the forward pass and the backward pass and take samples from each:

```
    def prob_h_given_v(self, visible, w, hb):
        return tf.nn.sigmoid(tf.matmul(visible, w) + hb)

    def prob_v_given_h(self, hidden, w, vb):
        return tf.nn.sigmoid(tf.matmul(hidden, tf.transpose(w)) + vb)

    def sample_prob(self, probs):
        return tf.nn.relu(tf.sign(probs - tf.random_uniform(tf.shape(probs))))
```

For the training, we need placeholders for the weights, hidden bias, and visible bias. We also need matrices for the previous and current weights, hidden biases, and visible biases:

```
    def train(self, X):
        _w = tf.placeholder("float", [self._input_size, self._output_size])
        _hb = tf.placeholder("float", [self._output_size])
        _vb = tf.placeholder("float", [self._input_size])

        prv_w = np.zeros([self._input_size, self._output_size], "float")
        prv_hb = np.zeros([self._output_size], "float")
        prv_vb = np.zeros([self._input_size], "float")

        cur_w = np.zeros([self._input_size, self._output_size], "float")
        cur_hb = np.zeros([self._output_size], "float")
        cur_vb = np.zeros([self._input_size], "float")
```

We will set a placeholder for the visible layer.

Next, we will take the initial input—the visible layer—and pass it through the three RBMs we trained earlier. This results in the output *forward*, which we will pass into the fourth RBM we train as part of this DBN class:

```
        v0 = tf.placeholder("float", [None, self._original_input_size])
        forwardOne = tf.nn.relu(tf.sign(tf.nn.sigmoid(tf.matmul(v0, \
                    self.rbmOne.w) + self.rbmOne.hb) - tf.random_uniform( \
                    tf.shape(tf.nn.sigmoid(tf.matmul(v0, self.rbmOne.w) + \
```

```
                    self.rbmOne.hb)))))
forwardTwo = tf.nn.relu(tf.sign(tf.nn.sigmoid(tf.matmul(forwardOne, \
                    self.rbmTwo.w) + self.rbmTwo.hb) - tf.random_uniform( \
                    tf.shape(tf.nn.sigmoid(tf.matmul(forwardOne, \
                    self.rbmTwo.w) + self.rbmTwo.hb)))))
forward = tf.nn.relu(tf.sign(tf.nn.sigmoid(tf.matmul(forwardTwo, \
                    self.rbmThree.w) + self.rbmThree.hb) - \
                    tf.random_uniform(tf.shape(tf.nn.sigmoid(tf.matmul( \
                    forwardTwo, self.rbmThree.w) + self.rbmThree.hb)))))
h0 = self.sample_prob(self.prob_h_given_v(forward, _w, _hb))
v1 = self.sample_prob(self.prob_v_given_h(h0, _w, _vb))
h1 = self.prob_h_given_v(v1, _w, _hb)
```

We will define the contrastive divergence like we did before:

```
positive_grad = tf.matmul(tf.transpose(forward), h0)
negative_grad = tf.matmul(tf.transpose(v1), h1)

update_w = _w + self.learning_rate * (positive_grad - negative_grad) / \
                    tf.to_float(tf.shape(forward)[0])
update_vb = _vb + self.learning_rate * tf.reduce_mean(forward - v1, 0)
update_hb = _hb + self.learning_rate * tf.reduce_mean(h0 - h1, 0)
```

Once we generate a full forward pass through this DBN—which includes the three RBMs we trained earlier plus the latest fourth RBM—we need to send the output of the fourth RBM's hidden layer back through the entire DBN.

This requires a backward pass through the fourth RBM as well as a backward pass through the first three. We will also use MSE as before. Here is how the backward pass occurs:

```
backwardOne = tf.nn.relu(tf.sign(tf.nn.sigmoid(tf.matmul(v1, \
                    self.rbmThree.w.T) + self.rbmThree.vb) - \
                    tf.random_uniform(tf.shape(tf.nn.sigmoid( \
                    tf.matmul(v1, self.rbmThree.w.T) + \
                    self.rbmThree.vb)))))
backwardTwo = tf.nn.relu(tf.sign(tf.nn.sigmoid(tf.matmul(backwardOne, \
                    self.rbmTwo.w.T) + self.rbmTwo.vb) - \
                    tf.random_uniform(tf.shape(tf.nn.sigmoid( \
                    tf.matmul(backwardOne, self.rbmTwo.w.T) + \
                    self.rbmTwo.vb)))))
backward = tf.nn.relu(tf.sign(tf.nn.sigmoid(tf.matmul(backwardTwo, \
                    self.rbmOne.w.T) + self.rbmOne.vb) - \
                    tf.random_uniform(tf.shape(tf.nn.sigmoid( \
                    tf.matmul(backwardTwo, self.rbmOne.w.T) + \
                    self.rbmOne.vb)))))

err = tf.reduce_mean(tf.square(v0 - backward))
```

Here is the actual training portion of the DBN class, again very similar to the RBM one earlier:

```
with tf.Session() as sess:
    sess.run(tf.global_variables_initializer())

    for epoch in range(self.epochs):
        for start, end in zip(range(0, len(X), self.batchsize), \
                range(self.batchsize,len(X), self.batchsize)):
            batch = X[start:end]
            cur_w = sess.run(update_w, feed_dict={v0: batch, _w: \
                                prv_w, _hb: prv_hb, _vb: prv_vb})
            cur_hb = sess.run(update_hb, feed_dict={v0: batch, _w: \
                                prv_w, _hb: prv_hb, _vb: prv_vb})
            cur_vb = sess.run(update_vb, feed_dict={v0: batch, _w: \
                                prv_w, _hb: prv_hb, _vb: prv_vb})
            prv_w = cur_w
            prv_hb = cur_hb
            prv_vb = cur_vb
        error = sess.run(err, feed_dict={v0: X, _w: cur_w, _vb: \
                            cur_vb, _hb: cur_hb})
        print ('Epoch: %d' % epoch,'reconstruction error: %f' % error)
    self.w = prv_w
    self.hb = prv_hb
    self.vb = prv_vb
```

Let's define functions to produce generated images from the DBN and show features.
These are similar to the RBM versions earlier, but we send the data through all four
RBMs in the DBN class instead of just through a single RBM:

```
def dbn_output(self, X):

    input_X = tf.constant(X)
    forwardOne = tf.nn.sigmoid(tf.matmul(input_X, self.rbmOne.w) + \
                            self.rbmOne.hb)
    forwardTwo = tf.nn.sigmoid(tf.matmul(forwardOne, self.rbmTwo.w) + \
                            self.rbmTwo.hb)
    forward = tf.nn.sigmoid(tf.matmul(forwardTwo, self.rbmThree.w) + \
                            self.rbmThree.hb)

    _w = tf.constant(self.w)
    _hb = tf.constant(self.hb)
    _vb = tf.constant(self.vb)

    out = tf.nn.sigmoid(tf.matmul(forward, _w) + _hb)
    hiddenGen = self.sample_prob(self.prob_h_given_v(forward, _w, _hb))
    visibleGen = self.sample_prob(self.prob_v_given_h(hiddenGen, _w, _vb))

    backwardTwo = tf.nn.sigmoid(tf.matmul(visibleGen, self.rbmThree.w.T) + \
                            self.rbmThree.vb)
    backwardOne = tf.nn.sigmoid(tf.matmul(backwardTwo, self.rbmTwo.w.T) + \
                            self.rbmTwo.vb)
    backward = tf.nn.sigmoid(tf.matmul(backwardOne, self.rbmOne.w.T) + \
                            self.rbmOne.vb)
```

```
    with tf.Session() as sess:
        sess.run(tf.global_variables_initializer())
        return sess.run(out), sess.run(backward)

def show_features(self, shape, suptitle, count=-1):
    maxw = np.amax(self.w.T)
    minw = np.amin(self.w.T)
    count = self._output_size if count == -1 or count > \
            self._output_size else count
    ncols = count if count < 14 else 14
    nrows = count//ncols
    nrows = nrows if nrows > 2 else 3
    fig = plt.figure(figsize=(ncols, nrows), dpi=100)
    grid = Grid(fig, rect=111, nrows_ncols=(nrows, ncols), axes_pad=0.01)

    for i, ax in enumerate(grid):
        x = self.w.T[i] if i<self._input_size else np.zeros(shape)
        x = (x.reshape(1, -1) - minw)/maxw
        ax.imshow(x.reshape(*shape), cmap=mpl.cm.Greys)
        ax.set_axis_off()

    fig.text(0.5,1, suptitle, fontsize=20, horizontalalignment='center')
    fig.tight_layout()
    plt.show()
    return
```

# How Training of a DBN Works

Each of the three RBMs we have trained already has its own weights matrix, hidden bias vector, and visible bias vector. During the training of the fourth RBM as part of the DBN, we will not adjust the weights matrix, hidden bias vector, and visible bias vector of those first three RBMs. Rather, we will use the first three RBMs as fixed components of the DBN. We will call upon the first three RBMs just to do the forward and backward passes (and use samples of the data these three generate).

During the training of the fourth RBM in the DBN, we will only adjust weights and biases of the fourth RBM. In other words, the fourth RBM in the DBN takes the output of the first three RBMs as given and performs forward and backward passes to learn a generative model that minimizes the reconstruction error between its generated images and the original images.

Another way to train the DBNs would be to allow the DBN to learn and adjust weights for all four RBMs as it performs forward and backward passes through the entire network. However, training of the DBN would be very computationally expensive (perhaps not so with computers of today but certainly by the standards of 2006, when DBNs were first introduced).

That being said, if we wish to perform more nuanced pretraining, we could allow the weights of the individual RBMs to be adjusted—one RBM at a time—as we perform batches of forward and backward passes through the network. We will not delve into this, but I encourage you to experiment on your own time.

## Train the DBN

We will now train the DBN. We set the original image dimensions as 784, the dimensions of the third RBM output as 500, and the desired dimensions of the DBN as 500. We will use a learning rate of 1.0, train for 50 epochs, and use a batch size of 200. Finally, we will call the first three trained RBMs as part of the DBN:

```
# Instantiate DBN Class
dbn = DBN(784, 500, 500, 1.0, 50, 200, rbm_list[0], rbm_list[1], rbm_list[2])
```

Now, let's train:

```
inputX = np.array(X_train)
error_list = []
error_list = dbn.train(inputX)
```

Figure 11-10 displays the reconstruction errors of the DBN over the course of the training.

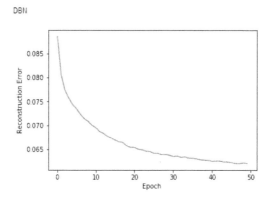

*Figure 11-10. Reconstruction errors of the DBN*

Figure 11-11 displays the learned features from the last layer of the DBN — the hidden layer of the fourth RBM.

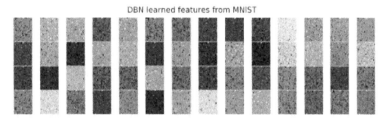

*Figure 11-11. Learned features of the fourth RBM in the DBN*

Both the reconstruction errors and the learned features look reasonable and similar to the ones from the individual RBMs we analyzed earlier.

# How Unsupervised Learning Helps Supervised Learning

So far, all the work we have done training the RBMs and the DBN involve unsupervised learning. We have not used any labels for the images at all. Instead, we have built generative models by learning relevant latent features from the original MNIST images provided in the 50,000 example training set. These generative models generate images that look reasonably similar to the original images (minimizing the reconstruction error).

Let's take a step back to understand the usefulness of such a generative model.

Recall that most of the data in the world is unlabeled. Therefore, as powerful and effective as supervised learning is, we need unsupervised learning to help make sense of all the unlabeled data that exists. Supervised learning is not enough.

To demonstrate the usefulness of unsupervised learning, imagine if instead of 50,000 labeled MNIST images in the training set, we had just a fraction—let's say we had only 5,000 labeled MNIST images. A supervised learning-based image classifer that had only 5,000 labeled images would not be nearly as effective as a supervised learning-based image classifier that had 50,000 images. The more labeled data we have, the better the machine learning solution.

How does unsupervised learning help in such a situation? One way unsupervised learning could help is by generating new labeled examples to help supplement the originally labeled dataset. Then, the supervised learning could occur on a much larger labeled dataset, resulting in a better overall solution.

## Generate Images to Build a Better Image Classifier

To simulate this benefit that unsupervised learning is able to provide, let's reduce our MNIST training dataset to just five thousand labeled examples. We will store the first five thousand images in a dataframe called `inputXReduced`.

Then, from these five thousand labeled images, we will generate new images from the generative model we just built using a DBN. And, we will do this 20 times over. In other words, we will generate five thousand new images 20 times to create a dataset that is 100,000 large, all of which will be labeled. Technically, we are storing the final hidden layer outputs not the reconstructed images directly, although we will store the reconstructed images, too, so we can evaluate them soon.

We will store these 100,000 outputs in a NumPy array called generatedImages:

```
# Generate images and store them
inputXReduced = X_train.loc[:4999]
for i in range(0,20):
    print("Run ",i)
    finalOutput_DBN, reconstructedOutput_DBN = dbn.dbn_output(inputXReduced)
    if i==0:
        generatedImages = finalOutput_DBN
    else:
        generatedImages = np.append(generatedImages, finalOutput_DBN, axis=0)
```

We will loop through the first five thousand labels from the training labels, called y_train, 20 times to generate an array of labels called labels:

```
# Generate a vector of labels for the generated images
for i in range(0,20):
    if i==0:
        labels = y_train.loc[:4999]
    else:
        labels = np.append(labels,y_train.loc[:4999])
```

Finally, we will generate the output on the validation set, which we will need to evaluate the image classifier we will build soon:

```
# Generate images based on the validation set
inputValidation = np.array(X_validation)
finalOutput_DBN_validation, reconstructedOutput_DBN_validation = \
    dbn.dbn_output(inputValidation)
```

Before we use the data we just generated, let's view a few of the reconstructed images:

```
# View reconstructed images
for i in range(0,10):
    example = i
    reconstructedX = pd.DataFrame(data=reconstructedOutput_DBN, \
                                  index=X_train[0:5000].index)
    view_digit(reconstructedX, y_train, example)
    view_digit(X_train, y_train, example)
```

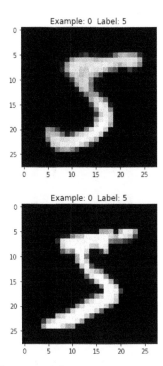

*Figure 11-12. First generated image of the DBN*

As you can see in Figure 11-12, the generated image is very similar to the original image—both display the digit five. Unlike the RBM-generated images we saw earlier, these are more similar to the original MNIST images, including the pixelated bits.

Let's view a few more images like this to compare the DBN-generated images with the original MNIST ones (see Figures 11-13 through 11-16).

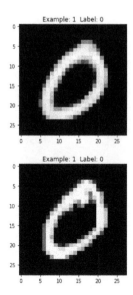

*Figure 11-13. Second generated image of the DBN*

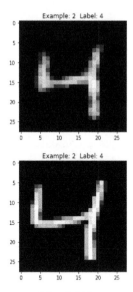

*Figure 11-14. Third generated image of the DBN*

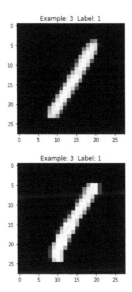

*Figure 11-15. Fourth generated image of the DBN*

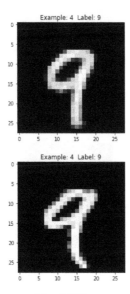

*Figure 11-16. Fifth generated image of the DBN*

Also note that the DBN model (as well as the RBM models) is generative and therefore the images are produced using a stochastic process. The images are not produced using a deterministic process, and, therefore, the images of a single example vary from one DBN run to another.

To simulate this, we will take the first MNIST image and use the DBN to generate a new one and do this 10 times over:

```
# Generate the first example 10 times
inputXReduced = X_train.loc[:0]
for i in range(0,10):
    example = 0
    print("Run ",i)
    finalOutput_DBN_fives, reconstructedOutput_DBN_fives = \
        dbn.dbn_output(inputXReduced)
    reconstructedX_fives = pd.DataFrame(data=reconstructedOutput_DBN_fives, \
                                        index=[0])
    print("Generated")
    view_digit(reconstructedX_fives, y_train.loc[:0], example)
```

As you see from Figures 11-17 through 11-21, all the generated images display the number five, but they vary from image to image even though they all were generated using the same original MNIST image.

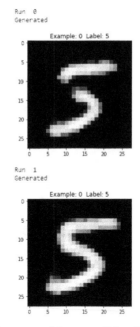

*Figure 11-17. First and second generated images of the digit five*

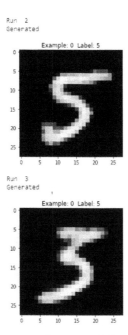

*Figure 11-18. Third and fourth generated images of the digit five*

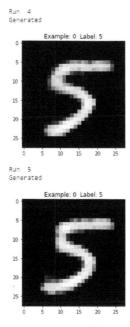

*Figure 11-19. Fifth and sixth generated images of the digit five*

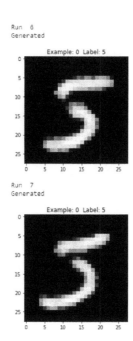

*Figure 11-20. Seventh and eighth generated images of the digit five*

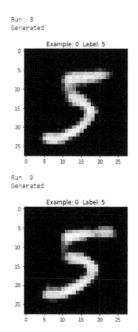

*Figure 11-21. Ninth and tenth generated images of the digit five*

# Image Classifier Using LightGBM

Now let's build an image classifier using a supervised learning algorithm we introduced earlier in the book: the gradient boosting algorithm *LightGBM*.

## Supervised Only

The first image classifier will rely on just the first five thousand labeled MNIST images. This is the reduced set from the original 50,000 labeled MNIST training set; we designed this to simulate real-world problems where we have relatively few labeled examples. Since we covered gradient boosting and the LightGBM algorithm in depth earlier in the book, we will not go into a lot of detail here.

Let's set the parameters for the algorithm:

```
predictionColumns = ['0','1','2','3','4','5','6','7','8','9']

params_lightGB = {
    'task': 'train',
    'application':'binary',
    'num_class':10,
    'boosting': 'gbdt',
    'objective': 'multiclass',
    'metric': 'multi_logloss',
    'metric_freq':50,
    'is_training_metric':False,
    'max_depth':4,
    'num_leaves': 31,
    'learning_rate': 0.1,
    'feature_fraction': 1.0,
    'bagging_fraction': 1.0,
    'bagging_freq': 0,
    'bagging_seed': 2018,
    'verbose': 0,
    'num_threads':16
}
```

Next, we will train on the 5,000 labeled MNIST training set (the reduced set) and validate on the 10,000 labeled MNIST validation set:

```
trainingScore = []
validationScore = []
predictionsLightGBM = pd.DataFrame(data=[], \
                      index=y_validation.index, \
                      columns=predictionColumns)

lgb_train = lgb.Dataset(X_train.loc[:4999], y_train.loc[:4999])
lgb_eval = lgb.Dataset(X_validation, y_validation, reference=lgb_train)
gbm = lgb.train(params_lightGB, lgb_train, num_boost_round=2000,
                valid_sets=lgb_eval, early_stopping_rounds=200)
```

```
loglossTraining = log_loss(y_train.loc[:4999], \
    gbm.predict(X_train.loc[:4999], num_iteration=gbm.best_iteration))
trainingScore.append(loglossTraining)

predictionsLightGBM.loc[X_validation.index,predictionColumns] = \
    gbm.predict(X_validation, num_iteration=gbm.best_iteration)
loglossValidation = log_loss(y_validation,
    predictionsLightGBM.loc[X_validation.index,predictionColumns])
validationScore.append(loglossValidation)

print('Training Log Loss: ', loglossTraining)
print('Validation Log Loss: ', loglossValidation)

loglossLightGBM = log_loss(y_validation, predictionsLightGBM)
print('LightGBM Gradient Boosting Log Loss: ', loglossLightGBM)
```

The following code shows the training and the validation log loss from this supervised-only solution:

```
Training Log Loss: 0.0018646953029132292
Validation Log Loss: 0.19124276982588717
```

The following code shows the overall accuracy of this supervised-only image classification solution:

```
predictionsLightGBM_firm = np.argmax(np.array(predictionsLightGBM), axis=1)
accuracyValidation_lightGBM = accuracy_score(np.array(y_validation), \
                                        predictionsLightGBM_firm)
print("Supervised-Only Accuracy: ", accuracyValidation_lightGBM)

Supervised-Only Accuracy: 0.9439
```

## Unsupervised and Supervised Solution

Now, instead of training on the five thousand labeled MNIST images, let's train on the 100,000 generated images from the DBN:

```
# Prepare DBN-based DataFrames for LightGBM use
generatedImagesDF = pd.DataFrame(data=generatedImages,index=range(0,100000))
labelsDF = pd.DataFrame(data=labels,index=range(0,100000))

X_train_lgb = pd.DataFrame(data=generatedImagesDF,
                        index=generatedImagesDF.index)
X_validation_lgb = pd.DataFrame(data=finalOutput_DBN_validation,
                            index=X_validation.index)

# Train LightGBM
trainingScore = []
validationScore = []
predictionsDBN = pd.DataFrame(data=[],index=y_validation.index,
                            columns=predictionColumns)

lgb_train = lgb.Dataset(X_train_lgb, labels)
lgb_eval = lgb.Dataset(X_validation_lgb, y_validation, reference=lgb_train)
```

```
gbm = lgb.train(params_lightGB, lgb_train, num_boost_round=2000,
                valid_sets=lgb_eval, early_stopping_rounds=200)

loglossTraining = log_loss(labelsDF, gbm.predict(X_train_lgb, \
                           num_iteration=gbm.best_iteration))
trainingScore.append(loglossTraining)

predictionsDBN.loc[X_validation.index,predictionColumns] = \
    gbm.predict(X_validation_lgb, num_iteration=gbm.best_iteration)
loglossValidation = log_loss(y_validation,
    predictionsDBN.loc[X_validation.index,predictionColumns])
validationScore.append(loglossValidation)

print('Training Log Loss: ', loglossTraining)
print('Validation Log Loss: ', loglossValidation)

loglossDBN = log_loss(y_validation, predictionsDBN)
print('LightGBM Gradient Boosting Log Loss: ', loglossDBN)
```

The following code displays the log loss of this unsupervised-enchanced image classification solution:

```
Training Log Loss: 0.004145635328203315
Validation Log Loss: 0.16377638170016542
```

The following code shows the overall accuracy of this unsupervised-enchanced image classification solution:

```
DBN-Based Solution Accuracy: 0.9525
```

As you see, the solution improves by nearly one percentage point, which is considerable.

# Conclusion

In Chapter 10, we introduced the first class of generative models called restricted Boltzmann machines. In this chapter, we built upon this concept by introducing more advanced generative models known as deep belief networks, which are comprised of multiple RBMs stacked on top of each other.

We demonstrated how DBNs work—in a purely unsupervised manner, the DBN learns the underlying structure of data and uses its learning to generate new synthetic data. Based on how the new synthetic data compares to the original data, the DBN improves its generative ability so much so that the synthetic data increasingly resembles the original data. We also showed how synthetic data generated by DBNs could supplement existing labeled datasets, improving the performance of supervised learning models by increasing the size of the overall training set.

The semisupervised solution we developed using DBNs (unsupervised learning) and gradient boosting (supervised learning) outperformed the purely supervised solution in the MNIST image classifaction problem we had.

In Chapter 12, we introduce one of the latest advances in unsupervised learning (and generative modeling, more specifically) known as generative adversarial networks.

# Generative Adversarial Networks

We have already explored two types of generative models: RBMs and DBNs. In this chapter, we will explore *generative adversarial networks (GANs)*, one of the latest and most promising areas of unsupervised learning and generative modeling.

## GANs, the Concept

GANs were introduced by Ian Goodfellow and his fellow researchers at the University of Montreal in 2014. In GANs, we have two neural networks. One network known as the *generator* generates data based on a model it has created using samples of real data it has received as input. The other network known as the *discriminator* discriminates between the data created by the generator and data from the true distribution.

As a simple analogy, the generator is the counterfeiter, and the discriminator is the police trying to identify the forgery. The two networks are locked in a zero-sum game. The generator is trying to fool the discriminator into thinking the synthetic data comes from the true distribution, and the discriminator is trying to call out the synthetic data as fake.

GANs are unsupervised learning algorithms because the generator can learn the underlying structure of the true distribution even when there are no labels. The generator learns the underlying structure by using a number of parameters significantly smaller than the amount of data it has trained on—a core concept of unsupervised learning that we have explored many times in previous chapters. This constraint forces the generator to efficiently capture the most salient aspects of the true data distribution. This is similar to the representation learning that occurs in deep learning. Each hidden layer in the neutral network of a generator captures a representation of the underlying data—starting very simply—and subsequent layers pick up more complicated representations by building on the simpler preceding layers.

Using all these layers together, the generator learns the underlying structure of the data and attempts to create synthetic data that is nearly identical to the true data. If the generator has captured the essence of the true data, the synthetic data will appear real.

## The Power of GANs

In Chapter 11, we explored the ability to use synthetic data from an unsupervised learning model (such as a deep belief network) to improve the performance of a supervised learning model. Like DBNs, GANs are very good at generating synthetic data.

If the objective is to generate a lot of new training examples to help supplement existing training data—for example, to improve accuracy on an image recognition task—we can use the generator to create a lot of synthetic data, add the new synthetic data to the original training data, and then run a supervised machine learning model on the now much larger dataset.

GANs can also excel at anomaly detection. If the objective is to identify anomalies—for example, to detect fraud, hacking, or other suspicious behavior—we can use the discriminator to score each instance in the real data. The instances that the discriminator ranks as "likely synthetic" will be the most anomalous instances and also the ones most likely to represent malicious behavior.

# Deep Convolutional GANs

In this chapter, we will return to the MNIST dataset we used in previous chapters and apply a version of GANs to generate synthetic data to supplement the existing MNIST dataset. We will then apply a supervised learning model to perform image classification. This is yet another version of semisupervised learning.

As a side note, you should now have a much deeper appreciation for semisupervised learning. Because much of the world's data is unlabeled, the ability of unsupervised learning to efficiently help label data by itself is very powerful. As part of such semisupervised machine learning systems, unsupervised learning enhances the potential of all successful commercial applications of supervised learning to date.

Even outside of applications in semisupervised systems, unsupervised learning has potential on a standalone basis because it learns from data without any labels and is one of the fields of AI that has the greatest potential to help the machine learning community move from narrow AI to more AGI applications.

The version of GANs we will use is called *deep convolutional generative adversarial networks (DCGANs)*, which were first introduced in late 2015 by Alec Radford, Luke Metz, and Soumith Chintala.[1]

DCGANs are an unsupervised learning form of *convolution neural networks (CNNs)*, which are commonly used—and with great success—in supervised learning systems for computer vision and image classification. Before we delve into DCGANs, let's explore CNNs first, especially how they are used for image classification in supervised learning systems.

# Convolutional Neural Networks

Compared to numerical and text data, images and video are considerably more computationally expensive to work with. For instance, a 4K Ultra HD image has dimensions of 4096 x 2160 x 3 (26,542,080) in total. Training a neural network on images of this resolution directly would require tens of millions of neurons and result in very long training times.

Instead of building a neural network directly on the raw images, we can take advantage of certain properties of images, namely that pixels are related to other pixels that are close by but not usually related to other pixels that are far away.

*Convolution* (from which convolutional neural networks derive their name) is the process of filtering the image to decrease the size of the image without losing the relationships among pixels.[2]

On the original image, we apply several filters of a certain size, known as the *kernel size*, and move these filters with a small step, known as the *stride*, to derive the new reduced pixel output. After the convolution, we reduce the size of the representation further by taking the max of the pixels in the reduced pixel output, one small area at a time. This is known as *max pooling*.

We perform this convolution and max pooling several times to reduce the complexity of the images. Then, we flatten the images and use a normal fully connected layer to perform image classification.

Let's now build a CNN and use it to perform image classification on the MNIST dataset. First, we will load the necessary libraries:

```
'''Main'''
import numpy as np
import pandas as pd
```

---

1 For more on DCGANs, take a look at the official paper on the topic (*https://arxiv.org/abs/1511.06434*).

2 For more on convolution layers, read "An Introduction to Different Types of Convolutions in Deep Learning" (*http://bit.ly/2GeMQfu*).

```
import os, time, re
import pickle, gzip, datetime

'''Data Viz'''
import matplotlib.pyplot as plt
import seaborn as sns
color = sns.color_palette()
import matplotlib as mpl
from mpl_toolkits.axes_grid1 import Grid

%matplotlib inline

'''Data Prep and Model Evaluation'''
from sklearn import preprocessing as pp
from sklearn.model_selection import train_test_split
from sklearn.model_selection import StratifiedKFold
from sklearn.metrics import log_loss, accuracy_score
from sklearn.metrics import precision_recall_curve, average_precision_score
from sklearn.metrics import roc_curve, auc, roc_auc_score, mean_squared_error

'''Algos'''
import lightgbm as lgb

'''TensorFlow and Keras'''
import tensorflow as tf
import keras
from keras import backend as K
from keras.models import Sequential, Model
from keras.layers import Activation, Dense, Dropout, Flatten, Conv2D, MaxPool2D
from keras.layers import LeakyReLU, Reshape, UpSampling2D, Conv2DTranspose
from keras.layers import BatchNormalization, Input, Lambda
from keras.layers import Embedding, Flatten, dot
from keras import regularizers
from keras.losses import mse, binary_crossentropy
from IPython.display import SVG
from keras.utils.vis_utils import model_to_dot
from keras.optimizers import Adam, RMSprop
from tensorflow.examples.tutorials.mnist import input_data
```

Next, we will load the MNIST datasets and store the image data in a 4D tensor since Keras requires image data in this format. We will also create one-hot vectors from the labels using the to_categorical function in Keras.

For use later, we will create Pandas DataFrames from the data, too. And, let's reuse the view_digit function from earlier in the book to view the images:

```
# Load the datasets
current_path = os.getcwd()
file = '\\datasets\\mnist_data\\mnist.pkl.gz'
f = gzip.open(current_path+file, 'rb')
train_set, validation_set, test_set = pickle.load(f, encoding='latin1')
f.close()
```

```
X_train, y_train = train_set[0], train_set[1]
X_validation, y_validation = validation_set[0], validation_set[1]
X_test, y_test = test_set[0], test_set[1]

X_train_keras = X_train.reshape(50000,28,28,1)
X_validation_keras = X_validation.reshape(10000,28,28,1)
X_test_keras = X_test.reshape(10000,28,28,1)

y_train_keras = to_categorical(y_train)
y_validation_keras = to_categorical(y_validation)
y_test_keras = to_categorical(y_test)

# Create Pandas DataFrames from the datasets
train_index = range(0,len(X_train))
validation_index = range(len(X_train),len(X_train)+len(X_validation))
test_index = range(len(X_train)+len(X_validation),len(X_train)+ \
                   len(X_validation)+len(X_test))

X_train = pd.DataFrame(data=X_train,index=train_index)
y_train = pd.Series(data=y_train,index=train_index)

X_validation = pd.DataFrame(data=X_validation,index=validation_index)
y_validation = pd.Series(data=y_validation,index=validation_index)

X_test = pd.DataFrame(data=X_test,index=test_index)
y_test = pd.Series(data=y_test,index=test_index)

def view_digit(X, y, example):
    label = y.loc[example]
    image = X.loc[example,:].values.reshape([28,28])
    plt.title('Example: %d  Label: %d' % (example, label))
    plt.imshow(image, cmap=plt.get_cmap('gray'))
    plt.show()
```

Now let's build the CNN.

We will call Sequential() in Keras to begin the model creation. Then, we will add two convolution layers, each with 32 filters of a kernel size of 5 x 5, a default stride of 1, and a ReLU activation. Then, we perform max pooling with a pooling window of 2 x 2 and a stride of 1. We also perform dropout, which you may recall is a form of regularization to reduce overfitting of the neural network. Specifically, we will drop 25% of the input units.

In the next stage, we add two convolution layers again, this time with 64 filters of a kernel size of 3 x 3. Then, we perform max pooling with a pooling window of 2 x 2 and a stride of 2. And, we follow this up with a dropout layer, with a dropout percentage of 25%.

Finally, we flatten the images, add a regular neural network with 256 hidden units, perform dropout with a dropout percentage of 50%, and perform 10-class classification using the softmax function:

```
model = Sequential()

model.add(Conv2D(filters = 32, kernel_size = (5,5), padding = 'Same',
            activation ='relu', input_shape = (28,28,1)))
model.add(Conv2D(filters = 32, kernel_size = (5,5), padding = 'Same',
            activation ='relu'))
model.add(MaxPooling2D(pool_size=(2,2)))
model.add(Dropout(0.25))


model.add(Conv2D(filters = 64, kernel_size = (3,3), padding = 'Same',
            activation ='relu'))
model.add(Conv2D(filters = 64, kernel_size = (3,3), padding = 'Same',
            activation ='relu'))
model.add(MaxPooling2D(pool_size=(2,2), strides=(2,2)))
model.add(Dropout(0.25))


model.add(Flatten())
model.add(Dense(256, activation = "relu"))
model.add(Dropout(0.5))
model.add(Dense(10, activation = "softmax"))
```

For this CNN training, we will use the *Adam optimizer* and minimize the cross-entropy. We will also store the accuracy of the image classification as the evaluation metric.

Now let's train the model for one hundred epochs and evaluate the results on the validation set:

```
# Train CNN
model.compile(optimizer='adam',
            loss='categorical_crossentropy',
            metrics=['accuracy'])

model.fit(X_train_keras, y_train_keras,
        validation_data=(X_validation_keras, y_validation_keras), \
        epochs=100)
```

Figure 12-1 displays the accuracy over the one hundred epochs of training.

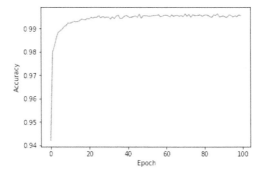

*Figure 12-1. CNN results*

As you can see, the CNN we just trained has a final accuracy of 99.55%, better than any of the MNIST image classification solutions we have trained so far throughout this book.

# DCGANs Revisited

Let's now turn back to deep convolutional generative adversarial networks once again. We will build a generative model to produce synthetic MNIST images that are very similar to the original MNIST ones.

To produce near-realistic yet synthetic images, we need to train a generator that generates new images from the original MNIST images and a discriminator that judges whether those images are believably similar to the original ones or not (essentially performing a bullshit test).

Here is another way to think about this. The original MNIST dataset represents the original data distribution. The generator learns from this original distribution and generates new images based off what it has learned, and the discriminator attempts to determine whether the newly generated images are virtually indistinguishable from the original distribution or not.

For the generator, we will use the architecture presented in the Radford, Metz, and Chintala paper presented at the ICLR 2016 conference, which we referenced earlier (Figure 12-2).

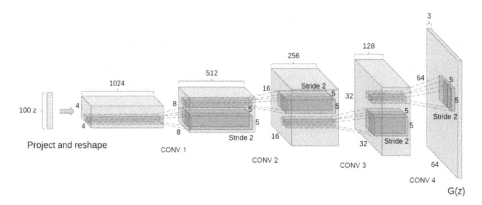

*Figure 12-2. DCGAN generator*

The generator takes in an initial *noise vector*, shown as a 100 x 1 noise vector here denoted as *z*, and then projects and reshapes it into a 1024 x 4 x 4 tensor. This *project and reshape* action is the opposite of convolution and is known as *transposed convolution* (or *deconvolution* in some cases). In transposed convolution, the original process of convolution is reversed, mapping a reduced tensor to a larger one.[3]

After the initial transposed convolution, the generator applies four additional deconvolution layers to map to a final 64 x 3 x 3 tensor.

Here are the various stages:

100 x 1 → 1024 x 4 x 4 → 512 x 8 x 8 → 256 x 16 x 16 → 128 x 32 x 32 → 64 x 64 x 3

We will apply a similar (but not exact) architecture when designing a DCGAN on the MNIST dataset.

## Generator of the DCGAN

For the DCGAN we design, we will leverage work done by Rowel Atienza and build on top of it.[4] We will first create a class called *DCGAN*, which we will use to build the generator, discriminator, discriminator model, and adversarial model.

Let's start with the generator. We will set several parameters for the generator, including the dropout percentage (default value of 0.3), the depth of the tensor (default value of 256), and the other dimensions (default value of 7 x 7). We will also use batch

---

3 For more on convolution layers, check out "An Introduction to Different Types of Convolutions in Deep Learning" (*http://bit.ly/2GeMQfu*), also referenced earlier in the chapter.

4 For the original code base, visit Rowel Atienza's GitHub page (*http://bit.ly/2DLp4G1*).

---

normalization with a default momentum value of 0.8. The initial input dimensions are one hundred, and the final output dimensions are 28 x 28 x 1.

Recall that both dropout and batch normalization are regularizers to help the neural network we design avoid overfitting.

To build the generator, we call the `Sequential()` function from Keras. Then, we will add a dense, fully connected neural network layer by calling the `Dense()` function. This will have an input dimension of 100 and an output dimension of 7 x 7 x 256. We will perform batch normalization, use the ReLU activation function, and perform dropout:

```
def generator(self, depth=256, dim=7, dropout=0.3, momentum=0.8, \
              window=5, input_dim=100, output_depth=1):
    if self.G:
        return self.G
    self.G = Sequential()
    self.G.add(Dense(dim*dim*depth, input_dim=input_dim))
    self.G.add(BatchNormalization(momentum=momentum))
    self.G.add(Activation('relu'))
    self.G.add(Reshape((dim, dim, depth)))
    self.G.add(Dropout(dropout))
```

Next, we will perform *upsampling* and *transposed convolution* three times. Each time, we will halve the depth of the output space from 256 to 128 to 64 to 32 while increasing the other dimensions. We will maintain a convolution window of 5 x 5 and the default stride of one. During each transposed convolution, we will perform batch normalization and use the ReLU activation function.

Here is what this looks like:

$100 \rightarrow 7 \times 7 \times 256 \rightarrow 14 \times 14 \times 128 \rightarrow 28 \times 28 \times 64 \rightarrow 28 \times 28 \times 32 \rightarrow 28 \times 28 \times 1$

```
    self.G.add(UpSampling2D())
    self.G.add(Conv2DTranspose(int(depth/2), window, padding='same'))
    self.G.add(BatchNormalization(momentum=momentum))
    self.G.add(Activation('relu'))

    self.G.add(UpSampling2D())
    self.G.add(Conv2DTranspose(int(depth/4), window, padding='same'))
    self.G.add(BatchNormalization(momentum=momentum))
    self.G.add(Activation('relu'))

    self.G.add(Conv2DTranspose(int(depth/8), window, padding='same'))
    self.G.add(BatchNormalization(momentum=momentum))
    self.G.add(Activation('relu'))
```

Finally, the generator will output a 28 x 28 image, which has the same dimensions as the original MNIST image:

```
    self.G.add(Conv2DTranspose(output_depth, window, padding='same'))
    self.G.add(Activation('sigmoid'))
```

```
self.G.summary()
return self.G
```

# Discriminator of the DCGAN

For the discriminator, we will set the default dropout percentage to 0.3, the depth as 64, and the alpha for the LeakyReLU function as 0.3.[5]

First, we will load a 28 x 28 x 1 image and perform convolution using 64 channels, a filter of 5 x 5, and a stride of two. We will use LeakyReLU as the activation function and perform dropout. We will continue this process three more times, doubling the depth of the output space each time while decreasing the other dimensions. For each convolution, we will use the LeakyReLU activation function and dropout.

Finally, we will flatten the images and use the sigmoid function to output a probability. This probability designates the discriminator's confidence in calling the input image a real (where 0.0 is fake and 1.0 is real).

Here is what this looks like:

28 x 28 x 1 → 14 x 14 x 64 → 7 x 7 x 128 → 4 x 4 x 256 → 4 x 4 x 512 → 1

```
def discriminator(self, depth=64, dropout=0.3, alpha=0.3):
    if self.D:
        return self.D
    self.D = Sequential()
    input_shape = (self.img_rows, self.img_cols, self.channel)
    self.D.add(Conv2D(depth*1, 5, strides=2, input_shape=input_shape,
        padding='same'))
    self.D.add(LeakyReLU(alpha=alpha))
    self.D.add(Dropout(dropout))

    self.D.add(Conv2D(depth*2, 5, strides=2, padding='same'))
    self.D.add(LeakyReLU(alpha=alpha))
    self.D.add(Dropout(dropout))

    self.D.add(Conv2D(depth*4, 5, strides=2, padding='same'))
    self.D.add(LeakyReLU(alpha=alpha))
    self.D.add(Dropout(dropout))

    self.D.add(Conv2D(depth*8, 5, strides=1, padding='same'))
    self.D.add(LeakyReLU(alpha=alpha))
    self.D.add(Dropout(dropout))

    self.D.add(Flatten())
```

---

5 LeakyReLU (*https://keras.io/layers/advanced-activations/*) is an advanced activation function that is similar to the normal ReLU but allows a small gradient when the unit is not active. It is becoming a preferred activation function for image machine learning problems.

---

```
self.D.add(Dense(1))
self.D.add(Activation('sigmoid'))
self.D.summary()
return self.D
```

## Discriminator and Adversarial Models

Next, let's define the discriminator model (i.e., the police detecting the fakes) and the adversarial model (i.e., the counterfeiter learning from the police). For both the adversarial and the discriminator model, we will use the RMSprop optimizer, define the loss function as binary cross-entropy, and use accuracy as our reported metric.

For the adversarial model, we use the generator and discriminator networks we defined earlier. For the discriminator model, we use just the discriminator network:

```
def discriminator_model(self):
    if self.DM:
        return self.DM
    optimizer = RMSprop(lr=0.0002, decay=6e-8)
    self.DM = Sequential()
    self.DM.add(self.discriminator())
    self.DM.compile(loss='binary_crossentropy', \
                    optimizer=optimizer, metrics=['accuracy'])
    return self.DM

def adversarial_model(self):
    if self.AM:
        return self.AM
    optimizer = RMSprop(lr=0.0001, decay=3e-8)
    self.AM = Sequential()
    self.AM.add(self.generator())
    self.AM.add(self.discriminator())
    self.AM.compile(loss='binary_crossentropy', \
                    optimizer=optimizer, metrics=['accuracy'])
    return self.AM
```

## DCGAN for the MNIST Dataset

Now let's define the DCGAN for the MNIST dataset. First, we will initialize the MNIST_DCGAN class for the 28 x 28 x 1 MNIST images and use the generator, discriminator model, and adversarial model from earlier:

```
class MNIST_DCGAN(object):
    def __init__(self, x_train):
        self.img_rows = 28
        self.img_cols = 28
        self.channel = 1

        self.x_train = x_train

        self.DCGAN = DCGAN()
```

```
        self.discriminator = self.DCGAN.discriminator_model()
        self.adversarial = self.DCGAN.adversarial_model()
        self.generator = self.DCGAN.generator()
```

The train function will train for a default two thousand training epochs and use a batch size of 256. In this function, we will feed batches of images into the DCGAN architecture we just defined. The generator will generate images, and the discriminator will call out images as real or fake. As the generator and discriminator duke it out in this adversarial model, the synthetic images become more and more similar to the original MNIST images:

```
def train(self, train_steps=2000, batch_size=256, save_interval=0):
    noise_input = None
    if save_interval>0:
        noise_input = np.random.uniform(-1.0, 1.0, size=[16, 100])
    for i in range(train_steps):
        images_train = self.x_train[np.random.randint(0,
            self.x_train.shape[0], size=batch_size), :, :, :]
        noise = np.random.uniform(-1.0, 1.0, size=[batch_size, 100])
        images_fake = self.generator.predict(noise)
        x = np.concatenate((images_train, images_fake))
        y = np.ones([2*batch_size, 1])
        y[batch_size:, :] = 0

        d_loss = self.discriminator.train_on_batch(x, y)

        y = np.ones([batch_size, 1])
        noise = np.random.uniform(-1.0, 1.0, size=[batch_size, 100])
        a_loss = self.adversarial.train_on_batch(noise, y)
        log_mesg = "%d: [D loss: %f, acc: %f]" % (i, d_loss[0], d_loss[1])
        log_mesg = "%s  [A loss: %f, acc: %f]" % (log_mesg, a_loss[0], \
                                                    a_loss[1])
        print(log_mesg)
        if save_interval>0:
            if (i+1)%save_interval==0:
                self.plot_images(save2file=True, \
                    samples=noise_input.shape[0],\
                    noise=noise_input, step=(i+1))
```

Let's also define a function to plot the images generated by this DCGAN model:

```
def plot_images(self, save2file=False, fake=True, samples=16, \
                noise=None, step=0):
    filename = 'mnist.png'
    if fake:
        if noise is None:
            noise = np.random.uniform(-1.0, 1.0, size=[samples, 100])
        else:
            filename = "mnist_%d.png" % step
        images = self.generator.predict(noise)
    else:
        i = np.random.randint(0, self.x_train.shape[0], samples)
```

```
            images = self.x_train[i, :, :, :]

    plt.figure(figsize=(10,10))
    for i in range(images.shape[0]):
        plt.subplot(4, 4, i+1)
        image = images[i, :, :, :]
        image = np.reshape(image, [self.img_rows, self.img_cols])
        plt.imshow(image, cmap='gray')
        plt.axis('off')
    plt.tight_layout()
    if save2file:
        plt.savefig(filename)
        plt.close('all')
    else:
        plt.show()
```

# MNIST DCGAN in Action

Now that we have defined the MNIST_DCGAN call, let's call it and begin the training process. We will train for 10,000 epochs with a batch size of 256:

```
# Initialize MNIST_DCGAN and train
mnist_dcgan = MNIST_DCGAN(X_train_keras)
timer = ElapsedTimer()
mnist_dcgan.train(train_steps=10000, batch_size=256, save_interval=500)
```

The following code displays the loss and the accuracy of the discriminator and the adversarial model:

```
0:  [D loss: 0.692640, acc: 0.527344] [A loss: 1.297974, acc: 0.000000]
1:  [D loss: 0.651119, acc: 0.500000] [A loss: 0.920461, acc: 0.000000]
2:  [D loss: 0.735192, acc: 0.500000] [A loss: 1.289153, acc: 0.000000]
3:  [D loss: 0.556142, acc: 0.947266] [A loss: 1.218020, acc: 0.000000]
4:  [D loss: 0.492492, acc: 0.994141] [A loss: 1.306247, acc: 0.000000]
5:  [D loss: 0.491894, acc: 0.916016] [A loss: 1.722399, acc: 0.000000]
6:  [D loss: 0.607124, acc: 0.527344] [A loss: 1.698651, acc: 0.000000]
7:  [D loss: 0.578594, acc: 0.921875] [A loss: 1.042844, acc: 0.000000]
8:  [D loss: 0.509973, acc: 0.587891] [A loss: 1.957741, acc: 0.000000]
9:  [D loss: 0.538314, acc: 0.896484] [A loss: 1.133667, acc: 0.000000]
10: [D loss: 0.510218, acc: 0.572266] [A loss: 1.855000, acc: 0.000000]
11: [D loss: 0.501239, acc: 0.923828] [A loss: 1.098140, acc: 0.000000]
12: [D loss: 0.509211, acc: 0.519531] [A loss: 1.911793, acc: 0.000000]
13: [D loss: 0.482305, acc: 0.923828] [A loss: 1.187290, acc: 0.000000]
14: [D loss: 0.395886, acc: 0.900391] [A loss: 1.465053, acc: 0.000000]
15: [D loss: 0.346876, acc: 0.992188] [A loss: 1.443823, acc: 0.000000]
```

The initial accuracy of the discriminator fluctuates wildly but remains considerably above 0.50. In other words, the discriminator is initially very good at catching the poorly constructed counterfeits from the generator. Then, as the generator becomes better at creating counterfeits, the discriminator struggles; its accuracy drops close to 0.50:

```
9985: [D loss: 0.696480, acc: 0.521484] [A loss: 0.955954, acc: 0.125000]
9986: [D loss: 0.716583, acc: 0.472656] [A loss: 0.761385, acc: 0.363281]
9987: [D loss: 0.710941, acc: 0.533203] [A loss: 0.981265, acc: 0.074219]
9988: [D loss: 0.703731, acc: 0.515625] [A loss: 0.679451, acc: 0.558594]
9989: [D loss: 0.722460, acc: 0.492188] [A loss: 0.899768, acc: 0.125000]
9990: [D loss: 0.691914, acc: 0.539062] [A loss: 0.726867, acc: 0.464844]
9991: [D loss: 0.716197, acc: 0.500000] [A loss: 0.932500, acc: 0.144531]
9992: [D loss: 0.689704, acc: 0.548828] [A loss: 0.734389, acc: 0.414062]
9993: [D loss: 0.714405, acc: 0.517578] [A loss: 0.850408, acc: 0.218750]
9994: [D loss: 0.690414, acc: 0.550781] [A loss: 0.766320, acc: 0.355469]
9995: [D loss: 0.709792, acc: 0.511719] [A loss: 0.960070, acc: 0.105469]
9996: [D loss: 0.695851, acc: 0.500000] [A loss: 0.774395, acc: 0.324219]
9997: [D loss: 0.712254, acc: 0.521484] [A loss: 0.853828, acc: 0.183594]
9998: [D loss: 0.702689, acc: 0.529297] [A loss: 0.802785, acc: 0.308594]
9999: [D loss: 0.698032, acc: 0.517578] [A loss: 0.810278, acc: 0.304688]
```

## Synthetic Image Generation

Now that the MNIST DCGAN has been trained, let's use it to generate a sample of synthetic images (Figure 12-3).

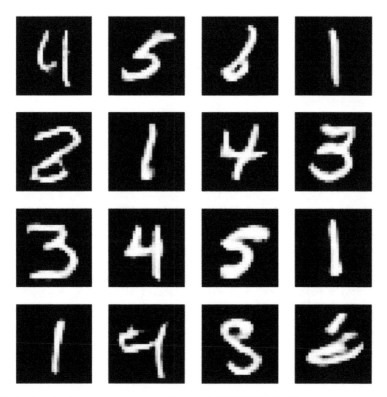

*Figure 12-3. Synthetic images generated by the MNIST DCGAN*

These synthetic images—while not entirely indistinguishable from the real MNIST dataset—are eerily similar to real digits. With more training time, the MNIST DCGAN should be capable of generating synthetic images that more closely resemble those of the real MNIST dataset and could be used to supplement the size of that dataset.

While our solution is reasonably good, there are many ways to make the MNIST DCGAN perform better. The paper "Improved Techniques for Training GANs" (*https://arxiv.org/pdf/1606.03498.pdf*) and the accompanying code (*https://github.com/openai/improved-gan*) delves into more advanced methods to improve GAN performance.

# Conclusion

In this chapter, we explored deep convolutional generative adversarial networks, a specialized form of generative adversarial networks that perform well on image and computer vision datasets.

GANs are a generative model with two neural networks locked in a zero-sum game. One of the networks, the generator (i.e., the counterfeiter), is generating synthetic data from real data, while the other network, the discriminator (i.e, the police), is calling the counterfeits fake or real.[6] This zero-sum game in which the generator learns from the discriminator leads to an overall generative model that generates pretty realistic synthetic data and generally gets better over time (i.e., as we train for more training epochs).

GANs are relatively new—they were first introduced by Ian Goodfellow et al. in 2014.[7] GANs are currently mainly used to perform anomaly detection and generate synthetic data, but they could have many other applications in the near future. The machine learning community is barely scratching the surface with what is possible, and, if you decide to use GANs in applied machine learning systems, be ready to experiment a lot.[8]

In Chapter 13, we will conclude this part of the book by exploring temporal clustering, which is a form of unsupervised learning for use with time series data.

---

6 For additional information, check out the OpenAI blog's generative models post (*https://blog.openai.com/generative-models/*).

7 For more on this, take a look at this seminal paper (*https://arxiv.org/abs/1406.2661*).

8 For some tips and tricks, read this post on how to refine GANs (*https://github.com/soumith/ganhacks*) and improve performance (*http://bit.ly/2G2FJHq*).

# CHAPTER 13

# Time Series Clustering

So far in this book, we have worked mostly with *cross-sectional data*, in which we have observations for entities at a single point in time. This includes the credit card dataset with transactions that happened over two days and the MNIST dataset with images of digits. For these datasets, we applied unsupervised learning to learn the underlying structure in the data and to group similar transactions and images together without using any labels.

Unsupervised learning is also very valuable for work with *time series data*, in which we have observations for a single entity at different time intervals. We need to develop a solution that can learn the underlying structure of data across time, not just for a particular moment in time. If we develop such a solution, we can identify similar time series patterns and group them together.

This is very impactful in fields such as finance, medicine, robotics, astronomy, biology, meteorology, etc., since professionals in these fields spend a lot of time analyzing data to classify current events based on how similar they are to past events. By grouping current events together with similar past events, these professionals are able to more confidently decide on the right course of action to take.

In this chapter, we will work on clustering time series data based on pattern similarity. Clustering time series data is a purely unsupervised approach and does not require annotation of data for training, although annotated data is necessary for validating the results as with all other unsupervised learning experiments.

There is a third group of data that combines cross-sectional and time series data. This is known as *panel* or *longitudinal* data.

# ECG Data

To make the time series clustering problem more tangible, let's introduce a specific real-world problem. Imagine we were working in healthcare and had to analyze electrocardiogram (EKG/ECG) readings. ECG machines record the electrical activity of the heart over a period of time using electrodes placed over the skin. The ECG measures activity over approximately 10 seconds, and the recorded metrics help detect any cardiac problems.

Most ECG readings record normal heartbeat activity, but the abnormal readings are the ones healthcare professionals must identify to react preemptively before any adverse cardiac event—such as cardiac arrest—occurs. The ECG produces a line graph with peaks and valleys so the task of classifying a reading as normal or abnormal is a straightforward pattern recognition task, well suited for machine learning.

Real-world ECG readings are not so cleanly displayed, making classification of the images into these various buckets difficult and error-prone.

For example, variations in the *amplitude* of the waves (the height of the center line to the peak or trough), the *period* (the distance from one peak to the next), the *phase shift* (horizontal shifting), and the *vertical shift* are challenges for any machine-driven classification system.

# Approach to Time Series Clustering

Any approach to time series clustering will require us to handle these types of distortions. As you may recall, clustering relies on distance measures to determine how close in space data is to other data so that similar data can be grouped together into distinct and homogeneous clusters.

Clustering time series data works similarly, but we need a distance measure that is scale- and shift-invariant so that similar time series data is grouped together regardless of trivial differences in amplitude, period, phase shift, and vertical shift.

## k-Shape

One of the state-of-the-art approaches to time series clustering that meets this criteria is *k-shape*, which was first introduced at ACM SIGMOD in 2015 by John Paparrizos and Luis Gravano.[1]

*k*-shape uses a distance measure that is invariant to scaling and shifting to preserve the shapes of time series sequences while comparing them. Specifically, *k*-shape uses a

---

[1] The paper is publicly available here (*http://www.cs.columbia.edu/~jopa/kshape.html*).

normalized version of cross-correlation to compute cluster centroids and then, in every iteration, updates the assignment of time series to these clusters.

In addition to being invariant to scaling and shifting, $k$-shape is domain-independent and scalable, requiring minimal parameter tuning. Its iterative refinement procedure scales linearly in the number of sequences. These characteristics have made it one of the most powerful time series clustering algorithms available today.

By this point, it should be clear that $k$-shape operates similarly to $k$-means: both algorithms use an iterative approach to assign data to groups based on the distance between the data and the centroid of the nearest group. The critical difference is in how $k$-shape calculates distances—it uses shaped-based distance that relies on cross-correlations.

# Time Series Clustering Using k-Shape on ECGFiveDays

Let's build a time series clustering model using $k$-shape.

In this chapter, we will rely on data from the UCR time series collection. Because the file size exceeds one hundred megabytes, it is not accessible on GitHub. You will need to download the files from the UCR Time Series website (*http://bit.ly/2CXPcfq*).

This is the largest public collection of class-labeled time series datasets, numbering—85 in total. These datasets are from multiple domains, so we can test how well our solution does across domains. Each time series belongs to only one class, so we also have labels to validate the results of our time series clustering.

## Data Preparation

Let's begin by loading the necessary libraries:

```
'''Main'''
import numpy as np
import pandas as pd
import os, time, re
import pickle, gzip, datetime
from os import listdir, walk
from os.path import isfile, join

'''Data Viz'''
import matplotlib.pyplot as plt
import seaborn as sns
color = sns.color_palette()
import matplotlib as mpl
from mpl_toolkits.axes_grid1 import Grid

%matplotlib inline

'''Data Prep and Model Evaluation'''
```

```
from sklearn import preprocessing as pp
from sklearn.model_selection import train_test_split
from sklearn.model_selection import StratifiedKFold
from sklearn.metrics import log_loss, accuracy_score
from sklearn.metrics import precision_recall_curve, average_precision_score
from sklearn.metrics import roc_curve, auc, roc_auc_score, mean_squared_error
from keras.utils import to_categorical
from sklearn.metrics import adjusted_rand_score
import random

'''Algos'''
from kshape.core import kshape, zscore
import tslearn
from tslearn.utils import to_time_series_dataset
from tslearn.clustering import KShape, TimeSeriesScalerMeanVariance
from tslearn.clustering import TimeSeriesKMeans
import hdbscan


'''TensorFlow and Keras'''
import tensorflow as tf
import keras
from keras import backend as K
from keras.models import Sequential, Model
from keras.layers import Activation, Dense, Dropout, Flatten, Conv2D, MaxPool2D
from keras.layers import LeakyReLU, Reshape, UpSampling2D, Conv2DTranspose
from keras.layers import BatchNormalization, Input, Lambda
from keras.layers import Embedding, Flatten, dot
from keras import regularizers
from keras.losses import mse, binary_crossentropy
from IPython.display import SVG
from keras.utils.vis_utils import model_to_dot
from keras.optimizers import Adam, RMSprop
from tensorflow.examples.tutorials.mnist import input_data
```

We will use the *tslearn* package to access the Python-based *k*-shape algorithm. tslearn has a similar framework as Scikit-learn but is geared toward work with time series data.

Next, let's load the training and test data from the ECGFiveDays dataset, which was downloaded from the UCR Time Series archive. The first column in this matrix has the class labels, while the rest of the columns are the values of the time series data. We will store the data as X_train, y_train, X_test, and y_test:

```
# Load the datasets
current_path = os.getcwd()
file = '\\datasets\\ucr_time_series_data\\'
data_train = np.loadtxt(current_path+file+
                        "ECGFiveDays/ECGFiveDays_TRAIN",
                        delimiter=",")
X_train = to_time_series_dataset(data_train[:, 1:])
y_train = data_train[:, 0].astype(np.int)
```

```
data_test = np.loadtxt(current_path+file+
                        "ECGFiveDays/ECGFiveDays_TEST",
                        delimiter=",")
X_test = to_time_series_dataset(data_test[:, 1:])
y_test = data_test[:, 0].astype(np.int)
```

The following code shows the number of time series, the number of unique classes, and the length of each time series:

```
# Basic summary statistics
print("Number of time series:", len(data_train))
print("Number of unique classes:", len(np.unique(data_train[:,0])))
print("Time series length:", len(data_train[0,1:]))

Number of time series: 23
Number of unique classes: 2
Time series length: 136
```

There are 23 time series and 2 unique classes, and each time series has a length of 136. Figure 13-1 shows a few examples of each class; now we know what these ECG readings look like:

```
# Examples of Class 1.0
for i in range(0,10):
    if data_train[i,0]==1.0:
        print("Plot ",i," Class ",data_train[i,0])
        plt.plot(data_train[i])
        plt.show()
```

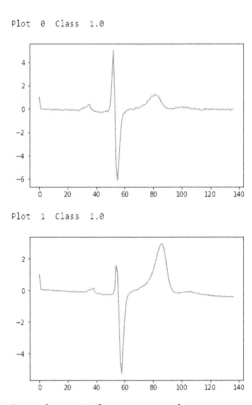

*Figure 13-1. ECGFiveDays class 1.0—first two examples*

Plot 4 Class 1.0

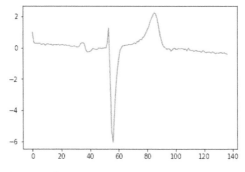

Plot 7 Class 1.0

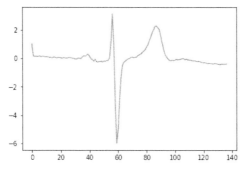

*Figure 13-2. ECGFiveDays class 1.0—second two examples*

Here is the code to plot results from `Class 2.0`:

```
# Examples of Class 2.0
for i in range(0,10):
    if data_train[i,0]==2.0:
        print("Plot ",i," Class ",data_train[i,0])
        plt.plot(data_train[i])
        plt.show()
```

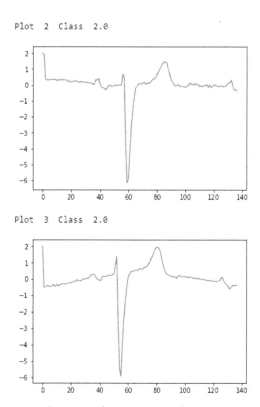

*Figure 13-3. ECGFiveDays class 2.0—first two examples*

Plot 5 Class 2.0

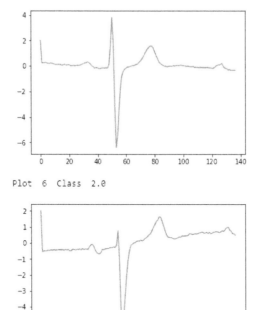

Plot 6 Class 2.0

*Figure 13-4. ECGFiveDays class 2.0—second two examples*

To the naked, untrained eye, the examples from class 1.0 and class 2.0 seem indistinguishable, but these observations have been annotated by domain experts. The plots
are noisy with distortions. There are also differences in amplitude, period, phase shift,
and vertical shift that make classification a challenge.

Let's prepare the data for the *k*-shape algorithm. We will normalize the data to have a
mean of zero and standard deviation of one:

```
# Prepare the data - Scale
X_train = TimeSeriesScalerMeanVariance(mu=0., std=1.).fit_transform(X_train)
X_test = TimeSeriesScalerMeanVariance(mu=0., std=1.).fit_transform(X_test)
```

# Training and Evaluation

Next, we will call the *k*-shape algorithm and set the number of clusters as 2, the max iterations to perform as one hundred, and the number of rounds of training as one hundred:[2]

```
# Train using k-Shape
ks = KShape(n_clusters=2, max_iter=100, n_init=100,verbose=0)
ks.fit(X_train)
```

To measure the goodness of the time series clustering, we will use the *adjusted Rand index*, a measure of the similarity between two data clusterings adjusted for the chance grouping of elements. This is related to the accuracy measure.[3]

Intuitively, the Rand index measures the number of agreements in cluster assignments between the predicted clusterings and the true clusterings. If the model has an adjusted Rand index with a value close to 0.0, it is purely randomly assigning clusters; if the model has an adjusted Rand index with a value close to 1.0, the predicted clusterings match the true clusterings exactly.

We will use the Scikit-learn implementation of the adjusted Rand index called the *adjusted_rand_score*.

Let's generate clustering predictions and then calculate the adjusted Rand index:

```
# Make predictions and calculate adjusted Rand index
preds = ks.predict(X_train)
ars = adjusted_rand_score(data_train[:,0],preds)
print("Adjusted Rand Index:", ars)
```

Based on this run, the adjusted Rand index is 0.668. If you perform this training and prediction several times, you will notice the adjusted Rand index will vary a bit but remains well above 0.0 at all times:

```
Adjusted Rand Index: 0.668041237113402
```

Let's predict on the test set and calculate the adjusted Rand index for it:

```
# Make predictions on test set and calculate adjusted Rand index
preds_test = ks.predict(X_test)
ars = adjusted_rand_score(data_test[:,0],preds_test)
print("Adjusted Rand Index on Test Set:", ars)
```

The adjusted Rand index is considerably lower on the test set, barely above 0. The cluster predictions are nearly chance assignments—the time series are being grouped based on similarity with little success:

---

2 For more on the hyperparameters, refer to the official *k*-shape documentation (*http://bit.ly/2Gfg0L9*).

3 Consult Wikipedia for more information on the Rand index (*https://en.wikipedia.org/wiki/Rand_index*).

```
Adjusted Rand Index on Test Set: 0.0006332050676187496
```

If we had a much larger training set to train our *k*-shape-based time series clustering model, we would expect better performance on the test set.

# Time Series Clustering Using k-Shape on ECG5000

Instead of the `ECGFiveDays` dataset, which has only 23 observations in the training set and 861 in the test set, let's use a much larger dataset of ECG readings. The `ECG5000` dataset (also available on the UCR Time Series archive) has five thousand ECG readings (i.e., time series) in total across the train and test sets.

## Data Preparation

We will load in the datasets and make our own train and test split, with 80% of the five thousand readings in the custom train set and the remaining 20% in the custom test set. With this much larger training set, we should be able to develop a time series clustering model that has much better performance, both on the train set and, most importantly, on the test set:

```python
# Load the datasets
current_path = os.getcwd()
file = '\\datasets\\ucr_time_series_data\\'
data_train = np.loadtxt(current_path+file+
                        "ECG5000/ECG5000_TRAIN",
                        delimiter=",")

data_test = np.loadtxt(current_path+file+
                       "ECG5000/ECG5000_TEST",
                       delimiter=",")

data_joined = np.concatenate((data_train,data_test),axis=0)
data_train, data_test = train_test_split(data_joined,
                                test_size=0.20, random_state=2019)

X_train = to_time_series_dataset(data_train[:, 1:])
y_train = data_train[:, 0].astype(np.int)
X_test = to_time_series_dataset(data_test[:, 1:])
y_test = data_test[:, 0].astype(np.int)
```

Let's explore this dataset:

```python
# Summary statistics
print("Number of time series:", len(data_train))
print("Number of unique classes:", len(np.unique(data_train[:,0])))
print("Time series length:", len(data_train[0,1:]))
```

The following code displays the basic summary statistics. There are four thousand readings in the training set, which are grouped into five distinct classes, and each time series has a length of 140:

```
Number of time series: 4000
Number of unique classes: 5
Time series length: 140
```

Let's also consider how many of the readings belong to each of these classes.

The counts per class are shown in Figure 13-5. Most of the readings fall in class 1, followed by class 2. Significantly fewer readings belong to clases 3, 4, and 5.

Let's take the average time series reading from each class to get a better sense of how the various classes look.

```
# Display readings from each class
for j in np.unique(data_train[:,0]):
    dataPlot = data_train[data_train[:,0]==j]
    cnt = len(dataPlot)
    dataPlot = dataPlot[:,1:].mean(axis=0)
    print(" Class ",j," Count ",cnt)
    plt.plot(dataPlot)
    plt.show()
```

Class 1 (Figure 13-5) has a sharp trough followed by a sharp peak and stabilization. This is the most common type of reading.

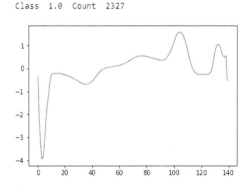

*Figure 13-5. ECG5000 class 1.0*

Class 2 (Figure 13-6) has a sharp trough followed by a recovery and then an even sharper and lower trough with a partial recovery. This is the second most common type of reading.

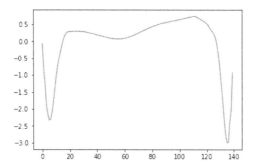

*Figure 13-6. ECG5000 class 2.0*

Class 3 (Figure 13-7) has a sharp trough followed by a recovery and then an even sharper and lower trough with no recovery. There are a few examples of these in the dataset.

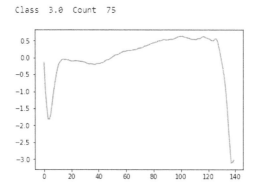

*Figure 13-7. ECG5000 class 3.0*

Class 4 (Figure 13-8) has a sharp trough followed by a recovery and then a shallow trough and stabilization. There are a few examples of these in the dataset.

Class 4.0 Count 156

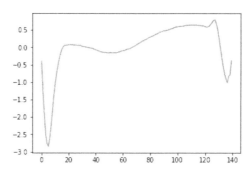

*Figure 13-8. ECG5000 class 4.0*

Class 5 (Figure 13-9) has a sharp trough followed by an uneven recovery, a peak, and then an unsteady decline to a shallow trough. There are very few examples of these in the dataset.

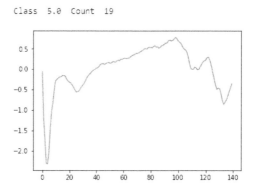

*Figure 13-9. ECG5000 class 5.0*

## Training and Evaluation

As before, let's normalize the data to have a mean of zero and standard deviation of one. Then, we will fit the *k*-shape algorithm, setting the number of clusters to five this time. Everything else remains the same:

```
# Prepare data - Scale
X_train = TimeSeriesScalerMeanVariance(mu=0., std=1.).fit_transform(X_train)
X_test = TimeSeriesScalerMeanVariance(mu=0., std=1.).fit_transform(X_test)

# Train using k-Shape
ks = KShape(n_clusters=5, max_iter=100, n_init=10,verbose=1,random_state=2019)
ks.fit(X_train)
```

Let's evaluate the results on the training set:

---

```
# Predict on train set and calculate adjusted Rand index
preds = ks.predict(X_train)
ars = adjusted_rand_score(data_train[:,0],preds)
print("Adjusted Rand Index on Training Set:", ars)
```

The following code shows the adjusted Rand index on the training set. It is considerably stronger at 0.75:

```
Adjusted Rand Index on Training Set: 0.7499312374127193
```

Let's evaluate the results on the test set, too:

```
# Predict on test set and calculate adjusted Rand index
preds_test = ks.predict(X_test)
ars = adjusted_rand_score(data_test[:,0],preds_test)
print("Adjusted Rand Index on Test Set:", ars)
```

The adjusted Rand index on the test set is much higher, too. It is 0.72:

```
Adjusted Rand Index on Test Set: 0.7172302400677499
```

By increasing the training set to four thousand time series (from 23), we have a considerably better-performing time series clustering model.

Let's explore the predicted clusters some more to see just how homogeneous they are. For each predicted cluster, we will evaluate the distribution of true labels. If the clusters are well-defined and homogeneous, most of the readings in each cluster should have the same true label:

```
# Evaluate goodness of the clusters
preds_test = preds_test.reshape(1000,1)
preds_test = np.hstack((preds_test,data_test[:,0].reshape(1000,1)))
preds_test = pd.DataFrame(data=preds_test)
preds_test = preds_test.rename(columns={0: 'prediction', 1: 'actual'})

counter = 0
for i in np.sort(preds_test.prediction.unique()):
    print("Predicted Cluster ", i)
    print(preds_test.actual[preds_test.prediction==i].value_counts())
    print()
    cnt = preds_test.actual[preds_test.prediction==i] \
                    .value_counts().iloc[1:].sum()
    counter = counter + cnt
print("Count of Non-Primary Points: ", counter)
```

The following code displays the homogeneity of the clusters:

```
ECG 5000 k-shape predicted cluster analysis

Predicted Cluster 0.0
    2.0   29
    4.0   2
    1.0   2
    3.0   2
```

```
    5.0   1
    Name: actual, dtype: int64

Predicted Cluster 1.0
    2.0   270
    4.0   14
    3.0   8
    1.0   2
    5.0   1
    Name: actual, dtype: int64

Predicted Cluster 2.0
    1.0   553
    4.0   16
    2.0   9
    3.0   7
    Name: actual, dtype: int64

Predicted Cluster 3.0
    2.0   35
    1.0   5
    4.0   5
    5.0   3
    3.0   3
    Name: actual, dtype: int64

Predicted Cluster 4.0
    1.0   30
    4.0   1
    3.0   1
    2.0   1
    Name: actual, dtype: int64

Count of Non-Primary Points: 83
```

The majority of the readings within each predicted cluster belong to just one true label class. This highlights just how well defined and homogeneous the *k*-shape-derived clusters are.

# Time Series Clustering Using k-Means on ECG5000

For the sake of completeness, let's compare the results of *k*-shape with results from *k*-means. We will use the *tslearn* library to perform the training and evaluate using the adjusted Rand index as before.

We will set the number of clusters as five, the number of max iterations for a single run as one hundred, the number of independent runs as one hundred, the metric distance as Euclidean, and the random state as 2019:

```
# Train using Time Series k-Means
km = TimeSeriesKMeans(n_clusters=5, max_iter=100, n_init=100, \
```

```
                        metric="euclidean", verbose=1, random_state=2019)
km.fit(X_train)

# Predict on training set and evaluate using adjusted Rand index
preds = km.predict(X_train)
ars = adjusted_rand_score(data_train[:,0],preds)
print("Adjusted Rand Index on Training Set:", ars)

# Predict on test set and evaluate using adjusted Rand index
preds_test = km.predict(X_test)
ars = adjusted_rand_score(data_test[:,0],preds_test)
print("Adjusted Rand Index on Test Set:", ars)
```

The *TimeSeriesKMean* algorithm runs even faster than *k*-shape using the Euclidean distance metric. But the results are not as good:

```
Adjusted Rand Index of Time Series k-Means on Training Set: 0.5063464656715959
```

The adjusted Rand index on the training set is 0.506:

```
Adjusted Rand Index of Time Series k-Means on Test Set: 0.4864981997585834
```

The adjusted Rand index on the test set is 0.486.

# Time Series Clustering Using Hierarchical DBSCAN on ECG5000

Finally, let's apply *hierarchical DBSCAN*, which we explored earlier in the book, and evaluate its performance.

We will run *HDBSCAN* with its default parameters and evaluate performance using the adjusted Rand index:

```
# Train model and evaluate on training set
min_cluster_size = 5
min_samples = None
alpha = 1.0
cluster_selection_method = 'eom'
prediction_data = True

hdb = hdbscan.HDBSCAN(min_cluster_size=min_cluster_size, \
                      min_samples=min_samples, alpha=alpha, \
                      cluster_selection_method=cluster_selection_method, \
                      prediction_data=prediction_data)

preds = hdb.fit_predict(X_train.reshape(4000,140))
ars = adjusted_rand_score(data_train[:,0],preds)
print("Adjusted Rand Index on Training Set:", ars)
```

The adjusted Rand index on the training set is an impressive 0.769:

```
Adjusted Rand Index on Training Set using HDBSCAN: 0.7689563655060421
```

Let's evaluate on the test set:

```
# Predict on test set and evaluate
preds_test = hdbscan.prediction.approximate_predict( \
            hdb, X_test.reshape(1000,140))
ars = adjusted_rand_score(data_test[:,0],preds_test[0])
print("Adjusted Rand Index on Test Set:", ars)
```

The adjusted Rand index on the test set is an equally impressive 0.720:

```
Adjusted Rand Index on Test Set using HDBSCAN: 0.7200816245545564
```

# Comparing the Time Series Clustering Algorithms

HDBSCAN and *k*-shape performed similarly well on the ECG5000 dataset, while *k*-means performed worse. However, we cannot draw strong conclusions by evaluating the performance of these three clustering algorithms on a single time series dataset.

Let's run a larger experiment to see how these three clustering algorithms stack up against one another.

First, we will load all the directories and files in the UCR Time Series Classification folder so we can iterate through them during the experiment. There are 85 datasets in total:

```
# Load the datasets
current_path = os.getcwd()
file = '\\datasets\\ucr_time_series_data\\'

mypath = current_path + file
d = []
f = []
for (dirpath, dirnames, filenames) in walk(mypath):
    for i in dirnames:
        newpath = mypath+"\\"+i+"\\"
        onlyfiles = [f for f in listdir(newpath) if isfile(join(newpath, f))]
        f.extend(onlyfiles)
    d.extend(dirnames)
    break
```

Next, let's recycle the code for each of the three clustering algorithms and use the list of datasets we just prepared to run a full experiment. We will store the training and test adjusted Rand indices by dataset and measure the time it takes each clustering algorithm to complete the entire experiment of 85 datasets.

# Full Run with k-Shape

The first experiment uses *k*-shape.

```
# k-Shape Experiment
kShapeDF = pd.DataFrame(data=[],index=[v for v in d],
                        columns=["Train ARS","Test ARS"])

# Train and Evaluate k-Shape
class ElapsedTimer(object):
    def __init__(self):
        self.start_time = time.time()
    def elapsed(self,sec):
        if sec < 60:
            return str(sec) + " sec"
        elif sec < (60 * 60):
            return str(sec / 60) + " min"
        else:
            return str(sec / (60 * 60)) + " hr"
    def elapsed_time(self):
        print("Elapsed: %s " % self.elapsed(time.time() - self.start_time))
        return (time.time() - self.start_time)

timer = ElapsedTimer()
cnt = 0
for i in d:
    cnt += 1
    print("Dataset ", cnt)
    newpath = mypath+"\\"+i+"\\"
    onlyfiles = [f for f in listdir(newpath) if isfile(join(newpath, f))]
    j = onlyfiles[0]
    k = onlyfiles[1]
    data_train = np.loadtxt(newpath+j, delimiter=",")
    data_test = np.loadtxt(newpath+k, delimiter=",")

    data_joined = np.concatenate((data_train,data_test),axis=0)
    data_train, data_test = train_test_split(data_joined,
                                    test_size=0.20, random_state=2019)

    X_train = to_time_series_dataset(data_train[:, 1:])
    y_train = data_train[:, 0].astype(np.int)
    X_test = to_time_series_dataset(data_test[:, 1:])
    y_test = data_test[:, 0].astype(np.int)

    X_train = TimeSeriesScalerMeanVariance(mu=0., std=1.) \
                            .fit_transform(X_train)
    X_test = TimeSeriesScalerMeanVariance(mu=0., std=1.) \
                            .fit_transform(X_test)

    classes = len(np.unique(data_train[:,0]))
    ks = KShape(n_clusters=classes, max_iter=10, n_init=3,verbose=0)
```

```
ks.fit(X_train)

print(i)
preds = ks.predict(X_train)
ars = adjusted_rand_score(data_train[:,0],preds)
print("Adjusted Rand Index on Training Set:", ars)
kShapeDF.loc[i,"Train ARS"] = ars

preds_test = ks.predict(X_test)
ars = adjusted_rand_score(data_test[:,0],preds_test)
print("Adjusted Rand Index on Test Set:", ars)
kShapeDF.loc[i,"Test ARS"] = ars

kShapeTime = timer.elapsed_time()
```

It takes approximately an hour to run the $k$-shape algorithm. We've stored the adjusted Rand indices and will use these to compare $k$-shape with $k$-means and HBDSCAN soon.

The time we measured for $k$-shape is based on the hyperparameters we set for the experiment as well as the local hardware specifications for the machine on which the experiments were run. Different hyperparameters and hardware specifications could result in dramatically different experiment times.

## Full Run with k-Means

Next up is $k$-means:

```
# k-Means Experiment - FULL RUN
# Create dataframe
kMeansDF = pd.DataFrame(data=[],index=[v for v in d], \
                        columns=["Train ARS","Test ARS"])

# Train and Evaluate k-Means
timer = ElapsedTimer()
cnt = 0
for i in d:
    cnt += 1
    print("Dataset ", cnt)
    newpath = mypath+"\\"+i+"\\"
    onlyfiles = [f for f in listdir(newpath) if isfile(join(newpath, f))]
    j = onlyfiles[0]
    k = onlyfiles[1]
    data_train = np.loadtxt(newpath+j, delimiter=",")
    data_test = np.loadtxt(newpath+k, delimiter=",")

    data_joined = np.concatenate((data_train,data_test),axis=0)
    data_train, data_test = train_test_split(data_joined, \
                                    test_size=0.20, random_state=2019)
```

```
X_train = to_time_series_dataset(data_train[:, 1:])
y_train = data_train[:, 0].astype(np.int)
X_test = to_time_series_dataset(data_test[:, 1:])
y_test = data_test[:, 0].astype(np.int)

X_train = TimeSeriesScalerMeanVariance(mu=0., std=1.) \
                            .fit_transform(X_train)
X_test = TimeSeriesScalerMeanVariance(mu=0., std=1.) \
                            .fit_transform(X_test)

classes = len(np.unique(data_train[:,0]))
km = TimeSeriesKMeans(n_clusters=5, max_iter=10, n_init=10, \
                    metric="euclidean", verbose=0, random_state=2019)
km.fit(X_train)

print(i)
preds = km.predict(X_train)
ars = adjusted_rand_score(data_train[:,0],preds)
print("Adjusted Rand Index on Training Set:", ars)
kMeansDF.loc[i,"Train ARS"] = ars

preds_test = km.predict(X_test)
ars = adjusted_rand_score(data_test[:,0],preds_test)
print("Adjusted Rand Index on Test Set:", ars)
kMeansDF.loc[i,"Test ARS"] = ars

kMeansTime = timer.elapsed_time()
```

It takes less than five minutes for *k*-means to run through all 85 datasets:

## Full Run with HDBSCAN

Finally, we have HBDSCAN:

```
# HDBSCAN Experiment - FULL RUN
# Create dataframe
hdbscanDF = pd.DataFrame(data=[],index=[v for v in d], \
                        columns=["Train ARS","Test ARS"])

# Train and Evaluate HDBSCAN
timer = ElapsedTimer()
cnt = 0
for i in d:
    cnt += 1
    print("Dataset ", cnt)
    newpath = mypath+"\\"+i+"\\"
    onlyfiles = [f for f in listdir(newpath) if isfile(join(newpath, f))]
    j = onlyfiles[0]
    k = onlyfiles[1]
    data_train = np.loadtxt(newpath+j, delimiter=",")
    data_test = np.loadtxt(newpath+k, delimiter=",")
```

```
data_joined = np.concatenate((data_train,data_test),axis=0)
data_train, data_test = train_test_split(data_joined, \
                            test_size=0.20, random_state=2019)

X_train = data_train[:, 1:]
y_train = data_train[:, 0].astype(np.int)
X_test = data_test[:, 1:]
y_test = data_test[:, 0].astype(np.int)

X_train = TimeSeriesScalerMeanVariance(mu=0., std=1.) \
                            .fit_transform(X_train)
X_test = TimeSeriesScalerMeanVariance(mu=0., std=1.) \
                            .fit_transform(X_test)

classes = len(np.unique(data_train[:,0]))
min_cluster_size = 5
min_samples = None
alpha = 1.0
cluster_selection_method = 'eom'
prediction_data = True

hdb = hdbscan.HDBSCAN(min_cluster_size=min_cluster_size, \
                    min_samples=min_samples, alpha=alpha, \
                    cluster_selection_method= \
                        cluster_selection_method, \
                    prediction_data=prediction_data)

print(i)
preds = hdb.fit_predict(X_train.reshape(X_train.shape[0], \
                                X_train.shape[1]))
ars = adjusted_rand_score(data_train[:,0],preds)
print("Adjusted Rand Index on Training Set:", ars)
hdbscanDF.loc[i,"Train ARS"] = ars

preds_test = hdbscan.prediction.approximate_predict(hdb,
                    X_test.reshape(X_test.shape[0], \
                                X_test.shape[1]))
ars = adjusted_rand_score(data_test[:,0],preds_test[0])
print("Adjusted Rand Index on Test Set:", ars)
hdbscanDF.loc[i,"Test ARS"] = ars

hdbscanTime = timer.elapsed_time()
```

It takes less than 10 minutes for HBDSCAN to run through all 85 datasets.

## Comparing All Three Time Series Clustering Approaches

Now let's compare all three clustering algorithms to see which fared the best. One approach is to calculate the average adjusted Rand indices on the training and test sets, respectively, for each of the clustering algorithms.

Here are the scores for each of the algorithms:

```
k-Shape Results

Train ARS    0.165139
Test ARS     0.151103

k-Means Results

Train ARS    0.184789
Test ARS     0.178960

HDBSCAN Results

Train ARS    0.178754
Test ARS 0.158238
```

The results are fairly comparable, with *k*-means having the highest Rand indices, followed closely by *k*-shape and HDBSCAN.

To validate some of these findings, let's count how many times each algorithm placed first, second, or third across all the 85 datasets:

```
# Count top place finishes
timeSeriesClusteringDF = pd.DataFrame(data=[],index=kShapeDF.index, \
                           columns=["kShapeTest", \
                                "kMeansTest", \
                                "hdbscanTest"])

timeSeriesClusteringDF.kShapeTest = kShapeDF["Test ARS"]
timeSeriesClusteringDF.kMeansTest = kMeansDF["Test ARS"]
timeSeriesClusteringDF.hdbscanTest = hdbscanDF["Test ARS"]

tscResults = timeSeriesClusteringDF.copy()

for i in range(0,len(tscResults)):
    maxValue = tscResults.iloc[i].max()
    tscResults.iloc[i][tscResults.iloc[i]==maxValue]=1
    minValue = tscResults .iloc[i].min()
    tscResults.iloc[i][tscResults.iloc[i]==minValue]=-1
    medianValue = tscResults.iloc[i].median()
    tscResults.iloc[i][tscResults.iloc[i]==medianValue]=0

# Show results
tscResultsDF = pd.DataFrame(data=np.zeros((3,3)), \
            index=["firstPlace","secondPlace","thirdPlace"], \
            columns=["kShape", "kMeans","hdbscan"])
tscResultsDF.loc["firstPlace",:] = tscResults[tscResults==1].count().values
tscResultsDF.loc["secondPlace",:] = tscResults[tscResults==0].count().values
tscResultsDF.loc["thirdPlace",:] = tscResults[tscResults==-1].count().values
tscResultsDF
```

*k*-shape had the most first place finishes, followed by HDBSCAN. *k*-means had the most second place finishes, performing neither the best but also not the worst on the majority of the datasets (Table 13-1).

*Table 13-1. Comparison summary*

|  | kShape | kMeans | hbdscan |
|---|---|---|---|
| firstPlace | 31.0 | 24.0 | 29.0 |
| secondPlace | 19.0 | 41.0 | 26.0 |
| thirdPlace | 35.0 | 20.0 | 30.0 |

Based on this comparison, it is hard to conclude that one algorithm universally trounces all the others. While *k*-shape has the most first place finishes, it is considerably slower than the other two algorithms.

And, *k*-means and HDBSCAN both hold their own, winning first place on a healthy number of datasets.

# Conclusion

In this chapter, we explored time series data for the first time in the book and demonstrated the power of unsupervised learning to group time series patterns based on their similarity to one another and without requiring any labels. We worked with three clustering algorithms in detail—*k*-shape, *k*-means, and HDBSCAN. While *k*-shape is regarded as the best of the bunch today, the other two algorithms perform quite well, too.

Most importantly, the results from the 85 time series datasets we worked with highlight the importance of experimentation. As with most machine learning, no single algorithm trounces all other algorithms. You must constantly expand your breadth of knowledge and experiment to see which approaches work best for the problem at hand. Knowing what to apply when is the hallmark of a good data scientist.

Hopefully you will be better equipped to solve more of the problems you face going forward with the many different unsupervised learning approaches you've learned throughout this book.

# CHAPTER 14

# Conclusion

Artificial intelligence is in the midst of a hype cycle not seen in the tech world since the advent of the internet age 20 years ago.[1] However, that does not mean the hype is not warranted or—to some degree—justified.

While the AI and machine learning work in prior decades was mostly theoretical and academic in nature—with few successful commercial applications—the work in this space over the past decade has been much more applied and industry-focused, led by the likes of Google, Facebook, Amazon, Microsoft, and Apple.

The focus on developing machine learning applications for narrowly defined tasks (i.e., weak or narrow AI) rather than on more ambitious tasks (i.e., strong or AGI) has made the field much more attractive to investors that want to achieve good returns on a shorter 7- to 10-year time frame. More attention and capital from investors, in turn, has made the field more successful, both in progress toward narrow AI as well as in laying the building blocks for strong AI.

Of course, capital is not the only catalyst. The rise of big data, the advancements in computer hardware (especially the rise of GPUs, led by Nvidia, for training deep neural networks), and the breakthroughs in algorithm research and development have played equally meaningful roles in contributing to the recent successes of AI.

Like all hype cycles, the current cycle may lead to some disappointment eventually, but so far the progress in the field has astonished many in the science community and has captured the imagination of an increasingly mainstream audience.

---

1 According to PitchBook (*http://bit.ly/2Rwwocm*), venture capital investors invested over $10.8 billion in AI and machine learning companies in 2017, up from $500 million in 2010 and nearly double the $5.7 billion invested in 2016.

# Supervised Learning

To date, supervised learning has been responsibile for the majority of the commercial successes in machine learning. These successes can be broken down by data type:

- With images, we have optical character recognition, image classification, and facial recognition, to name a few. For example, Facebook automatically tags faces in new photographs based on how similar the faces look to previously labeled faces, leveraging Facebook's database of existing photographs.

- With video, we have self-driving cars, which are already operating on roads across the United States today. Major players such as Google, Tesla, and Uber have invested very heavily into autonomous vehicles.

- With speech, we have speech recognition, fueled by assistants such as Siri, Alexa, Google Assistant, and Cortana.

- With text, we have the classic example of email spam filtering but also machine translation (i.e., Google Translate), sentiment analysis, syntax analysis, entity recognition, language detection, and question answering. On the back of these successes, we have seen a proliferation of chatbots in the past few years.

Supervised learning also performs well at time series prediction, which has many applications in fields such as finance, healthcare, and ad tech. Of course, supervised learning applications are not restricted to working with only one data type at a time. For example, video captioning systems combine image recognition with natural language processing to apply machine learning on videos and generate text captions.

# Unsupervised Learning

Unsupervised learning has not had nearly as many successes to date as supervised learning has had, but its potential is immense. Most of the world's data is unlabeled. To apply machine learning at scale to tasks that are more ambitious in scope than the ones supervised learning has already solved, we will need to work with both labeled and unlabeled data.

Unsupervised learning is very good at finding hidden patterns by learning the underlying structure in unlabeled data. Once hidden patterns are uncovered, unsupervised learning can group the hidden patterns based on similarity such that similar patterns are grouped together.

Once the patterns are grouped this way, humans can sample a few patterns per group and provide meaningful labels. If the groups are well-defined (i.e., the members are homogeneous and distinctly different from members in other groups), the few labels that humans provide by hand can be applied to the other (yet unlabeled) members of the group. This process leads to very fast and efficient labeling of previously unlabeled data.

In other words, unsupervised learning enables the successful application of supervised learning methods. This synergy between unsupervised learning and supervised learning—also known as semisupervised learning—may fuel the next wave in successful machine learning applications.

## Scikit-Learn

These themes from unsupervised learning should be very familar to you by now. But let's review everything we've covered so far.

In Chapter 3, we explored how to use dimensionality reduction algorithms to reduce the dimensionality of data by learning the underlying structure, keeping only the most salient features, and mapping the features into a lower dimensional space.

Once the data is mapped to a lower dimensional space, it becomes much easier to uncover the hidden patterns in the data. In Chapter 4, we demonstrated this by building an anomaly detection system, separating normal credit card transactions from abnormal ones.

In this lower dimensional space, it is also easier to group similar points together; this is known as clustering, which we explored in Chapter 5. A successful application of clustering is group segmentation, separating items based on how similar they are to one another and how different they are to others. We performed this on borrowers filing loan applications in Chapter 6. Chapters 3 through 6 concluded the unsupervised learning using Scikit-Learn portion of the book.

In Chapter 13, we expanded clustering to time series data for the first time and explored various time series clustering methods. We performed many experiments and highlighted just how important it is to have a wide arsenal of machine learning methods available because no one method works best for all datasets.

## TensorFlow and Keras

Chapters 7 through 12 explored unsupervised learning using TensorFlow and Keras.

First, we introduced neural networks and the concept of representation learning. In Chapter 7, we used autoencoders to learn new, more condensed representations from original data—this is yet another way unsupervised learning learns the underlying structure in data to extract insight.

In Chapter 8, we applied autoencoders to the credit card transaction dataset to build a fraud detection solution. And, very importantly, we combined an unsupervised approach with a supervised approach in Chapter 9 to improve the standalone unsupervised learning-based credit card fraud detection solution we built in Chapter 8, highlighting the potential synergy between unsupervised and supervised learning models.

In Chapter 10, we introduced generative models for the first time, starting with the restricted Boltzmann machine. We used these to build a movie recommender system, a very light version of the type of recommender systems used by the likes of Netflix and Amazon.

In Chapter 11, we moved from shallow to deep neural networks, and we built a more advanced generative model by stacking multiple restricted Boltzmann machines together. With this so-called deep belief network, we generated synthetic images of digits to augment the existing MNIST dataset and build a better image classification system. Again, this highlights the potential of using unsupervised learning to improve a supervised solution.

In Chapter 12, we moved to another class of generative models—the one most in vogue today—called generative adversarial networks. We used these to generate more synthetic images of digits similar to those in the MNIST image dataset.

# Reinforcement Learning

In this book, we did not cover reinforcement learning in any detail, but it is yet another area of machine learning that is receiving increased attention, especially after its recent successes in fields such as board and video game playing.

Most notably, Google DeepMind introduced its Go software *AlphaGo* to the world a few years ago, and AlphaGo's historic victory against the then-world champion Go player Lee Sedol in March 2016—a feat many expected would take another entire decade for AI to achieve—helped show the world just how much progress had been made in the field of AI.

More recently, Google DeepMind has blended reinforcement learning with unsupervised learning to develop an even better version of its AlphaGo software. Called *AlphaGo Zero*, this software does not use data from human games at all.

Such successes from marrying different branches of machine learning corroborate a major theme of this book—the next wave of successes in machine learning will be led by finding ways to work with unlabeled data to improve existing machine learning solutions that today rely heavily on labeled datasets.

# Most Promising Areas of Unsupervised Learning Today

We will conclude this book with the present and possible future state of unsupervised learning. Today, unsupervised learning has several successful applications in industry;

at the top of this list are anomaly detection, dimensionality reduction, clustering, efficient labeling of unlabeled datasets, and data augmentation.

Unsupervising learning excels in identifying newly emerging patterns, especially when future patterns look very different from past patterns; in some fields, labels of past patterns have limited value in catching future patterns of interest. For example, anomaly detection is used for identifying fraud of all types—credit card, debit card, wire, online, insurance, etc.—and for flagging suspicious transactions related to money laundering, terrorist financing, and human trafficking.

Anomaly detection is also used in cybersecurity solutions to identify and stop cyber-attacks. Rules-based systems struggle to catch new types of cyber-attacks so unsupervised, learning is becoming a staple in this field. Anomaly detection also excels at highlighting data quality issues; with anomaly detection, data analysts can pinpoint and address bad data capture much more efficiently.

Unsupervised learning also helps address one of the major challenges in machine learning: the curse of dimensionality. Data scientists typically have to select a subset of features to use in analyzing data and in building machine learning models because the full set of features is too large, making computation difficult if not intractable. Unsupervised learning enables data scientists to not only work with the original feature set but also to supplement it with additional feature engineering—without fear of running into major computational challenges during model building.

Once the original plus engineered feature set is ready, data scientists apply dimensionality reduction to remove redundant features and keep the most salient, uncorrelated ones for analysis and model building. This type of data compression is also useful as a preprocessing step in supervised machine learning systems (especially with video and images).

Unsupervised learning also helps data scientists and business people answer questions such as which customers are behaving in the most uncommon ways (i.e., in a way that is very different from the majority of customers). This insight comes from clustering similar points together, helping analysts perform group segmentation. Once distinct groups are identified, humans can explore what makes the groups special and distinctly different from other groups. Insight from this exercise could be applied to gain a deeper business understanding of what is happening and to improve corporate strategy.

Clustering makes labeling unlabeled data considerably more efficient. Because similar data is grouped together, a human needs to label only a few of the points per cluster. Once a few points within each cluster are labeled, the other not-yet-labeled points could adopt the labels from the labeled points.

Finally, generative models can generate synthetic data to supplement existing datasets. We demonstrated this with our work on the MNIST dataset. The ability to create lots of new synthetic data—of many different data types such as images and text—is very powerful and is just beginning to be explored earnestly.

# The Future of Unsupervised Learning

We are still very early in the current AI wave. Of course there have been major successes to date, but a lot of the AI world is built on hype and promise. There is a lot of potential that has yet to be realized.

The successes to date have been in mostly narrowly defined tasks led by supervised learning. As the current wave of AI matures, the hope is that we move from narrow AI tasks (such as image classification, machine translation, speech recognition, question-and-answer bots) to more ambitious strong AI (chatbots that can understand meaning in human language and converse naturally in the way a human would, robots that make sense of the physical world around them and operate in it without relying heavily on labeled data, self-driving cars that develop super-human driving performance, and AI that can exhibit human-level reasoning and creativity).

Many regard unsupervised learning as the key to developing AI of the strong type. Otherwise, AI will be shackled by the limits of how much labeled data we have.

One thing humans excel in—from birth—is learning to perform tasks without requiring many examples. For instance, a toddler is able to differentiate a cat from a dog with just a handful of examples. Today's AI needs many more examples/labels. Ideally, the AI could learn to separate images of different classes (i.e., a cat vs. a dog) with as few labels as possible, perhaps as little as one or none. To perform this type of *one shot* or *zero shot* learning will require more progress in the realm of unsupervised learning.

Also, most AI today is not creative. It is merely optimizing pattern recognition based on labels it has trained on. To build AI that is intuitive and creative, researchers will need to build AI that can make sense of lots of unlabeled data to find patterns that even humans would have not previously found.

Fortunately, there are some promising signs that AI is advancing ever so gradually to a stronger AI type.

Google DeepMind's AlphaGo software is a case in point. The first version of AlphaGo to beat a human professional Go player (in October 2015) relied on data from past Go games played by humans and machine learning methods such as reinforcement learning (including the ability to look many moves ahead and determine which move improves the odds of winning most significantly).

This version of AlphaGo was very impressive, beating one of the world's best Go players, Lee Sedol, in a high-profile best of five series in Seoul, South Korea, in March 2016. But the latest version of AlphaGo is even more remarkable.

The original AlphaGo relied on data and human expertise. The latest version of AlphaGo, called *AlphaGo Zero*, learned how to play and win Go from scratch, purely through self play.[2] In other words, AlphaGo Zero did not rely on any human knowledge and achieved superhuman performance, beating the previous AlphaGo version one hundred to zero.[3]

Starting from knowing nothing about Go, AlphaGo Zero accumulated thousands of years of human knowledge in Go play in a matter of days. But then it progressed further, beyond the realm of human-level proficiency. AlphaGo Zero discovered new knowledge and developed new unconventional winning strategies.

In other words, AlphaGo exercised creativity.

If AI continues to advance, fueled by the ability to learn from little to no prior knowledge (i.e., little to no labeled data), we will be able to develop AI that is capable of creativity, reasoning, and complex decision making, areas that have so far been the sole domain of humans.[4]

# Final Words

We have just scratched the surface of unsupervised learning and its potential, but I hope you have a better appreciation of what unsupervised learning is capable of and how it could be applied to machine learning systems you design.

At the very least, you should have a conceptual understanding of and hands-on experience using unsupervised learning to uncover hidden patterns, gain deeper business insight, detect anomalies, cluster groups based on similarity, perform automatic feature extraction, and generate synthetic datasets from unlabeled datasets.

The future of AI is full of promise. Go build it.

---

2 "AlphaGo Zero: Learning from Scratch" (*https://deepmind.com/blog/alphago-zero-learning-scratch/*) provides an in-depth introduction to AlphaGo Zero.

3 For additional information, check out the *Nature* article "Mastering the Game of Go Without Human Knowledge" (*https://www.nature.com/articles/nature24270*).

4 OpenAI has also had some notable successes in applying unsupervised learning for language understanding (*http://bit.ly/2GfhHrZ*), both of which are essential building blocks for strong AI.

# Index

## H

HDBSCAN (hierarchical DBSCAN), 146, 165, 315
hidden layers, 170
hidden Markov models, 23
hierarchical clustering
    agglomerative, 138
    evaluating cluster results, 141
    group segmentation, 161-164
    overview of, 18, 138
    Z matrix (dendrogram), 139
Hinton, Geoffrey, 231, 251
holdout set, 4
hyperbolic tangent (tanh) activation function, 170, 183
hyperparameter optimization, 171, 198

## I

identity function, 173, 187, 198
implicit data, 233
incremental PCA, 16, 80
independent component analysis (ICA), 17, 94, 118-120, 122
independent variables, 3
inertia, 18, 130
input layers, 170
input variables, 3
instance-based learning, 12
interpretability, 11
inverse_transform function, 107, 110, 116, 118
isometric mapping (Isomap), 16, 87

## J

Johnson-Lindenstrauss lemma, 85
Jupyter Notebook
    activating, 30
    resources for learning, xvi

## K

k-fold cross-validation, 40, 220
k-means clustering
    accuracy of, 133
    evaluating clustering results, 131
    goal of, 130
    group segmentation, 158
    k-means inertia, 130
    number of principal components and, 134
    on original dataset, 136

overview of, 18
    on time series data, 300
k-nearest neighbors (KNN), 12
k-shape algorithm, 300, 312
Keras
    Dense(), 291
    installing, 29
    overview of, 172
    role in unsupervised learning, 325
    Sequential(), 287, 291
    to_categorical function, 286
kernel PCA, 16, 82, 110-112
kernel size, 285
Kullback–Leibler divergence, 91, 244

## L

labeled versus unlabeled data, xv, 7
LabelEncoder, 155
latent Dirichlet allocation (LDA), 17
layer one predictions, 61
lazy learners, 12
learned representation, 169
learning rates, 185
Lending Club data, 149
LightGBM
    image classifier using, 279-281
    installing, 29
    model creation and evaluation, 54-56
linear activation function, 170, 182
linear methods
    linear regression algorithm, 11
    logistic regression algorithm, 12, 40-43
linear projection dimensionality reduction, 15, 74
locally linear embedding (LLE), 90
logistic regression algorithm, 12, 40-43
longitudinal data, 299
loss functions, 174, 184

## M

machine learning (see also machine learning example project)
    applied AI, xii
    classic vs. using neural networks, 170
    commercial applications for, xiii, 323
    critical developments in, xii
    ecosystem for, 3-26
    history of, xi
    major milestones in applied AI, xiii-xv

## About the Author

**Ankur A. Patel** is the vice president of data science at 7Park Data, a Vista Equity Partners portfolio company. At 7Park Data, Ankur and his data science team use alternative data to build data products for hedge funds and corporations and develop machine learning as a service (MLaaS) for enterprise clients. MLaaS includes natural language processing, anomaly detection, clustering, and time series prediction. Prior to 7Park Data, Ankur led data science efforts in New York City for Israeli artificial intelligence firm ThetaRay, one of the world's pioneers in applied unsupervised learning.

Ankur began his career as an analyst at J.P. Morgan, and then became the lead emerging markets sovereign credit trader for Bridgewater Associates, the world's largest global macro hedge fund. He later founded and managed R-Squared Macro, a machine learning-based hedge fund, for five years. Ankur is a graduate of the Woodrow Wilson School at Princeton University and the recipient of the Lieutenant John A. Larkin Memorial Prize.

## Colophon

The animal on the cover of *Hands-On Unsupervised Learning Using Python* is a common wombat *(Vombatus ursinus)*, also known as the coarse-haired or bare-nosed wombat. Though its scientific name includes *ursinus*, which is Latin for bear, wombats are marsupials like koalas and kangaroos. Wild wombats are found only on Australia's mainland and Tasmania. They make themselves at home in coastal forests, woodlands, and grasslands, where they dig burrows with their claws.

Wombats have short, thick fur; short, thick legs; a bald snout; and small ears. Like all marsupials, wombats have pouches for their young, but the wombat's pouch faces backward. A joey's face can peek out from between its mother's hind legs. This adaptation prevents the messy burrowing process from showering a joey in dirt. When born, a joey is bald and about the size of a jellybean. Gestation takes one month, but the young stay with their mothers for over one year for warmth and nutrients.

Adult common wombats average 44 pounds and 3 feet long. They live about 15 years in the wild and produce offspring once every two years. Wombats use their continuously growing incisors to graze on a variety of grasses and roots throughout the night. They are a nocturnal species, though they will come out to enjoy the sun during cold spells.

It was recently discovered that female wombats will nip at the backside of male wombats when they are ready to mate. A bite on the rear doesn't hurt a wombat because the skin of their posterior is tough. In fact, if a wombat finds itself pursued by a predator, it will turn around or dive into a burrow, exposing this thickest end to danger.

They may walk with a waddle, but a threatened wombat can run up to 25 miles per hour.

Many of the animals on O'Reilly covers are endangered; all of them are important to the world. To learn more about how you can help, go to *animals.oreilly.com*.

The cover illustration is by Karen Montgomery, based on a black and white engraving from Lydekker's *Royal Natural History*. The cover fonts are Gilroy Semibold and Guardian Sans. The text font is Adobe Minion Pro; the heading font is Adobe Myriad Condensed; and the code font is Dalton Maag's Ubuntu Mono.

# O'REILLY®

# There's much more
# where this came from.

Experience books, videos, live online
training courses, and more from O'Reilly
and our 200+ partners—all in one place.

Learn more at oreilly.com/online-learning

Milton Keynes UK
Ingram Content Group UK Ltd.
UKHW030109291123
433441UK00010B/455

9 781492 035640